CHARLES I's
EXECUTIONERS

CHARLES I's EXECUTIONERS

CIVIL WAR, REGICIDE AND THE REPUBLIC

JAMES HOBSON

PEN & SWORD
HISTORY

AN IMPRINT OF PEN & SWORD BOOKS LTD.
YORKSHIRE – PHILADELPHIA

First published in Great Britain in 2020 by
PEN AND SWORD HISTORY
An imprint of
Pen & Sword Books Ltd
Yorkshire – Philadelphia

ISBN 978 1 52676 184 2

A CIP catalogue record for this book is available from the British Library.

Typeset in Times New Roman 11.5/14 by
SJmagic DESIGN SERVICES, India.
Printed and bound in the UK by TJ Books Limited.

Pen & Sword Books Limited incorporates the imprints of Atlas, Archaeology,
Aviation, Discovery, Family History, Fiction, History, Maritime, Military, Military
Classics, Politics, Select, Transport, True Crime, Air World, Frontline Publishing,
Leo Cooper, Remember When, Seaforth Publishing, The Praetorian Press,
Wharncliffe Local History, Wharncliffe Transport, Wharncliffe True Crime and
White Owl.

For a complete list of Pen & Sword titles please contact
PEN & SWORD BOOKS LIMITED
47 Church Street, Barnsley, South Yorkshire, S70 2AS, England
E-mail: enquiries@pen-and-sword.co.uk
Website: www.pen-and-sword.co.uk

Or
PEN AND SWORD BOOKS
1950 Lawrence Rd, Havertown, PA 19083, USA
E-mail: Uspen-and-sword@casematepublishers.com
Website: www.penandswordbooks.com

Contents

Introduction

How many names on a piece of paper are needed to execute your king? The answer in January 1649 was fifty-nine. Their signatures and seals were affixed to a piece of parchment, with each subsequent column of names more crammed in than the last, yet with space left unused in the last column. Why would they leave a space *and* arrange the signatures to allow more?

So, even the arrangement is an enigma. Did they want more names, or did they feel that they had enough? It was certainly enough to behead Charles I and set up a government without a monarch for the first and last time in British history. Some people today have cast doubt on the use of the word 'revolution' to characterise the events of the civil war, but how else would you describe the trial and execution of the king and the abolition of the monarchy and House of Lords in a period of six months in 1649?

Who were the fifty-nine men who started this process? In short, they were puritans, politicians, soldiers, lawyers, bureaucrats and merchants. Some were opportunists, some were cowards, some were filled with spite and personal ambition, while others sacrificed themselves for a cause that dominated their lives. Some men acted on the noblest motivations of political and religious duty, inspired by a deep and intensive examination of their conscience, while others were greedy, weak, cynical and superficial. Most were army officers or MPs, or both. Some of them have claimed their place in British history, but the majority – a clear majority – remain completely unknown, and seem to merit no more than passing mentions in even the most comprehensive histories of the civil war.

This book is based on the belief that each regicide can tell us something important about the English Civil War and its aftermath. None of these men deserve to be footnotes, or called 'deedless', as some Victorian historians claimed. Committing regicide is the greatest of political statements. These fifty-nine organised and supported the only coup d'état in British history, and the only judicial execution of a monarch. The document they signed is not a work of fiction or the result of coercion. Indeed, lack of coercion was a more obvious characteristic. They had plenty of opportunities to shrink away from the ultimate act, and to do so without any risk to themselves. They may have been a very mixed bunch, but their determination to see events through makes them a cohort worth studying, both as individuals and in groups of like-minded people.

The fact that regicide was not unprecedented does not detract from the historical significance of the event. Sometimes monarchs are killed by their own people, sometimes in their own country, in public view and with a form of judicial process; but *all* these things happening at the same time creates a unique event. The 1649 execution was a transparent act, done with righteousness and at least the facade of confidence. Charles was never deposed; he was the lawful king until the end. The last words he would have heard were 'Your Majesty', and they came from a plebeian headsman.

There were 135 High Commissioners selected by the Parliament and army leaders, of which about seventy took an active part in the trial, and only fifty-nine signed the death warrant. Those who refused to take part were not punished, although there was some psychological pressure applied while signatures were being collected. After the restoration, individuals made their excuses; threats of violence were part of their mitigation, but, as the book will show, there was not much substance to it. The execution warrant was largely signed by people who, at the time, wished to sign it. Their level of determination, their motives and the strength of their feeling, however, varied considerably.

Each name, even those that have been forgotten, represents another reason why the king was executed. It is true that this book tries to treat them more equally than they deserve in order to establish why they would have wished to be remembered as regicides. The plan is to find at least one interesting thing about each of them which can help answer the question: why did it happen?

This is not a book of mini-biographies. Such a book would not only repeat itself tediously but would also fail to get over some of the common characteristics between the men that help to explain events. A biography, no matter how thin, would not be possible for many of the regicides. The evidence is often scarce and tainted by the centuries of hatred and resentment. Information about character and personality is rare and not always reliable; but it has been pounced on when it is available. Because of the available sources, this is a book about men. Women mattered in the civil war, however, and the absence of evidence is not evidence of absence. Where women made a difference, their story has been told, if it was known.

Some regicides are so pivotal that they have their own chapter, but they are mostly grouped based on their shared characteristics. Pains have been taken to make the groupings work, but they are never one hundred per cent convincing. Some apparent groupings turned out to be illusions. For example, there were six Sussex regicides, but there was nothing about Sussex that united them, apart from their Puritanism. A group consisting of Puritans would have fifty-plus members. That Sussex was more Puritan than most was not a categorisation that shone any light on their motivations and actions. Buckinghamshire was another Puritan county but their regicides could not hang together in the same group, despite the fact that they lived close together and were members of the same extended families.

The book uses the word 'regicide' in the strict sense, referring to those who signed the death warrant. This is not the approach taken by most historians today or by most people at the time. When the monarchy was restored in 1660, eighty, not fifty- nine, were exempted from pardon, and among those additional names were men like Hugh Peters, a firebrand Puritan preacher, John Cook, a republican lawyer and Daniel Axtell and Francis Hacker, who organised the security for the trial and execution. They are mentioned only briefly in this book, but strictly speaking deserve the title of regicide more than many who signed the warrant.

Other important people have been excluded, but appear in the text because they helped create the conditions for the fifty-nine to sign the warrant: Denzil Holles, Arthur Hesilrige, Thomas Fairfax, John Pym and, of course, Charles I, King of England, who was as responsible as anyone for the execution. In order to identify the king killers and avoid clunky formulations like 'future' or 'soon-to-be' regicides, I have used this key word to identify them *before* the event as well as after.

The focus on the fifty-nine and their personal motivations should not be interpreted as denying that the civil war had deep-rooted causes: the opposite is the case, as the political and economic undercurrents can be seen in their biographies. This book is most definitely not the history of 'great' men – a clear majority were not very great, and a fair number were scoundrels – but it deals with all fifty-nine regicides and allocates 500–3,000 words on each, depending on their importance. The problem here is that their relative degrees of significance are compressed – for instance, Henry Ireton is more than six times as important as Humphrey Edwards – but at least the opposite, more common problem of completely ignoring most of the king killers has been addressed. Highlighting the parts played by more obscure characters also challenges the myth that the civil war was 'Cromwell v Charles I'. Cromwell has a part in this book, but it is an abbreviated biography, making it very different to most books on the civil war and execution of the king.

This is ultimately a book about religion and politics. Most of these fifty-nine had motivations that could be defined as religious or political. When asked whether the conflict was a war of religion or war of liberty, the poet Andrew Marvell suggested that it was an impossible question to answer as 'whichsover was at the top, the other was at the bottom'. That idea runs through the whole book.

Chapter 1

The Morning Stars of the Regicide

John Alured, John Moore, John Blakiston, James Temple,
Peregrine Pelham

Some regicides did not live much longer than the man they executed. Over ten per cent of those who signed the execution warrant in 1649 were dead within four years. This is no more than actuarial logic, as some regicides were born in the 1590s and would be nearing the end of their lives by 1650. They did not enjoy the fame of the others, nor were they remembered much when the monarchy was restored. They mattered, though, and had they lived longer, most would have mattered more. They shared the same profile, character and reaction to religious and political events. Taken as a group, it is possible to sketch out a kind of 'composite' regicide, a set of characteristics that most of them possessed, and by doing that trace some of the causes of the civil war and the execution.

Our first regicide is **John Alured** of Hull who died in 1651 at the relatively young age of forty-four. He was a brave and principled man but was a relative unknown. He comes first in this story because he seems to possess most of the characteristics and background that drove men to the regicide conclusion. He is our 'archetype'.

Firstly, he was a Puritan; unhappy with the religious policies of Charles I and his bishops, particularly William Laud, Archbishop of Canterbury from 1633. This was overwhelmingly the case throughout our story. Nearly all regicides were Puritans, but, of course, not all Puritans were regicides. European Protestant churches had dispensed with bishops during the sixteenth-century reformation, but in England they were an important part of the monarch's ability to enforce national religious discipline. That discipline included ceremonies that, to some, smacked of Catholicism. Religious practices were insufficiently pure,

1

hence the term 'Puritan', a name invented by their enemies. Their preferred term was 'the Godly', or 'the Elect'. They hated the religious changes of Charles and Laud. The Alured family were in that number, and had been solidly Puritan for three generations. There had always been discontent with the compromise religious settlement of Elizabeth I from the beginning.

Most of our regicides were born into their Puritanism, though some developed their views in later life, often during some form of personal crisis. Alured seemed to have managed to do both. According to the godly minister Thomas Shephard, who married Alured to Mary Darley in November 1631, Alured was a 'profane young gentleman', before and during his nuptials, but who was helped by the family chaplain and his new wife to a new religious awakening.[1]

Thomas Shephard had had his own crisis. In his last year at the Puritan powerhouse of Emmanuel College, Cambridge, he nearly died, but was saved 'by the Lord calling him and toward the end of this year when I was most vile (after I had been next unto the gates of Death by the small pox the year before) the Lord began to Call me home to the fellowship of his grace.' This type of conversion probably happened to many other regicides, but for most of them the evidence is lacking.

Shephard hated bishops, believing himself to be persecuted by the Archbishop of York, Richard Neile, and Alured would have shared this opinion. Presbyterianism – those Puritans desiring church government by local elders rather than officials selected from above – were the main opposition to the king in the first stage of the civil war. Most of our regicides went beyond Presbyterianism. Many belonged to independent congregations who wanted the right to worship outside the Church of England. Some were separatists, believing the Church to be corrupt and wanting no contact with it. The majority of the fifty-nine were Independents, or separatists, rather than merely Presbyterians, and Alured was no exception.

Many of our regicides were influenced by charismatic men preaching radical religious views. Alured was influenced by Shephard, and later in the 1640s he was a member of Philip Nye's congregation (who wanted a plain and simpler worship and the right to be left alone). Nye was a famous theologian, important during the civil war and afterwards, and he supported the need for a degree of religious toleration. Nye's work would lead to toleration for all religious groups that did not threaten social harmony. Alured's exact views are not known, but many regicides with the same influences agreed with Nye's conclusion. Many regicides, perhaps even the majority, believed in tolerance of sincere Protestants who differed over details but shared fundamental beliefs, an idea ahead of its time in the 1650s.

Cutting off a king's head and declaring a commonwealth without a monarch or an assembly of aristocrats suggests that the regicides were republicans. In the true definition of the word, only a dozen or so actively hated the concept of rule by a single person. Our regicides were mostly opposed to Charles I as a king rather than kingship in general. Their opposition to the king was based on religion. They had concluded that he was a danger to the Protestant church, and many believed that the king's defeat in war was God's witness against him. Some millenarians believed that the execution of the king anticipated the reign of Jesus on earth. Alured was not a millenarian; those who believed in the immediate creation of a heaven on earth tended to shout it from the rooftops.

The religious views that motivated the regicides may seem alien to us, but they solve an important problem. Most of them were not social and political revolutionaries. Like Alured, they were influential, propertied men with immense power, mostly in their localities, so it is hard to uncover their true motivation without a real understanding of their faith. By 1648 England was a country in economic, political and social crisis, but it was religion that moved them rather than the ideologies that drove the later French or Russian revolutionaries.

Alured may have been some kind of republican, probably of the pragmatic kind. On the day of the king's execution, 30 January, he was named to the Commons committee for repealing the past legislation of Charles I. This could have been an attempt to lay the foundations for a republican form of government, but may simply have been an attempt to remove the influence of a bad king and a tainted dynasty. For most of the regicides it was the latter. On the morning of the execution, the regicides had not abolished the office of king.

Many of the regicides were involved in transatlantic trade and looked across the ocean for their financial and spiritual fulfilment, usually to the West Indies and the New World. Most commercial trading ports, with the exception of Bristol, were solidly for Parliament when war came. Alured became an investor in the Providence Island Company. They were interested in the Americas as a place where Charles and his bishops could not influence their religion or interfere with their livelihood. Many Puritans emigrated. Some came back in the 1640s to fight the king, and a small number became regicides. Some fled there after the Restoration. Alured's mentor Thomas Shephard tried to emigrate in 1632. His first attempt led to a shipwreck off the coast of Norfolk and subsequent rescue by a women called Mrs Corbet, almost certainly a relative of the local regicide of the same name. He did manage to get to the New World. Like most Puritans, he did not doubt God for making him endure terrible conditions while crossing the Atlantic, but praised Him for sparing them from drowning.

Many, but not all, of those who became regicides started their struggle against the king before the fighting started in England in 1642. Alured supported the Scots in their war against the king in 1639 when Charles tried to impose the kind of Catholic-looking religious changes on Scotland. He did this not through any love for the Scots, but the fear that England was next. Fear and suspicion of Scotland runs through the lives of most regicides, even when the Scots fought against the king between 1644 and 1646. The Scots were Presbyterians, the union was recent, and the execution was an English affair. All fifty-nine were English or Welsh.

Alured was reported to Charles' Privy Council and given a bond of £2,000 on good behaviour and ordered to stay in London, showing how wealthy his family were and the fact that he was regarded as more dangerous in his native Yorkshire than the capital.

When war came our regicides fell into two groups: recruiters and recruited. Most of them were gentlemen who became officers who spent their own money on equipping themselves and their men. Others simply joined the army as volunteers. On the outbreak of civil war in 1642, Alured was commissioned as a captain of horse under the Earl of Essex, but his main field of operations was in Yorkshire under Fernando, Lord Fairfax, the father of Thomas Fairfax, who became the most important military commander of the civil war.

Alured spent most of the First Civil War as a soldier in Lord Fairfax's northern Parliamentarian army, and is known to have fought at Adwalton Moor in 1643, and possibly at the more famous battle of Marston Moor in 1644. Many of our regicides were promoted into senior positions in the army in 1644–45, when the New Model Army was created. Alured was promoted regularly by Fairfax in full knowledge of his religious beliefs and did indeed become a colonel in 1645.

Most of our regicides were, or later became, Members of Parliament, and the pattern tells us much about their social status. Some were members in 1640 (or earlier if they were older); others took their father's seats in the 1640s, so were essentially in the same class. Some lower status regicides were recruited in 1645–47 after proving themselves to be an ally of Parliament through fighting or other war work. Alured was an MP in 1640, confirming his position as a higher status regicide.

Some regicides were national figures while some were mostly local ones, even if they secured a seat in the Westminster Parliament. Alured did enter London with the victorious Parliamentary army in 1646, but like most regicides his war was mostly local and regional. Like many of the 'regional regicides', he was a committee man in the war too, collecting the customs in Hull and exercising other administrative tasks during the war, or at least taking the responsibility for them if not physically present to do the work.

Regicides also fall into two distinct groups in another sense: those who became richer because of war, and those who became poorer. Alured probably became poorer, owing to his own personal bad luck and the habit of Parliament of reneging on its obligations. Many regicides had their houses destroyed by enemy action, but Alured's county seat in Hull, Charterhouse, was destroyed by his patron and ally, Thomas Fairfax, during the first siege of Hull in 1643. His house had come into the family's possession after the dissolution of the monasteries.[2] Like many of the Puritan gentry, they had benefited greatly from the Reformation that they claimed to despise. The house's location, on the northern boundary of the city, made it easy for the Royalists to occupy and use as a siege point, and it was consequently demolished.

Although the family were able to sell the surrounding gardens, the site was later cleared and the Alureds never recovered. The family's losses were later recognised by the House of Commons, who agreed to pay £5,000 in compensation, but often this money was never paid or was honoured only years later. On his deathbed in August, it was reported to the House of Commons that Alured was now owed £8,769. The increase may well have been the thousands of pounds of his own money spent supplying the Parliamentary forces of Yorkshire. On 28 August 1651 an ally in the Commons asked for it to be paid but Alured died soon after. On 20 November 1651 his widow, Mary, petitioned for the money, but was equally unsuccessful. Alured was by no means the only regicide with a strong and resilient wife who worked hard in petitioning for justice for their family when her husband was in danger.

Alured, like many Puritans fighting in Fairfax's northern army, would have been alarmed at the number of English Catholics the king was ready to employ in his defence. Most regicides were united by a fear of creeping Catholic practices in the Church and traitorous foreign influences. One regicide with specific knowledge of this was **John Moore.**

Moore (1599–1650) was from Liverpool, and the only Lancastrian to sign the death warrant. Lancashire was the only English county with an active network of Catholic families who had real power and influence. For other Puritans, the dangers of 'popery' were often theoretical until the civil war began, but for Moore and his family, it had always been part of everyday life and politics.

John Moore was a second-generation Puritan and republican. His father, Edward, held the same views and had spent four days in the Tower of London by order of King Charles. In the Commons in June 1626 Edward was bold enough to claim that 'we were born free and must continue free if the king would keep his kingdom'. This form of republicanism – allowing a monarch only if they were considerably less powerful than the House of Commons – was a more common variant than the small number of regicides who opposed the monarchy in principle. In 1631 Edward was involved in an altercation with Catholic William Norris. Moore senior was seriously injured in the swordfight, and the King's Court of Star Chamber – hated by father and son as an example of an over powerful monarchy – sent Norris to prison and protected Moore, which may well have elicited mixed feelings.

The Moore family was old and wealthy. John Moore was a major transatlantic merchant, with business activity in Barbados and the West Indies. Global trade was a growing feature of Stuart England. The place to make most money was in the East rather than the West, but the Levant and East India companies were government monopolies, where money and influence flowed to the Crown and its favourites. Families like the Moores looked to the New World, because in terms of both trade and faith the Stuarts could be excluded.

The Moores had to struggle to maintain their status. Liverpool was a place of divided loyalties, and religious and political tension, and the family's pre-eminence was challenged by a large number of Catholic families as well as the Earl of Derby, a Protestant but also a Royalist.[3] The Liverpool Puritans did well to gain one of the two seats in the 1641 Parliament, and John Moore became associated with those MPs who supported a vigorous prosecution of the war and opposed any compromise with the king. His appearances on House of Commons committees show his interests: on 5 December he protested against the monopolies that had directed trade to the king's friends; in February he was opposing superstition and idolatry (longhand for Catholicism); and in November he was hunting for recusants (strictly speaking, merely somebody who refused to submit to authority, but in reality, Catholics again).

He was a tolerable soldier as well as a parliamentary committee man. When the war started, he worked hard to take Lancashire for Parliament in the face of massive Royalist support in the county, taking Liverpool in May 1643. He was made a Colonel and Governor of Liverpool, but he lost the town to Prince Rupert. Moore escaped by sea, and never regained his reputation as a soldier even when Liverpool was back in Parliament's hands by October.

Prince Rupert, the nephew of Charles I, was a formidable asset to the Royalist cause, despite his youth (born 1619) or perhaps because of it. His success was based on recklessness and skill but he developed a reputation for cruelty after victory. When Liverpool was briefly taken, the regicide's father, Edward, was appalled. Rupert was guilty of 'putting all to the sword for many hours. Good Lord deliver us from the cruelty of bloodthirsty papists.' People were left naked and starving, according to contemporary sources.[4]

Men like the Moores were motivated by a fear of Catholics. The Catholic rebellion of November 1641 had led to the murder of Protestant settlers in Ireland. There was much anti-Catholic propaganda alongside the real suffering, and it increased the suspicion of the king, who many feared would use any army raised in England against Parliament rather than against the Irish rebels. Every single one of our regicides would have taken this into consideration, and for many of them the management of Ireland was to be an important part of their career, and, in some cases, would be their graveyard.

In 1642 John Moore had subscribed £600 to aid Protestants. Liverpool would have been filling up with refugees from the events in Ireland, which had helped provoke civil war. Other more famous regicides like

Edmund Ludlow had their awareness heightened by Protestant refugees coming into northern ports and the capital. It was a warning of what might happen to Protestants if they lost the fight, as they did temporarily in Liverpool in 1644.

Parliament reformed the army in 1645 with the Self-denying Ordinance, which effectively made people choose between their political and military roles; they could not have both. The regulation was aimed at Moore and men like him who had not been judged as particularly effective. He was relieved of his command and became a full-time administrator.

Like Alured and the vast majority of regicides, Moore opposed a settlement with the king after 1646. He was allowed to keep his seat when the army purged the Commons of the king's supporters in December 1648, and helped to organise security arrangements at King Charles' trial. Moore signed the death warrant as a republican and Puritan, and a representative of the merchant classes and the north of England. There seemed to have been a deliberate attempt to create a document that represented all strands of the political nation, and Moore was a useful addition.

We have some clues as to Moore's personality. Adam Martindale, his mild-mannered clerk, seemed to have a reasonable opinion of him, but called his family 'utterly intolerable, hell on earth and thieves'. As a man without great military victories or political triumphs, Moore was forgotten very quickly, but he stands as an example of a powerful force, without which the war and regicide would not have happened. Like many more famous regicides, he died in Ireland of a fever when fighting for the new commonwealth, showing his fear and hatred of Catholics to the last.

Fear of episcopal power, and the king's use of it, was a key motivation for **John Blakiston**. Blakiston was a keen regicide who did not miss a day of the trial, but outlived his monarch by a mere six months, dying at the age of forty-six in June 1649. Like Alured and Moore, it was the religious policies of King Charles and Archbishop Laud that estranged him from the religious establishment. Unlike them, Blakiston seemed to have come to this conclusion on his own. He was born in County Durham, a place where the Prince Bishops' rule was absolute. His father, Marmaduke, was a supporter of Laud and actively worked to increase the bishops' power and influence, becoming very wealthy with four lucrative church posts in Durham and Yorkshire. Some of the same advantages would have been available to the son – though his elder brother inherited much of his father's wealth – but John Blakiston rejected them and opted for struggle instead.

Blakiston may have had a mid-life spiritual crisis in 1631. He was prosecuted by the King's Court of High Commission in 1636, accused of five years' absence from church, which predated Laud. It was Laud who upset most Puritans so Blakiston was an early adopter in a hostile environment, which shows his determination. Blakiston was also in trouble with the king because of his feud with a man called Yeldard Alvey. He did not like Alvey's Laudian-inspired version of Protestantism, and had stopped going to services led by him.

The ecclesiastical record that eventually got him excommunicated has survived, and feels quite modern. The story goes that both Blakiston and Alvey were at the same wedding reception when Alvey apparently started to lecture Blakiston's wife, Susan, about religion. Blakiston seems to have verbally assaulted the vicar, accusing him of taking away his husband's power over his wife, and of 'seventy different kinds' of heresy, which was probably an exaggeration brought on by wounded spousal pride.

Alvey did have a reputation for enjoying such talks with attractive women, and his enemies sometimes suspected improper motives. Blakiston may well have been jealous; Blakiston's pedigree was grander than Alvey's and here he was, laying down the law on his faith to his own wife. Not only was it an unacceptable break with patriarchy, there may have been the inference that his wife, as the weaker vessel, would be easily swayed by the silver-tongued Alvey.

This is an important point that applies to many of the regicides, and most of the rebels against the king. They were not trying to overthrow the existing order, they were not trying to liberate society, and there was nothing about Puritanism that meant more freedom for women. None of the regicides believed in the equality of women, not even most of the radical Independent churches who mostly did not allow women to preach. When new forms of government were being discussed from 1647, nobody suggested votes for women.

Blakiston was not short of powerful religious friends in Newcastle, but was trumped when Alvey got Archbishop Laud involved. Having lost, Blakiston was (literally and metaphorically) unrepentant, seeing it as a punishment from God for not acting faster and more effectively, and vowing to follow his own light in opposition to the superstition that was 'rising up like hemlock'. He vowed to take action. So it seems clear why Blakiston was an eager member of the war party in 1642 as MP for Newcastle.[5]

Blakiston shared with many other regicides an interest in investing in the New World and in the governance of Ireland. He played an active part in the trial, and was one of a handful of key regicides who were specifically tasked with making it a safe and solemn occasion. His main contribution was redesigning the Great Seal of England. Monarchs signified their royal assent to public documents by affixing to them impressions of their Great or Broad Seals. The existing one in 1649, showing Charles on his throne and declaring him king and defender of the faith, was hardly suitable for a trial in which he was fighting for his life in a court on already shaky authority. A new one was designed with Parliament replacing one man as the symbol of authority.

The reason for Blakiston's death is unknown, but he clearly saw that it was imminent. His will was dated 1 June 1649 and he was reported dead by 6 June. Parliament gave his widow, Susan, £3,000, mostly from the estate of William Widdrington, who had fought for the king and was now in exile. Susan, who was older than Blakiston when they married, was still alive in 1660. This is known because the Royalists confiscated all her estates in May of that year.

None of our first three regicides were convinced that Protestantism would survive: Alured feared Catholic magnates; Moore was convinced of the malignity of Irish rebels; and Blakiston hated bishops. All three would have worried about the powerful Catholic nations of Europe, like the Spanish Empire, stuffed full of gold from its plundering of South America. The Thirty Years War, a constant backdrop to events in Britain before and during the civil war, was putting Protestantism in peril. The Stuart monarchy, represented by Charles I with his Catholic wife, Henrietta Maria, was doing nothing to help, and had prorogued Parliament for a decade after 1629 so that nothing could be done by MPs. Who would defend the true religion?

Enter **James Temple**. Even the most knowledgeable of historians would struggle to recognise his name. He is not a well-known regicide, and not even the best-known regicide named Temple; he had a less reputable distant relative called Peter (see Chapter 19). However, his story matters, not for what he did in the civil war or execution, but for his story beforehand, when he and people like him felt the need to defend Protestantism from its many enemies.

James Temple came from a Puritan Sussex background and showed his dedication to the cause very early in life. Sussex was not one of the most populous or prominent of the forty counties of England in the seventeenth century, yet it is overrepresented in the number of regicides it provided. Temple had moved to Sussex as a child, and like many of the regicides, his connection was indirect, proving that there was nothing in the soil that made them kill their king. The Royalist historian, Clarendon, admitted that the king's cause was unpopular there.[6]

Temple was not a prominent regicide, and was not even an important Sussex regicide, but he probably deserves more consideration than he receives. At the relatively tender age of twenty-one, he volunteered to defend French Protestants.[7] This was a very dangerous activity, and one that many of the gentry fretted about, but James Temple seems to have been a regicide who actually did something. Aged only nineteen, he took part in a botched expedition to rescue the French Protestants by relieving the siege of La Rochelle. Temple's older brother, John, was killed alongside 4,000 of the 7,000 English soldiers.

Temple is the only one of our regicides so far who lived until the Restoration, although he seemed to have died politically around 1650 when he was relieved of his governorship of Tilbury Fort after suspicion of corruption. He survived in 1660 by adopting the same tactics of other, more famous regicides (see Chapter 22) but is important mostly because he represented a real fear for the fate of the true faith against a powerful set of enemies; one that spurred many more prominent people into action.

Peregrine Pelham was a little like Blakiston and Moore. He was a prosperous merchant, importing wine and exporting metal from his base in Hull.[8] He was born in Bosham, Sussex, but lived most of his life in East Yorkshire. His background was more modest than most regicides. Most of the higher status regicides had a pre-war life story that included university (generally Cambridge) and the Inns of Court; a smaller number advanced through trade. Pelham's father thought it appropriate to apprentice him to a Hull merchant and Pelham moved up from successful businessmen to sheriff, alderman and MP. When he was chosen by the Hull burgesses as their MP in 1640, he was the second-most successful local businessman, replacing John Lister, the most successful one, who had just died.

Pelham did as much as more famous generals and politicians to secure a victory for Parliament. Hull was vital for both sides. It stored the weapons and armoury for the whole of the north of England, which had been used in 1639 to fight the Scots, so it was no accident that the king was demanding entrance to the city four months before the civil war in England even started. In April 1642, along with John Hotham, Pelham barred the king's entry into the city. Hotham, despite this act of bravery and ground-breaking precedent for disobedience, had to have his resolve stiffened by Pelham and the Yorkshire-trained bands, a volunteer militia body. He is our first regicide who used the power of the trained bands for political ends.

Pelham was well aware of his contribution: 'I kept the King out of Hull when he came in person (although I had not such instructions from the House) – where there was a very great magazine in which I suppose I saved the state above £100,000.' In a way, Pelham was being modest rather than boastful. The loss of Hull, its armoury and its strategic sea and river position could have produced an early victory for the Royalists. The Battle of Edgehill was the first pitched battle of the civil war and was a bloody and indecisive draw. The resources of the Hull armoury might have tipped the battle into the Royalists' favour, with significant consequences for the course of the war, if Pelham had not saved the town for Parliament.

One of the major sources for the more obscure king-killers is Mark Noble's book of 1798, *The Lives of the Regicides*. Noble's work was produced during the Napoleonic Wars. France had committed regicide and the subsequent war and threat of invasion had created economic, social and political upheaval – just as it had in the English Civil War – and the Tory cleric's book was a warning in the form of mini character assassinations. For the gentry regicides, those with some social status, his accusation was that they were unnatural, ungrateful (especially if the king had been good to them at some point) and ambitious. For those lower down the social scale, they were presented as the weak tool of other, more ruthless men, too stupid to achieve such results on their own, or just men whose sudden power went to their heads and allowed them to be greedy. For both kinds of regicide, Noble blamed family and religious demagogues, because of course he could not blame the king.

Pelham, according to Noble's schemata, was a weak tool of more competent evil men, and his 'whole family were inimical to the court'. When he entered Parliament he fell in with 'an ungovernable set of [the] unreasonable', who followed their own interests rather than that of their sovereign. Pelham put himself in the war party in parliament, worked hard and was effective. When John Hotham showed signs of vacillation and treachery to Parliament, Pelham was happy (with the help of his regicide ally, Alured) to support his execution, and that of his son the day before, adding to his agony.

Pelham was also a committed Parliamentarian. A large number of his letters were discovered in 1884, in which he writes to his small electorate, the burgesses of Hull, with real concern for their welfare, and with (mostly anecdotal and second-hand) descriptions of battles. He also continued to trade. In 1646 the House of Commons reported that Pelham had been persecuted by traders in the Netherlands regarding an unspecified act of criminality over a trade deal. The MPs reminded them that Pelham had parliamentary privilege.

Most regicides were created in three phases. In the early days of the war, they were usually members of the war party, who preferred to defeat the king before any negotiation. This was certainly the case with Pelham. His letters show distaste for the half-hearted way in which the war was being fought in the first three years, and a lack of respect for the Earl of Essex who was leading it.

Secondly, attitudes were hardened by events, as often happens in war. Pelham's fears that Charles could not be trusted were confirmed when the king's diplomatic correspondence was captured and published after the Battle of Naseby (1645). These letters showed a willingness to fight with the assistance of Irish Catholics in England and brought Pelham to the conclusion that only total military victory would suffice. The third stage is the Second Civil War of 1648, where Charles's restarting of the war was seen as betrayal, and his defeat interpreted as a message from the Almighty. At this point men like Pelham came to the desperate conclusion that the king had to die. Many of our regicides had the same experiences.

Pelham, like Blakiston, Moore and Alured, was a local man drawn into a national struggle that engulfed the country. There was always a tension between serving the two. In September 1649, with the king dead and a republic declared, the burgesses of Hull selected Pelham to be their mayor, perhaps unsurprisingly, considering the work-rate shown in his letters. But the House of Commons had other ideas. It was not willing to relinquish the services of a person who had been thought considerable enough to be appointed one of the king's judges, and proposed a particular order that 'the town should receive no prejudice in respect of their charters or liberties by his absence nor by his not coming down to be sworn into office on the appointed day'. The Commons then unilaterally appointed his deputy as temporary and then permanent mayor after his death in March 1650.

Unlike the vast majority of regicides, he seemed to have failed to use his power and influence to make money for himself. He died with no will, which suggests his death was sudden, or that there was nothing to distribute. He was owed over £7,000, and the Commons offered £500 to feed the surviving family and pay for his funeral. They formed a committee to see if more could be done. For a man who saved Parliament in 1642 and clearly worked harder than most, he probably deserved better.

Chapter 2

The Main Regicide
Henry Ireton

The prominence of Oliver Cromwell – as well as his own premature death – has consigned **Henry Ireton** (born 1611) to the margins of history. This is unwarranted, and is not what people believed at the time. When victims were chosen by the victorious Royalists for a grisly and humiliating post-mortem execution in 1661, Ireton, who had been dead for a decade, was still remembered with hatred. He mattered, and was arguably the most important regicide of all, especially if the history is framed around the period 1642 to 1649 only.

Royalists wanted revenge on the man who first envisioned the trial of the king. Ireton was that man, not Oliver Cromwell. Ireton showed more leadership, took more robust action, and supplied more of the intellectual arguments for the unprecedented judicial process than Cromwell. Ireton also mattered because he was the only man on earth who could influence Oliver Cromwell to any practical extent. Where Ireton went, Cromwell would follow, and it was that way round, at least until the execution of the king.

Ireton was ten years younger than Cromwell, and his life mirrored that of his more famous friend. Ireton went to Oxford and the Inns of Court in the 1620s but does not seem to have completed his degree or practised law for very long. This was less of a personal setback than it would be today; a year or so at university and a smattering of law to allow him to run his family estates was all that was needed.

What do we know about Ireton's personality? The hostile commentator Anthony Wood[1] says Ireton left university prematurely because he had the 'character of a stubborn and saucy fellow towards the seniors and therefore his company was not wanting'. Both friends and enemies agree that he was a formidable character, and very much a Puritan in

15

his religious views. Fellow believer, Lucy Hutchinson, wife of John Hutchinson, described Ireton as 'a very grave, serious, religious person', and she was somebody who rarely had kind words for anybody.

Ireton was probably the braver man before the civil war. He was opposing the power of bishops before the war through petitions and protest, and there is no evidence that Cromwell was doing such things. However, when the civil war started, neither man agonised much about military resistance to the king. Both were very quick to raise a troop of horse for Parliament a full two months before official hostilities started. Fellow regicide John Hutchinson did the same and both families were brave to do so. Ireton and Hutchinson's Nottinghamshire was far more supportive of the king than Cromwell's home county of Huntingdonshire, which was one of the reasons that King Charles chose Nottingham to raise his standard in August 1642. All three families rebelled despite being surrounded by powerful Royalists. In an age when fainter hearts would hang on to neutrality and then join the strongest side when that was no longer an option, these actions clearly marked out Cromwell, Ireton and the Hutchinsons as people of principle.

Ireton's military record was exemplary. He moved south to fight with the Earl of Essex after initially fighting in his home county. He became a soldier of national importance at the Battle of Gainsborough in 1643, the start of a lifetime's association with Cromwell. Ireton shared Cromwell's resolve to fight the war until the king was defeated, which was not common in the ranks of the Earl of Essex's army, or in the House of Commons in 1642 and 1643. When Cromwell criticised the half-hearted prosecution of the war by Manchester and Essex in 1644, Ireton supported him. Like most of the military regicides, the key year for Ireton was 1645, when he became one of the commanders of a regiment of the New Model Army.

Ireton played a vital part in the Battle of Naseby (1645), promoted by Fairfax on the eve of battle, at Cromwell's request. He nearly died on that day. A hostile source described it thus[2]: 'After a vigorous combat Ireton's wing was defeated by Prince Rupert. He himself received two wounds in the face and was made prisoner, but when Rupert by rashly pursuing the Parliamentarians lost the advantages of his success and when the valour and skill of Fairfax and Cromwell had turned the fortune of the day.'

Ireton was rescued by Cromwell and Fairfax at Naseby. Ireton's thigh was run through with a pike, and his face seared with a strike from a halberd (a 6-ft-foot long combined spear and battleaxe), and his horse shot under him. He was saved only when Cromwell's 'reckless' attack on Prince Rupert's forces allowed Ireton time to escape from his temporary imprisonment. There was a point of difference here: Ireton never had a reputation for tactical brilliance like Cromwell, but was never as rash on the battlefield as Cromwell.

The Battle of Naseby was a metaphor for the eventual defeat of the king: plenty of bravery on both sides, but more skill and discipline on the part of the Puritan armies, which saved the life of a future regicide on that day. The other hero of Naseby was the commander of the New Model Army, Thomas Fairfax, a man who at the time fought the king with the same belief as Ireton and Cromwell, but could not in the end follow them in taking the final step.

In 1646 the city of Oxford surrendered and the military defeat of the king was apparent. Ireton, like Cromwell and Fairfax, thought that they had achieved their war aims. It was at this point that Ireton married Cromwell's daughter, Bridget, at her father's headquarters at Holton, Oxfordshire. Ireton probably believed that his fighting days were over and he could settle into married life. He had been courting Bridget for a year and they were well matched. 'Biddy' was an intensely religious woman, concerned with the state of her soul to the point of unnecessary joylessness (according to her father anyway) and Ireton was as intelligent, reserved, and religiously-minded as his new wife. Physically he was tall, dark and moderately handsome, with bushy black hair and beard, which was striking and uncommon at the time.

So, the two men, whose views on religion were identical, and who had forged a friendship in war, were now related by marriage. Cromwell advised his daughter about her relationship with her new husband: 'That which is best worthy of love in thy husband is that of the image of Christ, which he bears; look on that and love it best.' It is no surprise that Cromwell expressed his views through the prism of religion, saying that the love of God should be valued far above the love that God had created for man. It is the type of thing that Ireton would also have said, although presumably not about himself. In the same correspondence, Cromwell teases his daughter by saying that he did not address a letter to Ireton because of the long intense reply that he would give: 'Dear Daughter, I write not to thy husband, partly to avoid trouble — for one line of mine begets many of his.' Cromwell has gone down in history as very serious and intense, and he thought Ireton was even more so, which says a lot.[3]

Both men shared the same confidence about how events would play out after the king's defeat. They had fought to ensure that Parliament could negotiate from a position of strength, and so expected that negotiations would produce a weakened monarchy. They also expected that the victorious army of 20,000 soldiers would be given their payment of arrears, immunity from prosecution, and a religious settlement that allowed Protestants to worship freely.

Their confidence was misplaced. There was not going to be such a settlement in 1646 because their military victory had decided nothing. Defeat on the battlefield did not stop Charles from being the legitimate monarch. It was not a war to depose him, but an attempt to rein him in, and Charles did not feel weakened by defeat. Monarchy was a divine trust; he would not jeopardise it by compromising with the enemy, not even a victorious one.

The soldiers had won the war, but negotiations with the king would be done by Parliament, not by the army. There was a Presbyterian majority in the Commons that wanted neither religious toleration nor harsh treatment of the monarch, and did not wish to support a ruinously expensive army now that the war had been won. From 1647 there was a concerted campaign to remove the leaders of the New Model Army apart from Fairfax, settle with the king and reduce the army by fifty per cent, sending the remainder of the soldiers to Ireland. All officers would have to sign a declaration that would prevent the religious toleration that many soldiers wanted.

Successful officers like Ireton had actually weakened their position by winning the war. The huge army was the main reason for the massive rise in taxation. Now it could be removed, both as a political force and a drain on the taxpayer, making Parliament more popular and more able to resist men like Ireton who supported the demands of the army yet relied on their continued existence for his own power.

In 1646 Charles had surrendered to the Scots and feigned a willingness to settle the Church on Presbyterian lines, which was the original demand of the Scots when they joined with the English in 1644 in the war against him. His plan was a crude attempt to play army and Parliament against each other and restart the war with the help of the Scots. By the end of 1646 the Scots had seen through his prevarication and sold him to the English Parliament. The House of Commons raised the £400,000 cost by selling bishops' land; one the few measures that both sides could agree on. The Scottish army withdrew from England, further emboldening the Commons to deal quickly and harshly with its now redundant standing army. Charles was back in Parliament's hands on 30 January 1647. Exactly two years later his head would fall into a basket as a traitor: a fate that almost no one wanted, or could have predicted, in 1647.

The dispute between army and Parliament was exacerbated when former army officers transferred to the new battlefield. Since 1642 the House of Commons had lost a third of its members through death, migration to the king's Parliament in Oxford, or expulsion. By 1645 the improving military situation meant the new members could be 'recruited', in the sense of filling the vacant seats, without any of the military implications. Ireton became MP for Appleby in the second wave of recruiter elections in October 1645. There were over 235 new MPs over the course of eighteen months. Many were Presbyterian 'moderates', but others were religious Independents and about twenty were army officers.

Many of the less important regicides, who were not the kind of people with the status to get elected to a normal pre-war Parliament, entered the political arena at this point. Forty-three of the regicides were MPs and the majority were 'recruiters'. After the frustrations of a bloody war and a failure to negotiate a peace, these men were angrier and less prone to compromise than those they had replaced. This explains why the 1649 execution warrant was dominated by army officers and the Members of Parliament who supported them.

Ireton threw himself wholeheartedly into the political struggle that was developing between Parliament and the army, which was almost as bitter as the war itself. An example of this was the meeting between a parliamentary delegation and the officers in Saffron Walden on 21 March 1647. The parliamentary commissioners were there to disband the army and sent a loyal minority to Ireland. The choice of this town was due to a parliamentary demand that the army keep at least twenty-five miles from London. There was good reason for this: the army's grievances were real and the attitudes in the ranks were hardening. Agitators had been elected by regiments to petition and new groups were appearing, demanding political reforms as well as economic justice for soldiers. A list of parliamentary demands was soon superseded by an army petition led by Ireton and other regicides, John Okey, Robert Lilburne, Thomas Pride and William Goffe.

Ireton must have been to the forefront, as a week later he was called to a parliamentary commission accused of collecting signatures by force. Ireton's chief accuser was Denzil Holles, a prominent Presbyterian opponent of the army, who had proposed in the Commons that those who collected signatures were the enemy of the state. In April 1647 the Commons had to prohibit a proposed duel between them. Holles went on to call them 'disturbers of the peace' and members of the 'vicious party': a kick in the teeth for those who had achieved peace with their own blood. To men like Ireton this was not the fruits of victory, but a bitter betrayal and defeat.

His friend Cromwell felt the same, but was inactive. In early 1647 he was having one of his regular bouts of depressive melancholy and real physical afflictions that laid him low for at least the first quarter of the year. Ireton became the driving force. In June 1647 the army physically took control of the king from the parliamentary semi-imprisonment he had enjoyed since February. This was a turning point. It is hard to work out who was behind it. Fairfax, the leading army commander, did not know. If Cromwell knew then it was surprising that he would choose to be in London when it happened, making himself vulnerable to Parliament's revenge. Ireton, therefore, was probably behind it.

Despite Ireton's apparently radical actions, he merely wanted a settlement with the king, not great social change. In August 1647 he and Cromwell formulated a settlement called the Heads of Proposals, which was much more generous than the one that the Presbyterians had offered the king. It allowed freedom of worship for Protestants, a maintained episcopacy with reduced powers, a council of state to deal with foreign affairs, and parliamentary oversight of the armed forces. He was being offered better terms than those proposed by either the Commons or the Scots, who both shared a narrow-minded Presbyterianism that could not countenance a settlement with bishops. Under Ireton's proposals, he would be treated like a king but not allowed to rule. It is what many MPs wanted, and it seemed like the basis for a settlement to many moderates. Charles thought otherwise.

This was the king's chance to secure an unlikely political victory after a military defeat. He felt under no duress and was feeling quite comfortable. Cromwell and Ireton allowed him to use the banned Church of England prayer book and to have his own chaplains. But Charles still saw himself as crucial to the constitution and therefore having the upper hand, and believed he could play each side against the other. This rather explained his confidence when addressing Ireton: 'You cannot be without me; you will fall to ruin if I do not sustain you.' Ireton knew what the king was trying to do, telling him: 'Sir, You have the intention to be arbiter between Parliament and us, and we mean to be it between Your Majesty and Parliament.' The King's reply was over-confident and complacent: 'I shall play my game as well as I can.' Ireton's riposte was a prediction of later events: 'If your majesty has a game to play, you must give us leave to play ours.' 'Ours' meant the army, not the MPs.

By 1647 there was a fourth power in the land: army radicals, called 'Levellers' by their enemies, whose influence in the ranks meant that their demands needed to be taken seriously by army 'grandees' like Ireton and Cromwell. They all met in debate at St Mary's Church, Putney, in October, in what was to be England's first debate about its governance. There was some agreement. Some Leveller demands were similar to the aspirations of Ireton and Cromwell, which is not a surprise as both were convinced of the need for a weakened monarchy with an attenuated hold on religious consciences.

The disagreements were about the depth of political representation. The Levellers' document 'The Agreement of the People' called for the vote for all men who were not servants, thus extending the vote to nearly half of the adults in the country, a level of representation not actually achieved until 1918. There was no demand from any of the ruling institutions for this level of democracy, and Ireton's reply at Putney was to reinforce the argument against the vote for the poor for the next 200 years: 'I think that no person hath a right to an interest or share in the disposing of the affairs of the kingdom, and in determining or choosing those that determine what laws we shall be ruled by here – no person hath a right to this that hath not a permanent fixed interest in this kingdom.'

In 1647 Ireton and Cromwell were social conservatives who wanted to settle with their king. The only 'right' they could offer the ordinary person was the natural right to life. Ireton believed that a king constrained by a parliament of propertied men would be enough, just like before the war. Ireton was going back to a time before the Stuarts, not (in his mind) recklessly forward to some utopian and impracticable future.

The Leveller view, eventually defeated by men like Cromwell and Ireton, has survived the centuries better than their vision. The 'Agreement of the People' demanded religious toleration by limiting the power of parliament: 'We do not empower our said representatives to [...] make any laws [...] about matters of faith, religion and God's law.' Some 144 years later, the new republican government of the USA came to the same conclusion in the first amendment to the constitution: 'Congress shall make no law respecting an establishment of religion, or prohibiting the free exercise thereof[4]'.

It was the Second Civil War that sealed the king's fate. While political discussions at Putney were taking place, Charles escaped from Hampton Court and, after his recapture, encouraged and condoned nationwide uprisings from his new prison on the Isle of Wight. This cynical and stubborn restarting of the war hardened hearts. When the first war finished in mid-1646, nobody in power – Presbyterian or Independent – thought another war was possible. The damage caused to a relatively poor country in a mere four years had been remarkable and tragic. Whether it was sky-high taxation, ruined towns and houses, rampant disease, refugees, food shortages made worse by poor harvests, and a death rate as bad, proportionally, as the First World War, the consequences of civil war were clear. Now the king, refusing to accept the defeat that was clearly God's judgement, was starting the misery all over again. When the King was defeated again in late 1648, it was now not just the Levellers who demanded that everyone be subject to the same laws.

Ireton spent most of October 1648 at Windsor Castle formulating a petition to Parliament demanding that the 'same fault may have the same punishment' in law. It was Ireton who was behind it, not Cromwell, and other key regicides such as Ludlow, Goffe, and Harrison were more influential than Cromwell in late 1648.

Cromwell did matter, however. He was the second military power in the land after Thomas Fairfax. Militarily, he came out as the hero of the Second Civil War, rather than Ireton or Fairfax, and masterminded the last crushing victory at Preston in August 1648. He needed Ireton to convince him to move against the king. Contemporary commentators saw this, even if we have forgotten. His consent would be needed, and only Ireton had the key combination of support in the army and the unconditional trust of Oliver Cromwell to get that agreement.

Where Ireton went, Cromwell would follow. Speaking in 1655, the Parliamentarian and lawyer Bulstrode Whitelocke – no friend of either man, but an astute chronicler of events – said, 'No one could prevail so much with Cromwell nor order him so far as Ireton.' He believed that the Ireton petition of October 1648 was the point of no return for the king.

There was still one bulwark defending the king, and that was Parliament. Despite the recruitment of some New Model Army officers, there was still a majority for a settlement with Charles. About twenty army officers had been fighting the Second Civil War, allowing Parliament to carry on without consulting them. For the second time, the army was being robbed of its victory.

Around November 1648, there were the first rumblings in the military about putting the king on trial. The *Army Remonstrance* demanded that the king be brought to justice on the basis that he was not above the law, and by waging war against the nation he had broken his contract with the people. Ireton's regiment was one of the six regiments that took part, and its petition was more strongly worded than most: 'justice should be done on the king, as if he were the humblest commoner.'

The *Remonstrance* also proposed a written constitution. Parliaments would have regular sittings independently of the wishes of the monarch, and there would be a wider voting entitlement based on a much larger (male) electorate. The present Parliament, which had been sitting for six years, would dissolve itself and new elections would be called. This was a limited constitutional monarchy that Charles would have hated.

It was presented to Parliament by another future regicide, Isaac Ewer, a man toughened in war and unmoved by Parliament's refusal to even consider the contents of the petition. The language was beginning to change, and it was ominous. The king was now 'Charles Stuart', the 'man of blood', and calls for justice led to calls for capital punishment, as the natural tariff for the crime committed. Even in November, however, the king's execution was still not the most likely outcome.

By December 1648 it was clear that a majority in Parliament still wished to settle with the king on terms little different from those offered before the second civil war. On 30 November the army reiterated its demands for payment and the recognition of their remonstrance. Some MPs, in a naive belief in the power of their own laws, considered declaring them rebels. On 2 December the army invaded Westminster. The next day was a Sunday and the godly army rested.

Thomas Fairfax was in charge of events, in theory. Ireton was the driving force, both in the actions taken and the ideology behind them.

On a cold winter morning, 6 December 1648, Thomas Pride and Lord Grey of Groby, armed with a list of MPs who wished to settle with the king and further armed with soldiers, excluded those who wanted a settlement, leaving what would be called a 'Rump Parliament' to its enemies. It was a carefully thought out list, divided into two levels of hostility amongst the MPs: 186 were sent away, and forty-five were temporarily arrested and confined.

This was a coup d'état, the only one in British history. It led to the abolition of the House of Lords, the trial and execution of the king and the creation of Britain's only ever republic. Henry Ireton was at the centre of it all; Cromwell was not even in London when it happened, and had not been so since May. Cromwell probably had his own plan to deal with the Commons but accepted Ireton's actions, both as a *fait accompli* and perhaps a better plan than purging the whole house and holding elections, which Ireton certainly considered.

By late December Cromwell had accepted the inevitability of a trial. 'The providence of God has cast this upon us,' he explained to the Commons. And it was providence; something beyond their control. In January 1649, when the 135 High Commissioners for the trial were announced, the first three were Fairfax, Cromwell and Ireton, in that order.

From our point of view in the twenty-first century, Ireton's military influence and his political views are easy to understand, but seeing events through the prism of religion is much harder. On 5 January, with the pressing need to set up a High Court of Justice, Ireton and army officers spent the day listening to the prophetess Elizabeth Poole, asking serious questions about the meaning of her religious visions.

From 1649 to 1651, Ireton loses his pre-eminent place as a regicide. Once again, his career shadowed that of his friend, Oliver Cromwell, as they both went abroad in 1649 to protect the new republic, which seemed to be taken by surprise by the course of events. Ireton's ship to Ireland – still called the *Charles* – was among the seventy-seven ships that followed Cromwell to Ireland two days later. Ireton took charge of military operations in Ireland after Cromwell left in May 1650. Cromwell allowed civilians to be killed without condemnation in Drogheda and Wexford, whereas Ireton, in his siege of Limerick, granted mercy to most of the Limerick defenders, but not the Bishop of Emly, who had long encouraged the people to fight for their country and their faith, and had refused a large bribe which the Cromwellian General had offered him if he would leave the city: 'The ecclesiastics were soon condemned; but, ere the Bishop was dragged to the gibbet, he turned to the dark and cruel man who had sacrificed so many lives, and poured such torrents of blood over the land, summoning him, in stern and prophetic tones, to answer at God's judgment-seat for the evils he had done'. The Bishop and his companion were executed (or martyred) on the Eve of All Saints, 31 October 1651.

It seemed that lack of self-care and overwork hastened Ireton's death in November 1651. Even his implacable enemy, Mark Noble, remarked on this. He seemed initially to have some form of severe fever. Fellow regicide Edmund Ludlow was in Ireland and suffered similarly, but Ludlow survived by not going back to work immediately. Ireton squandered his chance of recovery by riding around looking for a place for his army to escape the appalling wet weather, according to Noble.

When Cromwell received news of his friend's death he was bereft and insisted that he be brought home for a state funeral. Ireton's own funeral, like his career, was an eerie prediction of what was to come for Cromwell. Both had lavish funerals, with a solemn parade from Somerset House to the new vault in Westminster Abbey for the elite of the new regime. The Royalist John Evelyn witnessed the event in February 1652: 'the magnificent funeral of that arch-rebel, Ireton, carried in pomp [...] accompanied with divers regiments of soldiers, horse and foot; then marched the mourners, General Cromwell (his father-in -law), his mock-Parliament men, officers, and forty poor men in gowns, three led horses in housings of black cloth, two led in black velvet, and his charging horse, all covered over with embroidery and gold, on crimson velvet; then the guidons [pennants], ensigns, four heralds, carrying the arms of the State (as they called it).'

Evelyn could see the motive for the elaborate funeral. It was an attempt to legitimise the new state both by basing it on precedent (the funeral was partly based on that of James I) and burying the new elite in Westminster Abbey. It was a political funeral – displays of heraldic pomp and pride were not very 'puritan' – and a quiet night-time funeral with no fuss would have been preferred by Ireton himself.

Most historians assume that the body that was buried in 1652 and dug up again in 1661 was definitely that of Ireton. This seems debatable. Bodies were not routinely repatriated for burial after death abroad, and Ireton, whether he died of the plague or typhus, would not have found people willing to transport him. The original story is that Ireton was embalmed, in another echo of the Cromwell story. This seems difficult to prove, and his body did not show much evidence of that in 1661.

His early death changed history. He seemed to have been more of a republican than Cromwell. Mark Noble believed that, had he lived, he would have resisted the single person rule of his friend. Algernon Sydney went even further, 'If Ireton had not died, the Republic would have been established, and that he would have prevented Cromwell from aspiring to dominion.'

Mark Noble portrayed Ireton as cold-bloodedly vicious and scheming, the Cassius figure as opposed to Brutus in the assassination of Julius Caesar. In the legend, it was Cassius's persuasiveness that provided the rationale for assassination and pushed the hesitant Brutus into action. Cassius was as necessary as Brutus for the death of Caesar, and Ireton is very much the same type of figure. David Farr emphasises that, for the period between the spring of 1647 and the new year of 1649, 'one of the most important influences on Cromwell [...] after God, was Ireton.'[5]

Chapter 3

The Gentry Soldiers

Oliver Cromwell, Richard Deane, John Okey

The greatest of the regicides was **Oliver Cromwell**. This is a statement of the obvious today, but was not the case in the period up to 1649. Victory in the First Civil War (1642–1646) was a team effort, led not by Cromwell but his commander in the New Model Army, Thomas Fairfax. Fairfax was the mastermind behind the military defeat of the king, and was as strong as anybody when fighting for his soldiers' rights, but he baulked at execution. The regicide itself was the work of other men apart from Cromwell, and, as Chapter Two shows, he was not even the main instigator.

Cromwell was born in Huntingdon on 25 April 1599. His father, Robert, was a second son. They were gentry, but they lived modestly. His family were not natural opponents of the monarchy, nor particularly Puritan. His father's brother, Sir Oliver Cromwell, inherited the main family residence in Hinchingbrooke, and King James I was a regular and expensive guest there. Sir Oliver had to sell Hinchingbrooke in 1627, partly due to debts created by a generosity to the king that was never reciprocated, at least not in cash terms, and with it they relinquished their political influence in their county. Cromwell was a junior member of a family that was a fading force in East Anglia. His future looked, in the words of his biographer, Antonia Fraser, 'unremarkable but not unpleasant'.

A Puritan education was chosen for Cromwell under the instruction of a severe anti-Catholic schoolmaster, Thomas Beard of Huntingdon. This was followed by a traditional education at Cambridge and the Inns of Court, which may have been funded by the extended family. He married Elizabeth Bourchier in 1620, making a valuable connection with a wealthy trading family with links in London and Essex, and which was unrelated to the regicide of the same name.

Fast forward to 1640 and Cromwell is the MP for Cambridge, after an adulthood of mixed fortunes. He had returned to Huntingdon after marriage and performed the traditional duties of the gentry in local government. He fell out with them after some intemperate behaviour on his part, and then rather erratically sold most of his property and moved down the geographical and social scale to be a farmer in tiny, isolated St Ives. At this point he had some form of spiritual crisis and became, in his mind, much godlier. Due to his later fame, much of this was recorded. It was probably quite common among the regicides as an alternative path to their opposition to the king's religious policies, especially if there was no history of religious dissent in the family.

He starts to stand out in 1642 when he becomes an active proponent of war, months before other MPs. He raised a troop of horse in Huntingdon, like many similar gentry regicides, and rose through the ranks thanks to his military efficiency and godliness. He was present at the last moment of the Battle of Edgehill in 1642, but drew different conclusions to most about how the war should proceed. He was one of the first people to object to the idea that his side was fighting for 'King and Parliament' and that they were opposing a king ruled by evil advisors in order to reinstate the legal one. The Commons, trying to cover all bases, described its armed forces in a rather tortuous fashion; it was an 'Army employed for the Defence of the Protestant Religion, the Safety of his Majesties Person and of the Parliament, the Preservation of the Laws, Liberties, and Peace of the Kingdom, and Protection of his Majesties Subjects from Violence and Oppression.'[1] Many on the parliamentary side clung on to this idea of 'the king's two bodies' for the first few years of the war. Those who rejected it early were much more likely to become regicides four or five years later, and Cromwell was one of them.

Cromwell became a national figure in 1643 because of his military successes in East Anglia, especially at the Battle of Winceby in October. He worked with Thomas Fairfax for the first time, and won the battle because of the quality of his cavalry. This was one of his major contributions to the defeat of the king. Parliament had most of the advantages in the civil war; they controlled the navy, London, and the richest parts of the country. One of the king's few advantages was the quality and leadership of the cavalry, and it was Cromwell who took that away from him. When his men won at Winceby, it was not a personal

28

achievement, as he was shot from under his horse and played little part, but a victory for new thinking.

This new thinking included recruitment. Having rejected the concept of 'King and Parliament', he recruited men who wanted to win the war. He did not check people's religious views before recruiting them, only a desire to defeat the king mattered: 'The state in choosing men to serve it takes no notice of their opinions, if they be willing faithfully to serve it.' This was meritocratic and tolerant, but it was a tactic to win a war, not a belief in the equality of man.

Cromwell became famous at Marston Moor and Naseby. From 1646 Cromwell is central to the events of the civil wars, but not the kingpin. In military matters in 1646, he was second to Fairfax; in the political struggle of 1647 he was mostly second to Henry Ireton. Cromwell became the leading future regicide in 1648 when he led a military team that won the Second Civil War. Even then it was down to teamwork. The revolt was nationwide this time, and needed even more simultaneous military action.

The rise of Oliver Cromwell after 1649 meant that the other regicides have been viewed in relation to him. The new republic went on to conquer Ireland, bring Scotland to heel at Dunbar, and defeat Charles II at Worcester in 1651. Cromwell led this work. In April 1653 he used his power and prestige to dissolve the Rump Parliament, which had been created by Pride's Purge in 1649, on the grounds that it was corrupt, ineffective and self-perpetuating.

In December 1653 Cromwell became a single ruler under the new written constitution, the Instrument of Government, and he was deserted by the republicans whose main motivation in regicide was to end the rule of individuals. He was never able to prosper with his own Parliaments. His first one lasted for the statutory minimum time – for one term from 3 September 1654 until 22 January 1655 – before it was dissolved, having passed none of Cromwell's eighty-four proposed laws. Cromwell's two further Parliaments were fractious and unsuccessful. They were separated by a period of military rule known as the 'Major-generals', which was an attempt to secure the new state against Royalists and introduce the moral reformation that the Puritan in him wanted.

Cromwell died on 3 September 1658, and was succeeded as Lord Protector by his son, Richard, who was unable to hold together the warring coalitions or establish a new form of governance. These events are told through the experience of the other regicides in the following chapters.

There was no greater soldier for the regime than **Richard Deane** (1610–1653).[2] He fought in England, Ireland, Scotland and Wales, and was crucial to the success of major battles such as Naseby, Preston, Dunbar and Worcester. He also fought in the parliamentary navy. Deane's specialism was breaking down walls with cannon, and developing new tactics with artillery that broke sieges and enabled victory at Sherborne Castle, Truro and Oxford. Deane was also present with Oliver Cromwell at the siege of Basing House in 1645. He died early and was never a politician. He is, therefore, a relatively obscure figure, but there would never have been a Lord Protector Oliver Cromwell without his efforts.

Deane was a member of the gentry, though at the lower end of the group, like Cromwell. He does not seem to have followed the university/ Inns of Court route, and consequently little is known of his early life. The situation is made less clear by the usual attempt of hostile Royalist propaganda to impugn his background with claims of plebeian roots, both at the time and later. Deane's background was not so much misconstrued as completely made up by his enemies. Mark Noble claimed that Deane was a 'Hoyman's assistant' – a hoy being a modest boat carrying small amounts of freight – but this was not true. Noble tended to do this to lesser regicides, and any gaps in their personal background were filled with propaganda, which tells you much more about Noble than it does about Deane.

Deane's family were no friends of the king's religious policies. His mother was a member of the Puritan Wass family. Religion seemed to be Deane's motivation for taking up arms. A close relative was the Mayor of London, who, in 1628, tried to enforce the Sabbath against the resistance of the locals. Deane joined the Earl of Essex's army in September 1642 as a *matross* of artillery. This was a lowly job, assisting the gunner, which was another thing the Royalist propaganda would deride him for later. Among the 'Eighteen Gentlemen of the Ordinance' was an Edward Wass, almost certainly a member of his maternal family and the reason for Deane's appointment. Nepotism, as we might call it today, was one of the natural functions of the extended family in the seventeenth century.

The English Civil War may have been about lots of things, but equality of opportunity was not one of them.

Deane's original posting was due to connections, but his further promotion was based on merit, a common pattern during the turbulence of the civil war. He became an expert in artillery, which was to play a massive part in seventeenth-century warfare, and had become a commissioned officer by the time of the Battle of Edgehill. He was a member of the army of Robert Devereux, 'Old Robin', Earl of Essex, whose reputation for military efficiency was based on little more than his social status. Essex was one of the old guard who fought the war to weaken the king, but those of his ilk had fallen away by 1645.

Deane was present at a famous Parliamentarian defeat at the Battle of Lostwhithiel, in Cornwall, in August-September 1644, a debacle masterminded by 'Old Robin' himself. Essex recognised Deane as 'an honest, judicious and stout man' (stout in the sense of reliable), even when Deane told him that his military position was untenable. Edward Hyde, a Royalist and historian who was gracious enough to see credit in the other side, called him a 'bold and excellent officer'.

Much of Deane's artillery was lost at Lostwhithiel, although 2,500 cavalry had broken through the Royalist lines. Essex escaped by fishing boat and left his army to the Royalists, his undeserved reputation in tatters. Deane's reputation, meanwhile, grew. He became Comptroller of Ordinance, a position that implied responsibility and administrative competence, and continued to fight in some key battles. He was in command of the artillery at Naseby (14 June 1645) and during Fairfax's campaign in the west of England. In 1647, relatively late in the war for a future regicide, he was promoted to colonel and given a regiment. When the war broke out afresh in 1648 Deane went with Cromwell to Wales. As brigadier-general, his leading of the right wing at Preston contributed greatly to final victory against the forces of the king.

By 1647 Deane was seen very much as part of the Cromwellian party, but a follower, unlike Ireton. When Cromwell was ordered by Parliament to go to Ireland in order to get him away from politics, Deane was told to go as well, meaning that he, too, was seen as important enough to be neutralised. They both refused. In June 1647 Deane was present at Newmarket and is reputed to have kissed the king's hand, with Ireton and Cromwell both being present, while merely bowing.

Like Ireton and Cromwell, Deane was determined to support the army against those who would disband or disrespect it. His was one of the regiments that remonstrated against the king in November 1648: 'That the Parliament be desired [...] to consider his own act in taking the guilt of bloodshed upon himself; and accordingly to proceed against him as an enemy to the kingdom.' These would be either his words, or written with his approval.

Deane was one of the first to know Cromwell's mind about the necessity of a trial. He was present when leading lawyers told them that there was no legal justification for trying a king. When the king was sentenced to death, Deane was one of the three regicides tasked with finding the most secure location. He was one of the more determined and talented of their group.

After the war Deane played his part in the subjugation of Ireland. It was not a popular posting; Deane's regiment of foot was one of the three chosen at random (by a small child who matched each regiment with a piece of paper that was either blank or said 'Ireland'). This selection also picked out other regicides (Ireton, Scrope, Hewson and Ewer), which was to be expected as these military men were a power in the land in 1649. It cannot, therefore, be said that he volunteered to serve in Ireland, but he still went, and made his will.

In 1649 Deane was one of three people promoted into the high command of the navy. Their rank – Generals at Sea – explains their role exactly. None of them were experienced naval officers (although Deane may have had some naval training before 1640), but that was not the most important qualification. All were competent and loyal soldiers and they would be expected to take advice from more experienced seamen. His command at sea was interrupted in 1651, when, as major-general he was brought back to the army and took part in the Battle of Worcester. Later he was made president of the commission for the settlement of Scotland, with overall command of the military forces. In April 1653 Cromwell evicted the Rump, and the Generals at Sea had to decide how to react. Deane pledged his loyalty to Cromwell, and this was a great advantage to the new regime.

At the outset of the Battle of the Gabbard against the Dutch on 1 June 1653, Deane was killed. Noble reported that he was smashed in two by a cannonball. It seems that Deane was killed before the battle had really started, and his mangled corpse was covered with a cloak. It must have been a horrific injury if it was thought necessary to prevent the hardened parliamentary sailors from seeing it.

He received a hero's funeral, his body being laid in state at the Queen's House in Greenwich and then carried by barge and, 'attended with many other barges boats in mourning equipages as they slowly along the procession was saluted by the guns from the shipping at the Tower and ordnance planted for that purpose in the way to Westminster Abbey.'[3]

His body lay in state at Greenwich, and after a public funeral he was buried, assisted by Cromwell himself, in Henry VII's chapel at Westminster Abbey. He was disinterred at the Restoration. He was one of the elite of the new regime, and the scale of punishment shows his importance.

John Okey was one of the more socially modest regicides. He was from a prosperous family, but he was a sixth son who would therefore have had to fend for himself. The gentry route of university and the Inns of Court was closed, so instead, like many of the lesser gentry regicides, he became a London merchant. He was a ship's chandler before the civil war and used his transferrable skills as a quartermaster in Essex's army, joining at the bottom, as his social status demanded.

He had a successful career in the army before 1645, and when the New Model Army was formed, Okey was appointed colonel of a regiment of dragoons, a form of mounted infantry troopers capable of quickly advancing, attacking, and then withdrawing from an engagement. It was the only regiment of its kind in the whole parliamentary army.

His motivation, like many others, was religious. He was a Baptist. From a twenty-first century perspective, nothing could sound less dangerous than this moderate, mainstream, and thoughtful Protestant group, but in the seventeenth century the implications of the word were very different. Baptists (or 'Anabaptists', as a term of abuse) did not merely deny the validity of adult baptism. They were seen as a highly disruptive force in society, and they had form. The short-lived Anabaptist rebellion in Germany in 1534 had abolished money, distributed the wealth of the rich to the poor, vandalised cathedrals, destroyed monasteries and introduced compulsory rebaptism for adults. Even a century later, 'Anabaptist' was the preferred term of abuse when religious conservatives wanted to condemn somebody else's beliefs (similar to the twentieth-century usage of a word like 'commie'). When being abused by the ordinary people, they were called 'dippers'.

Those Baptists who came to England were persecuted by Tudor monarchs of both religions, united in their condemnation. It was still the most damning thing that you could say about anybody in the 1640s, despite clear theological differences between English Baptists and their counterparts of a century earlier. They now believed in separating themselves from the state, and using local lay preachers. Four other regicides (Lilburne, Ludlow, Hewson and Tichborne) have also been associated with this relatively small group of people, and their influence on the execution was disproportionate to their number.

Okey's religious views were similar to those of Oliver Cromwell, who himself was criticised for recruiting Baptists to his army. Okey knew the most famous Baptist, John Bunyan, who served in the New Model Army during the final years of the English Civil War. Bunyan's spiritual views were developed as a recruit in late 1644. Okey and Bunyan were both born in Bedfordshire and were members of the same local church in 1653.

Okey's regiment gained fame for their actions at the Battle of Naseby (1645), where his dragoons opened the fighting by firing into the right wing of the Royalist horse from a concealed position. They later delivered probably the first mounted charge by English dragoons, contributing to victory by breaking the morale of the king's infantry. Okey's reaction to Naseby was identical to Cromwell's: he was no more than the humble agent of the Lord, who was doing 'His' work. Their victory, 'should magnify the name of our God that did remember a poor handful of despised men, whom they had thought to have swallowed up before them.' He also attributed his regiment's tactical success to Cromwell, extending Cromwell's undeserved reputation for military genius, though this *enfilade* fire was a common tactic, known to all armies at the time. A battlefield tactician of today would attribute much of Okey's success to a failure of discipline on the part of the Royalist cavalry, but Okey saw it differently.

Okey was a marked man in the Commons because of his background and beliefs. He was one of the officers whose appointment to the New Model Army was blocked in 1644 because of his low status. Okey was captured by the Royalists at the second siege of Bristol, but was released after the city surrendered; another regicide who benefitted from the gentlemanly tactics of the first half of the war.

After the end of the First Civil War, Okey supported the army against Parliament for the same reasons as Cromwell, Ireton and Deane, but seemed more interested in practical protection for the soldiers, especially the regiments that Parliament wanted to disband. His own regiment was not noticeably radical, and he was not particularly associated with the Levellers (he was criticised by Leveller leader John Lilburne as lacking any conviction for political change). Okey was a religious rather than a political regicide. His main interests were a 'reformation of manners'.

During the Second Civil War in 1648 he played a vital part in putting down the Royalist rebellion, especially at the Battle of St Fagan's and the siege of Pembroke Castle. When Okey signed the death warrant he would have done it without hesitation. Charles was an enemy of religious freedom who could not be trusted: a man against whom God had witnessed. He did not serve in Ireland, but had he done so he would have fought with the fanaticism of Cromwell. He was also entrusted with what the Commonwealth called the 'pacification' of Scotland in 1651–1652, but which most neutral observers would have called occupation after the military defeat at Dunbar in 1650.

After his return from Scotland, there was a falling out with Oliver Cromwell. In February 1652 he filed a petition to Parliament calling for reforms to religious governance that would allow the better spread of the gospel, and for the dissolution of the Rump Parliament, which had made little progress in the kind of legal reforms that would allow congregations like his in Bedford to flourish. Cromwell seemed to have dissuaded him. When Cromwell himself scornfully dissolved the same Parliament a mere eight months later, Okey seemed to think he was a hypocrite, believing that Cromwell's reasons were more about power for himself.

Okey was a warm supporter of what was called later the 'Good Old Cause'. This originated with the soldiers who were fighting against the principle of the Stuart monarchy not just the poor behaviour of one monarch, and believed in the rule of a Parliament, without a single powerful person, that would protect fundamental rights. Many regicides signed with this republican motivation in their mind. When Cromwell turned against these ideas in 1653, they turned against him.

So, Okey's attitude to Cromwell as Lord Protector was hostile. Under the rule of Oliver Cromwell, the trappings of monarchy had been imposed on the country by a small group of army grandees with the kind of power over a huge standing army that was not even claimed by the king. In 1654 he signed the petition of the three colonels, drafted by the Leveller and republican John Wildman and Matthew Alured (brother of the regicide), which criticised Oliver Cromwell and the Protectorate. Okey's desire was for the return of a government based on a representative Parliament with no power for the single person, or a power that did not include a 'negative voice' (veto) in decisions made by the Commons: the 'Good Old Cause' in a nutshell.[4]

When Cromwell died, Okey took his chance. The rule of his son proved that a hereditary principle had returned to government. With his republican allies, Scot, Walton and Ludlow, he tried his very best to undermine the new Protectorate of Richard Cromwell. Okey refused to accept the new constitution, and organised a propaganda blitz with Ludlow. The 'betrayal' narrative of 1648 returned. Okey was reputed to have said: 'I see it will be a crime to be an army man – is the expense of our blood nothing?'

The arguments of 1648 were corrosive enough, but what made it worse was the solution of 1648 was also back in fashion: the return of the Rump Parliament. This, according to Okey and others, had been a free Parliament, which was a very generous description. It was one of the tragedies of the 'Good Old Cause' that it became synonymous with nostalgia about the Parliament of 1648–1653. That was the best they could think of. It was no more successful in 1659 in settling the country, and their republican views were as unpopular as they were a decade earlier. Okey wanted a 'free parliament' and plotted and planned to get one. A year later a free Parliament did indeed emerge, but it was full of vengeful Royalists.

Okey made no attempt to modify his position or help the opposition discretely as an insurance policy against the return of Charles II. As a member of a low status family, he had no friends or family on the Royalist side to put in a good word for him. This lack of ambiguity made the decision to flee the country easier for him. There was no reason to believe that he would not be exempted from the general pardon offered by Charles II. He went first to Germany and so forfeited his rights and was declared an outlaw.

His plan to evade 'justice' failed. In 1661, while in the Netherlands, Okey was arrested with regicides John Barkstead and Miles Corbet by Sir George Downing, the English ambassador to the Dutch court.

Downing was, in the words of Samuel Pepys, a 'perfidious rogue' and remarked that 'the entire world took notice of him for a most ungrateful villain'. To Andrew Marvell, Downing was 'Judas' (which does beg the question 'Who was Jesus?'). These comments seem fair. Downing had worked for the Cromwell government as an excellent spymaster, organising the surveillance of Royalists in the Netherlands. In 1660 Downing changed sides and did the same job for the king. He was regarded by both sides as an odious turncoat, a servile supporter of either side when the time was right.

Okey and the others wished to keep in contact with their families and provide them with money in their new precarious and dangerous situation, so they set up a dead letter box in Delft, organised by a local merchant and supporter, Abraham Kicke. Downing located Kicke through his spy connections, and with a mixture of bribery (£200) and threats to destroy his business, Downing persuaded Kicke to betray his close friend. Barkstead sent a letter to Kicke, on behalf of himself and Okey, suggesting a rendezvous with their wives, and Kicke replied with reassurances about their safety, which were lies. All three were captured.

Downing knew Okey, who had once been his commander, and his regiment had sponsored Downing's work in America. The street where the British prime minster lives is named after this dubious character, who acquired a large parcel of land in exchange for his work for the king.

The three prisoners were immediately sent to England, and as they had been previously outlawed, their trial turned entirely on the question of identity. Okey and his companions were executed by being hanged, drawn and quartered, the usual punishment under law for high treason, on 19 April 1662. He spent the minutes before his death berating the Life Guards who surrounded him. He told them to pray more and swear less.

The new king had agreed to return Okey's body to his wife, Mary, for burial in the family vault at Christ's Church, Stepney. This did not occur, however, as the new government learned that a sizeable number of people planned to attend Okey's funeral, and worried that this assembly might afford those opposed to the Restoration some sort of anti-government display. As many as 20,000 turned up, and the funeral was cancelled with 'with much harshness and many bitter words'. Okey's body was interred within the precincts of the Tower of London with a minimum of burial observance, which his wife had to organise.

Okey died well, in the sense that he did not squirm or wriggle at his trial and confessed himself satisfied with his cause. Samuel Pepys noticed this, but could not understand it. 'They looked very cheerful,' he noted, 'but I hear that they all died defending what they did to the king to be just, which was very strange.'

Okey saved many of the other regicides from a grisly death. By dying well, and having it published and broadcast, his execution became positive propaganda, and new Protestant martyrs were being created. It was now two years since the first executions, and fatigue, at least with the public, was starting to set in. Even some of the king's supporters were beginning to think that more grisly deaths would be counterproductive. The Cavalier Parliament had added another twenty names to the list of those already executed. These executions never happened, and the manner of Okey's death was one of the reasons.

Chapter 4

The Brewer, the Servant and the Cobbler?

Thomas Pride, Isaac Ewer, John Hewson

Most of the regicides were members of the gentry. Their level of wealth and influence varied but they shared key characteristics. They would be from a notable family with historical roots in their locality. They owned property and mostly lived on the work of others. The eldest male inherited the bulk of the property and was educated at university or the Inns of Court, or both. They were often related by marriage, or knew each other socially, and were part of an interconnected power structure. They were Justices of the Peace for their county and the higher level gentry were Members of Parliament. There were large differences in status and wealth between members of the same social group. In the previous chapter Okey was on the lowest rung because his family were in commerce; Cromwell stands in the middle as a second son, while Ireton is nearer the top because of his inheritance of landed property.

Most of the Parliamentarians came from this social group, but did the civil war put power into the hands of the less socially prestigious? Denzil Holles, a leader of the Presbyterian group in parliament, certainly thought so. In 1644, two years into the war, he was alarmed to note that 'most of the colonels [...] are tradesmen, tailors, goldsmiths, shoe makers and the like.' Holles was both exaggerating and being misleading. Goldsmiths and traders were the 'middling sort', while tailors and shoemakers where a step below them. There were not very many of them, but enough to panic men like Holles, and it was the war that created them.

We have three candidates as 'low status' regicides: Thomas Pride, the son of a Somerset farmer, date of birth uncertain, who died in a palace in Surrey; John Hewson, a cobbler who was eventually a member of Cromwell's reconstituted House of Lords (known as the 'Other House'); and Isaac Ewer, who married into the new Commonwealth's security services and missed out on wealth and influence by his early death fighting for the new Republic in 1650.

Thomas Pride is the only one of the three who has made it into the general history books, largely because a major event of the civil war is named after him. He was the face of the coup d'état in December 1648 when he was entrusted by the officer grandees to remove those MPs who were ready to settle with the king; an event known as Pride's Purge. The event, however, was not prompted by Pride. It was on the order of his superior, Henry Ireton, and another grandee, Thomas Grey, Lord Grey of Groby, who stood behind Pride and identified the people on the list who were to be excluded. Neither was the purge a one-off event. The regiments of regicides Hewson and Deane were involved in the mopping up operation on the day after but this example of army power will always have Pride's name on it because he was ordered to do it first.

This may give the impression that Pride was merely a tool of others. This was a conclusion that was encouraged by Royalists, who liked their regicides in binary groups: criminal masterminds or simple-minded ciphers, represented by their higher or lower status respectively. Pride was neither of these. When Charles II was restored in 1660, Pride was included in the initial list of those already dead who were to be dug up and posthumously executed. Royalists hated Pride. He was the perfect example of the kind of social mobility that only being on the winning side in a revolution could produce. They hated him for his low social status, adding presumption and unnaturalness to the other charge of treason, but they confirmed his importance by looking, unsuccessfully, for his corpse in an attempt to desecrate it. Therefore, he was ranked with Cromwell, Ireton and Bradshaw, even by his enemies.

Royalist propaganda claimed that he had been a brewer (or a drayman if they were feeling particularly vindictive). As pointed out in the biography of Thomas Pride,[1] the term 'brewer' was a common rejoinder employed by Royalists to criticise prominent figures of the Parliament. Cromwell, Horton, Cawley, and Waite were all accused of being brewers or innkeepers.

Why a brewer? It was a commonplace trade; a household occupation not to be confused with the prestigious position of the Bass and Whitbread families of the next century. Brewing did not have the éclat of guild organisations like the haberdashers and goldsmiths, and for Puritans, who claimed to control the poor behaviour of others, it was hypocritical. The real crime, of course, was to break out of the constraints of the 'Great Chain of Being' and rise beyond his status in life. Pride was one of the middling sort who wanted to be their own masters. Pride did that, and it was the war, and his commitment to it, that made it possible.

Pride *was* from a modest social background, but not as modest as the Royalists wished, or feared. He was originally apprenticed to a haberdasher. The family would have paid for their son's training, food and accommodation, so this was not a sign of poverty. He did move into the brewing industry, but the Royalist image of a brewer's draymen seems very wide of the mark. He was a brewing businessman rather than a brewer. The propaganda stuck because, from what we can glean from his personality, it seems that he was loud and overconfident, verging on boorishness, with a simple yeoman farmer's approach to life which was either straightforward or simple-minded depending on your viewpoint.

Throughout his life there were persistent rumours that he was illiterate. This suited his enemies just as much as the image of him plodding through the streets with a horse and cart, but it also has some basis in truth. On more than one occasion when a written document was required, he would call on someone else to do it. On his death in 1658, he left no books in his will. His very large signature on the execution warrant has been described as 'practised', as if writing was unfamiliar to him.

He was a Puritan. In 1629 he married Elizabeth Thomason, an ironmonger's daughter, and the ceremony was performed by William Gouge, the Puritan vicar of St Anne's Blackfriars since 1608. Gouge had been in trouble for not following the legally enforceable communion rites of the Church of England, and for his opposition to James I's 'Book of Sports', which sanctioned dancing and other recreational activities on the Sabbath when it was reissued in 1633, much to the disgust of Puritans.

So many regicides were influenced by men in pulpits who were not preaching automatic obedience to their king. The regicides (and, more generally, future soldiers of the New Model Army), would have their hearts hardened by the constant harassment of the church authorities, including breaking up of assemblies, mass arrests and imprisonments, and accusations of heresy. Pride experienced all of these things in the 1630s. He was later influenced – like so many London artisanal regicides – by

John Duppa, who rejected the whole structure of the Church of England, making Pride as much a Separatist as an Independent.

Pride joined the Orange Regiment of the London trained bands when the conflict began and was at the battle of Edgehill. He accepted a captaincy in Barclay's Regiment of Foot, paying for a company himself. After a gruelling apprenticeship in war in the south of England, facing deadly skirmishes, sieges, set battles and some of the worst artillery bombardments of the whole war, he was promoted to major in December 1643.

In 1644 Pride was in Cornwall, a Royalist county that would have seemed completely alien to a member of the metropolitan elite. Cornish was still spoken extensively, in some places exclusively, and most people were sincerely attached to the form of religious observance that they already had. Pride, like the regicide Deane, was present at an ignominious parliamentary defeat at Lostwhithiel. The battle was lost for two main reasons: the Parliamentary navy were stuck in Portsmouth due to adverse winds; and the Parliamentarians completely overestimated their support amongst the Cornish. Pride would have been part of a week of continuous fighting and skirmishing. To add insult to injury, his regiment was later accused of cowardice. At this point, Pride signed an Attestation of Officers,[2] refuting the implication and blaming officers with Royalist sympathies and Essex himself.

Like many of the New Model Army, he was fighting for religious freedom. He was a friend and comrade of William Goffe, also a future Cromwell loyalist, and their names are adjacent on the execution warrant. They were both Puritans, though the word is a catch-all term and can sometimes create an equivalence that is misleading. Pride was a Separatist, whilst Goffe was a radical millenarian awaiting the coming of Christ. They disagreed with each other, but could still work together to oppose the king. This toleration made them extremists twice over in the eyes of their enemies.

Their commanding officer, Harry Barclay, was a Scottish Presbyterian who declined to serve in the New Model Army in 1644, thus leaving more room for people like Goffe and Pride. Pride was identified as an ambitious, godly officer, evidenced by the reluctance of a less zealous House of Commons to appoint him to the New Model Army. By the end of 1645, however, Pride, and many like him, was in command of regiments despite the blocking attempts of Denzil Holles, who also took against Okey for the same reason.

In the second half of the civil war, Pride participated in the great 'trophy battles': at Naseby, commanding a reserve force without much incident and at the siege of Bristol, where he was a member of an under-strength regiment. He was first noticed by Cromwell at Dartmouth in 1646, and was at the later battles of Chepstow (described by Cromwell as a 'desperate business'), Preston (1648), and Dunbar (1650).

Set battles were important, but the ideas of men like Pride were also moulded by the less glamorous aspects of war-bombardments, street fighting, living and fighting in trenches, scaling ladders, spending cold nights on sentry duty, and sleeping outside in the rain. At the same time, people like Pride maintained their own faith without parishes, churches and clergy appointed by bishops and kings. They came to the conclusion that they had sacrificed enough in war, and therefore wanted the peace to be different, a sentiment which has been a powerful force for change throughout history.

Pride was now promoted to the second rank of political influencers in London: below Cromwell and Ireton, but still an important link between the Independent officers and the ordinary soldiers. Pride continued to be influential in the capital. In August 1647 his regiment entered London at the head of Fairfax's army – there was some talk of purging the Presbyterians even at that early point – and when Fairfax took the Tower of London, it was with the help of Pride's regiment.

When the military war finished, the political war between the Commons and army commenced. Pride probably becomes a national figure in March 1647 when he (and Ireton) were accused of collecting signatures by force and intimidation to oppose the disbanding of the army. Pride was the first to be called to the bar of the House of Commons, and attempts to intimidate him did not work. The Commons had no evidence and Pride lied, denying any involvement, despite the fact that Thomas Fairfax had already told the Commons of his complicity. Holles, who had complained about tradesman taking over the military, condemned Pride (and Ireton) as 'enemies of the state'. Such abuse was not much of a reward for risking life and injury in nasty skirmishes and pitched battles. Pride, and soldiers like him, felt betrayed.

Pride was determined to stay in business despite the war, and make money when his side won the peace. In August 1647 sixty-seven large brewers asked the Commons for the abolition of taxes on beer, and Pride was one of them. As a colonel, Pride was asking for the money to pay soldiers' arrears, but as a businessman he was not willing to pay the necessary tax, which was either hypocritical or eminently reasonable, depending on your point of view. It is surprising that he was able to run his business at all. His biographer suggests that the work would have been done by his wife, Elizabeth, another resourceful seventeenth-century woman who has been mostly lost to history.

Pride was always a businessman, even when he was a soldier, but he never really a politician. He was not at the Putney debates, and was not a Leveller or a social progressive. He was committed to religious toleration, the fair treatment of the nation's soldiers and, after the Second Civil War, subscribed to the view that the king was responsible for the country's misery.

When the peace was won again at the end of the Second Civil War, the Parliament brazenly continued negotiations with the king. On November 20 the Remonstrance of the Army was presented by the cavalry regiments of Cromwell, Ireton, Harrison and Whalley and the foot regiments of Deane and Pride, men who were nine weeks away from regicide. Pride's regiment was particularly demanding that Charles should face justice.

What did Pride do in the years after the execution? He had become one of the most influential regicides in the land, central to the operation of the new republic. He did attempt to make money, which may sound alarm bells, but probably shouldn't. It was part of a bigger picture, and Pride was certainly interested in more than making a profit. He was moving men and materiel for the cause, employing his peacetime skills. When he took on contracts he would insist on payment, but it seemed that the new Commonwealth was not an easy touch. So, when Pride asked for reimbursement of £1,400 for 2,000 soldiers that he had procured to go to Ireland, the government took the precaution of counting them, and finding a mere 1056, asked for the remainder before paying the bill.

He seemed genuinely interested in the welfare of the armed forces, the security of the new regime, religious toleration and a Puritan reformation of manners. In 1650 he became governor of St Bartholomew's Hospital, and insisted that army war veterans should be cared for by experienced nurses. He requisitioned rooms in London inns for their accommodation and took deer from Marylebone Park for their meals.

He lived in some splendour in a wing of St James's Palace, much to the Royalists' disgust, but did so with his men. His regiment became a security and logistics organisation after the execution. Based in Westminster, he was essentially the Common's armed guard. When the Duke of Hamilton was executed for his part in the Second Civil War, it was Pride's regiment that provided the security.

It wasn't just about money and war, however. In August 1649 Pride and William Goffe presented a petition to the Commons asking for the repeal of laws that prevented godly Protestants from worshipping as they wished. Pride endorsed the views of one radical pamphleteer who demanded the end of the death penalty for theft, using an argument from the Old Testament that property theft was not 'an eye for an eye'. Pride did not object to the death penalty in principle, something that he had already proved with his king.

Pride was unpopular among those who resented the course of events. He did not, for example, manage to be elected to the Honourable Company of Brewers. Some people thought that he had become too grand, and this was one of the few things that they could do to bring him down a peg. He was not involved in the actual fighting in Ireland, but would have had the same attitude as Cromwell, Ireton, Hewson and Moore.

He was involved in the war with England's northern neighbour. Scotland was a foreign country even after 1603 when they shared the same king, and was even more foreign in 1649. The execution warrant was a very English affair, with no consent and plenty of active opposition from the Scots. After the emergency in Ireland was resolved, it was the Scots who had to be subdued.

Pride was one of many regicides who played an active part. He was present at the battle of Dunbar in 1650, a victory for Cromwell's army under the most trying of conditions. The New Model Army had sent three regiments to defeat the Scots, with Pride commanding a Regiment of Foot and his old friend, William Goffe, taking charge of Cromwell's regiment, making Pride one of the most senior military men in the land. Dunbar must have reminded Pride of the debacle at Lostwhithiel. The English army was hemmed in on three sides, with their back to the sea, and could only be supplied by ship. There was a gradual process of attrition caused by disease and poor supplies. The Scots, who outnumbered the Parliamentary army and were safe behind fortified lines, had no reason to risk an attack. These were the similarities between the two battles, but the differences – the command of Oliver Cromwell and

John Lambert – were of far greater importance. Parliament launched a successful surprise attack, though Pride's biography believes that little of the success could be put down to him as he made some initial tactical mistakes. Nobody ever called Pride a great soldier, like some of the other regicides. Brave but not brilliant, he was a businessman by instinct and a soldier only through necessity.

Most regicides seem to have enriched themselves with the property of disgraced Royalists, which was sold off cheaply to the new rulers. In 1650 Pride bought 1,000 acres of valuable parkland around Henry VIII's Nonesuch Palace and resided in Worcester House, where he lived out his days, surrounded by souvenirs of his busy life, which he liked to show to visitors. He rests there to this day, exact location unknown, exempt from royal revenge.

Isaac Ewer is the lowest born of this trio. He did not follow, as far as we know, the normal route of most regicides, but came from a modest Essex family. In his last will and testament he describes himself as being 'but a serving – man' before the war, although he seemed to have been entrusted with minor administrative posts in his own county. In 1633 he married Joan Thurloe, whose brother, John, became the feared spymaster of the Cromwell regime. Thurloe was the executor of his will and lifelong friend. Ewer did not live to extract maximum advantage from this connection, which would have been an honourable and pragmatic thing to do in a society that did not condemn what we would call 'nepotism'.

He joined the civil war very quickly, but like other regicides who were at the bottom of the social scale, he was recruited into the army rather than being a recruiter himself. He was an active participant in the First Civil War. He joined the Parliamentary army in 1642 and ultimately rose to be a colonel of foot in December 1645, but his main significance came later.

Ewer was a hard, committed servant of Parliament, played a crucial role in the Second Civil War, and was trusted by Cromwell. When the Royalists retook Chepstow Castle in 1648, Cromwell initially moved against them, but then passed the work to Ewer, who commanded a train of artillery, seven companies of foot and troops of horse. There were only 120 defenders and the siege was entering its third week. Eventually, the walls were breached at a part of the castle that was later to be called

Marten's Tower, named after the regicide who was held prisoner there after the Restoration. This was the last chance for the governor, Sir Nicholas Kemys, to surrender. He not only failed to do this, but also tried to escape through the breach in the wall. As the conventions of war had been broken, Ewer had no compunction in having the captured Kemys shot out of hand, with a hundred or so of his men put to the sword.

Ewer's most memorable moment was his role at the siege of Colchester in the Second Civil War, and he formed one of the councils of war passing summary sentence on Sir Charles Lucas and Sir George Lisle. These two men had already compounded (paid a fine) for their role in earlier fighting. Strictly speaking they had broken their parole, a promise not to fight in exchange for their freedom. When Fairfax won the bitter battle after a three-month siege, he promptly had Lucas and Lisle executed by firing squad in the castle yard, and without any due process.

It was Ewer who presented to the House of Commons, on 20 November 1648, the 'Remonstrance of the Army', in which they insisted on Charles I being speedily brought to justice. The army expected, and received, a hostile response from Parliament and clearly believed Ewer was the man to face them down. While other soldiers insulted and threatened the MPs who were about to settle with the king, Ewer remained polite. It was the good humour of a man who knew that he would get his own way in the end.

Ten days later Ewer was trusted with another task for which absolute loyalty was needed. The king was still at Carisbrooke Castle on the Isle of Wight. Charles had realised that his sponsored rebellions of 1648 had failed. This depressed him, but not to the point that he would admit culpability or concern about the damage done. Colonel Hammond, Charles's captor on the island, could not comprehend what would happen to Charles next, despite letters from his cousin, Oliver Cromwell, asking him to consider why God had sent Charles continuous defeats on the battlefield. Fairfax dismissed Hammond and replaced him with Ewer, whose resolution to bring the king to justice had been fully formed by the Second Civil War. Ten days later Ewer was given the custody of the king at Hurst Castle, and was made governor. His selection for this task suggested efficiency and total loyalty.

Noble was highly dismissive of Ewer. As with many of the lower status regicides, he seems to get most of Ewer's ancestry wrong, and puts him into the 'vile creature of Cromwell' category. Perhaps he was half right. Ewer was no cipher, but he could seem cruel at times.

Ewer did not have long to live after he signed the death warrant (he was present every day of the trial, which most regicides did not manage). In April 1649 his regiment was ordered to Ireland and Ewer made his will. He was thirty-seven at the time. Like Ireton, Ewer died in Ireland. Like the regicide Hewson, he was present at Drogheda, one of the most controversial events of the war, led the storming of the town and worked with Ireton in the reduction of Waterford. He died, probably of the plague, in August 1649, and was buried in Ireland, but not shipped back to England, as Ireton (allegedly) was.

Ewer was certainly a stout servant of the Republic. Unlike many others, he does not seem to have enriched himself during the civil war. In 1658 Thurloe wrote to Henry Cromwell pleading for help for the two orphan boys. They had 'as much less estate behind him than the world may possibly think', and that the money voted by Parliament had never materialised. The apparent generosity of the Commons for fallen soldiers has to be tempered by the fact that the money would arrive in unreliable dribbles, or, in the case of Ewer, not at all.

John Hewson was of a lower social group than any regicides encountered so far. Before the war, Hewson had progressed – marginally – from a repairer of shoes (a cobbler) to a maker of shoes (a cordwainer). This was still remembered in 1658, when Hewson was raised to Cromwell's 'Other House', giving him the title of Lord Hewson. The Earl of Warwick and other aristocrats are said to have refused to recognise the Upper House because of Hewson's lowly birth. Noble called him 'a soldier of fortune and rose from the lowest situation'. The second half is fact, but he was a man of principle, something which men like Noble were incapable of recognising. Their world view told them that men like this, without experience or education, could not possibly understand the consequences of their actions when ordered to act by others.

He was more than a Puritan; he was a Separatist, like Pride. He had, rumour suggested, three sons who were 'Anabaptists'. He joined the civil war as early as possible and rose predominantly by merit, with his promotions due to bravery in the field. He prospered in the New Model Army because of his religious beliefs. Like Pride, he became a lieutenant colonel when the New Model Army was formed in 1645.

We have some indication of his personality. He was a brave soldier, pious and puritan, but with a strong hint of cruelty and fanaticism. By his own admission he was a 'child of wrath' in his youth, who was put on a Christian path by others. He was possibly another regicide turned puritan by spiritual crisis rather than family influence. He was not a political progressive. When Cromwell and Fairfax suppressed the Levellers, he aided them.

He was merciless and brave, risking his life to prevent the people of Kent enjoying their Christmas in 1647. When the people of Canterbury resisted the Puritan mayor's declaration that Christmas Day was to be treated as a working day, it was Hewson's regiment that was sent to restore order. When Hewson was sent to Maidstone to restore the Puritan version of 'order' in 1648, he faced vicious street fighting with Royalists, who lined the street with snipers and defended each building so that each house had to be captured in turn.

Hewson was at Drogheda with Oliver Cromwell. It was Cromwell who gave the order for 'no quarter' (no mercy) when the defenders refused to surrender, a reasonable convention of war at the time, but Hewson would have condoned the murder of civilians, which took place afterwards. At the siege of Kilkenny (1650) he lost an eye under musket fire.

Hewson was a man who welcomed confrontation, and was, therefore, either brave or committed, or bullying and intimidating, according to belief. As well as attacking Christmas, he rode through the streets of London on the day of the king's execution, forbidding any outward signs of mourning and he may have been the man responsible for finding a competent man to do the deed itself. The alleged executioner was William Hulet, a sergeant from Hewson's own regiment, and the implication was that Hewson had recruited him. The perpetrator kept his face covered, unlike the regicides themselves. Hulet was promoted soon afterwards. A witness heard Hewson offer £100 to anybody who would do it, and joked and boasted about it afterwards. He allegedly told a Captain Toogood that Hulet 'did the King's business for me upon the scaffold'.[3] Hulet was never convicted and neither was the more likely culprit, Richard Brandon. The authorities were convinced that it was Hulet, and the witnesses expected to be believed when they represented Hewson as heartless, cruel and conniving.

Hewson was a member of the rather unique Parliament of 1653, which replaced the Rump. It had various names: the 'Good Parliament', to distinguish it from the failures of the Rump; the 'Little Parliament' because it was a third of the size of a normal House of Commons (but more than twice the size of the Rump that existed in 1653); the 'Barebones[4] Parliament', after one of its godly members; and the most accurate name of all, the 'Nominated Parliament' because there were no elections held, the members being chosen by Cromwell and his Council of Officers, with some proposals from the godly Independent churches taken into account.

Its task was to make reforms in the areas where the Rump had manifestly failed to make any progress: the law, tithes and the support of the clergy, trade, education and the poor. Its laws would pave the way to a reformation of manners and the creation of a godly people. Hewson had by this point moved to oversee the occupation of Ireland, and earned his place because of that, but he would not have been there had he not already been reliable and godly. He would have had limited practical influence on discussions.

Another military representative and 'Barebones' member was Henry Cromwell, Oliver's second oldest son. Hewson and Henry Cromwell did not get on at all. Noble is correct, for a change, when he suggests that Hewson complained directly to the Lord Protector about his own son's behaviour, which is a remarkable comment on Hewson's character: brave and principled or arrogant and foolhardy, depending on your view, but clearly a man who was not afraid of confrontation.

Hewson was always an army man. In the dying days of the Commonwealth, Londoners were calling for a new set of elections, or a return of the Long Parliament that had purged in 1648. Either would have resulted in the return of the monarchy. Hewson was still supporting the attempt of a desperate and unpopular set of army officers who were trying to develop a republican settlement, a solution that was not wanted or required by anybody in the country. On 5 December 1659, apprentice boys rioted near the Royal Exchange and demanded a 'free and fair Parliament'. When fainter hearts had failed to suppress them, Hewson was sent in. The mob made their point about wanting to be ruled by their natural betters by throwing shoes and shouting, 'A cobbler! A cobbler!' At least two people were killed by Hewson's troopers, and a few days later a coroner's court was convened and Hewson was blamed. This was not the sort of public response that the godly men of the New Model were used to, but Hewson was still happy to confront his enemies on the streets of London, even when the cause was lost.

Hewson remained remembered and hated by Royalists. He died soon after fleeing the country, living in obscure poverty in Amsterdam. Some Royalists suggested digging him up and subjecting him to the same humiliation as Cromwell, Ireton and Bradshaw. For a man who started with a cobbler's shop, he had made quite an impression on history.

Chapter 5

The Metropolitan Militia Men

John Barkstead, Robert Tichborne, Owen Rowe, John Venn

With the exception of the three mentioned in the previous chapter, most regicides were members of the gentry. A smaller number of the 'middling sort', a step below the gentry, did become regicides, and they represent many thousands of similar men who helped defeat the king. This group can be characterised as follows: they lived in London; they were tradesman or skilled artisans and rose through apprenticeship and patronage rather than education. It would have been impossible for them to become MPs before the civil war; they were much more likely to be a member of a volunteer militia such as the London Trained Bands. They were from a class of people who strove to be prosperous through their own efforts. Many of them already had their own opinions on religion, which they wished to express. Civil war allowed them to express these opinions, and the political collapse of the establishment allowed them to take power. Four new regicides fall into this category: John Barkstead, Robert Tichborne, Owen Rowe and John Venn.[1]

When our four regicides joined the Trained Bands before the war, they were making a statement about themselves. The four were what we might term petty bourgeois: shopkeepers, tradesmen and merchants, ambitious for themselves and their community. Participation in the Trained Bands would have been theoretically compulsory for these four men, but it was easy to avoid. They must have enjoyed getting up early and practising with pike and musket. It was a commitment, and it marked them out as people who wanted to make a difference to their community.

Queen Elizabeth I had set up militias in the 1570s, and these were often dormant in peacetime and ineffective in war. The London Trained Bands were the exception. Without the Trained Bands there would have been no civil war and no regicide. In the prelude to war they were the only real military force in the country, and control of these part-time soldiers also meant control of London. By 1642 there was an army of 20,000, over which Charles had no influence. The Trained Bands formed the core of several of Parliament's armies during the early years of the war. It was the Trained Bands that originally secured Windsor for Parliament, leaving London on the same day as the Battle of Edgehill and coming back a few days later with £3,000 worth of silver plate.

One of those men present at Windsor, and who had plundered the establishment to provide cash for Parliament, was **John Barkstead**. He was from a modest social background, a constant supporter of Oliver Cromwell and rather a fearsome man. He had no legal or university education and had to work for a living. His exact date of birth is unknown, though it has been estimated at 1605 as he was still less than twenty-one when his father, Michael, made his will. The lack of a secure date of birth is another sign of lowly status. Prestigious families had 'gateway ancestors' who provided exact dates of birth.

Barkstead, like many of the lower-status regicides, was a skilled artisan worker. He was a goldsmith and silversmith like his father, and was one of those citizens who gained soldiering experience through the London Trained Bands. This was Barkstead's route into respectable society during peacetime, and his way into the ruling establishment during war.

What did these men feel strongly about, and what was their motivation for opposing the king? The answer is religion of course, but not the same type of religious dissatisfaction experienced by the high-status regicides, who were both rebels and members of the establishment at the same time. These London men were outsiders. Barkstead was a member of a Congregationalist Church opposed to the king's religious influence and which organised itself outside the Church of England. It was persecuted by the authorities. In this respect Barkstead was more like Pride and Hewson than Ireton and Cromwell.

Barkstead began his career under fellow metropolitan militia man John Venn, and like Venn, ended up as a military governor. Barkstead was governor of Reading from July 1644 until January 1647, and present at the Siege of Colchester (1648) during the Second Civil War. The furious attack on the town was repulsed three times and showed not only great courage on the part of the Parliamentarians but also their anger and frustration towards the Royalists who were causing needless suffering by provoking a fight that they could not win and which they had promised not to restart (a fair description of the king himself).

Barkstead was very unpopular with the Royalists and was far more famous then than he is now. This was due to a number of reasons. Despite identifying as a republican he seemed to be easily reconciled to each new form of government. He was rapacious as well as a hypocrite, and it seems that he used his position as Lieutenant of the Tower of London (after 1652) to extort money from imprisoned Royalists on a scale that was remarkably blatant, despite the fact that taking bribes was an acknowledged prerequisite of the post.

Thanks to his notoriety at the Tower of London, Barkstead was hated in the capital. In one piece of Royalist propaganda, an image shows Satan with his cabinet, which includes Barkstead as one of the members (alongside more famous regicides like Scot, Harrison, Bradshaw and Jones). It was said that even nefarious types thought Barkstead was a grasping villain. An anonymous pamphlet about him in 1659 was subtitled 'A Grand Pimp of Tyranny Portrayed'.

Cromwell, however, seems to have had confidence in him at all times. 'There was never a design on foot but we could hear of it out of the Tower,' said Cromwell. Barkstead gave him two weeks' prior notice of any rebellion, a much more valuable contribution to the stability of any regime than even brilliance on the battlefield. Barkstead seemed able to reconcile himself to every form of government organised by Cromwell and was consequently knighted. Becoming a major-general, and accepting all honours that came his way, also makes Barkstead a Cromwellian. As major-general in London he closed down the original Globe Theatre made famous by Shakespeare.

When King Charles II was restored in 1660, forty-one of the regicides were alive and had to decide what to do next. Barkstead fled abroad to Hanau, Germany, a free Protestant city with a history of welcoming refugees, and which specialised in gold and luxury items. Barkstead the goldsmith would feel at home. He became a burgess in the town. Noble, cynical as ever, believed that his welcoming reception was 'sufficient proof that they had taken much property with them'. Perhaps Barkstead was using the money he had extorted from prisoners during his efficient but ruthless reign at the Tower.

Barkstead showed his human side when he was lured from the safety of Germany to Holland to see his wife. While there, he was arrested by George Downing and forced to return to England. Barkstead's defence was that he was not the John Barkstead named in the oath, but this was made worse by the fact that the two other captured regicides used the same excuse.

Barkstead was executed in April 1662. His last words were a failure to apologise or repudiate the cause. He had constantly asked God if he had acted in malice and was assured that he had not. When he claimed to have made no personal gain, the crowd erupted and his later words were drowned out. They did not know the contents of Barkstead's conscience, but they knew the last statement was untrue. Thomas Burton, the MP, reported that Barkstead's severed head was put on a pole and placed on Traitors' Gate at the Tower, the place where he had wielded his power and robbed and terrorised Royalists. This was an echo of Ireton, Bradshaw and Cromwell, whose heads were placed on Westminster Hall, the place where they had impudently assumed the right to try and execute their king.

Another regicide without an impressive family tree is **Robert Tichborne**, born around 1610, and probably the eldest son of Richard Tichborne. Like John Barkstead, Robert followed his father's profession, in this case that of a linen draper. The interesting aspect of Tichborne's career was that he does not seem to have been either particular zealous or efficient, but still managed to prosper; a blessing that his betters had enjoyed for centuries, but was a new experience for a shopkeeper's son.

Robert Tichborne was involved in the London militia, and was a volunteer in the Honourable Artillery Company by 1636. The Honourable Artillery Company has a long and proud history, but a misleading name. 'Artillery' meant anything fired in the air during war with a bow or a gun. In the 1640s it was an important recruiting ground for both rebels and regicides. By 1643 he was a captain in the Yellow regiment of London Trained Bands. His enemies mocked his abilities as a soldier. According to one contemporary critic, he was 'fitter for a warm bed than to command a regiment'. Tichborne did take part in the siege of Gloucester, and although there are no stories of personal heroism, Gloucester was an example of the importance of the metropolitan militia. By late 1643 Parliament had been chased out of most of the north and west, except Hull and Gloucester. The king's decision to break the siege of Gloucester rather than head for London meant that Gloucester became crucial. Although the Parliamentary defence of the town was spirited, it was the Earl of Essex's five regiments of trained bands that saved the town. On seeing their approach, the Royalists, hungry and wet, moved away.

Tichborne would have been one of these militia men, showing determination and resilience rather than personal bravery. He was also present at the Battle of Newbury, where the Royalist forces from Gloucester intercepted Essex's army of Londoners. This was the last chance to destroy them, and the king failed. He played no part in the national fighting and was neither an MP in 1640 nor chosen in a recruiter election after the First Civil War[2].

Tichborne didn't need to be an MP, though, as he had a considerable power base. He was elected to the Common Council of London and served on the London Militia Committee. When the army first invaded London in their struggle with Parliament, it was Tichborne who was entrusted with the Tower of London, just as Barkstead was later. Here, he was second only to Fairfax as a colonel in charge of 600 soldiers. Noble commented that he commanded the city of London 'as he pleased'.

Despite his protestations of innocence in 1660, Tichborne had definitely picked a side in the war. He was one of the colonels criss-crossing Whitehall in January 1469 in preparation for the trial and execution. He (with Owen Rowe and John Blakiston) was tasked with preparing Westminster Hall for the process. In order to calm Judge Bradshaw's fear of attack on the day, Tichborne arranged for the soldiers to have extra weapons, procured from the Tower of London; a logical choice considering Tichborne's link with the Tower. It was because of his efforts that Colonel Hewson's regiment was able to ring the building with well-armed men, but it also meant that it did look very much like a law court.

There was some element of opportunism in his actions. Tichborne was the bureaucrat who swept in once the fighting had been done. He was both committed and ready to prosper personally – he had made money out of the sale of bishop's estates during the Long Parliament before 1648 – but this desire to make money did not conflict with his primary motivation. He was a prominent member of an independent Baptist congregation led by George Cockayne at Soper Lane, near Coleman

Street, St Pancras, and there seems to be an element of the millenarian Fifth Monarchy about him in this speech just after the execution:

> And truly his great and glorious workings in these our days doth seem to point out that time to be near at hand; when God himself doth shake the whole Earth and heavens [...] Now the World is so near an end, and to believe that glorious Reign of Christ at hand, will make much joy and settlement in the heart, though the present workings of God be to turn, and overturn things, yet all this serves to accomplish these glorious promises of his, in bringing forth this Righteous and peaceful Kingdome of Christ.

The Fifth Monarchist cult is dealt with in chapters twelve and thirteen. Its key belief is millenarianism: that God would put an end to a corrupt and sinful world in the fullness of time. Most Puritans had a kernel of millenarianism in them, believing that the amount of sin and wickedness on the earth made the reign of man unsustainable in the medium term, but Fifth Monarchists believed the time was near at hand and that it was the responsibility of those on earth to 'overturn' society to prepare for it.

When Tichborne made his remarks the king had been dead three weeks. Millenarians were waiting patiently, and Fifth Monarchists were waiting impatiently, for the reign of King Jesus to arrive.[3] While waiting for the 'rapture', Tichborne remained loyal, taking on jobs that gave him power in the capital. He was Sheriff of London in 1651, but also performed real service for the Commonwealth. He was also one of the eight commissioners sent to Scotland in October 1651 to settle the government of Scotland and prepare the way for the compulsory union with England. Tichborne was selected for the Nominated Assembly (the so-called 'Barebones Parliament') of 1653, as one of the members (inevitably) for London. Members were either chosen by Cromwell or a small number of leading army officers, or by the Independent churches of London. Tichborne could have been the selection of either.

Some of the more extreme religious radicals and Fifth Monarchists, men like Thomas Harrison and John Carew (see chapters thirteen and fourteen), thought the Nominated Assembly should introduce a form of Mosaic Law and abolish tithes (therefore also abolishing the national church). Tichborne can be discounted as an 'extreme' member of the Nominated Assembly (no more than thirty from 140) by the fact that he continued to be loyal when the experiment ended and Cromwell took control. Most Fifth Monarchists violently opposed Cromwell becoming Lord Protector, though Tichborne's loyalty was constant but arguably not very principled.

He was knighted in 1655, made Lord Mayor of London in 1656, and accepted the summons to Cromwell's newly reconstituted 'Other' House in December 1657. This was a form of government that would have chilled the heart of any real republican and dismayed any Fifth Monarchist who thought the imminent arrival of King Jesus would put an end to this form of vanity. He retained his original power base as a colonel in the Yellow regiment and a member of the London Militia Committee, and presented an address to the Lord Protector five months before Cromwell's death in 1658. When the government of Richard Cromwell fell and the Rump Parliament was returned, Tichborne, never an MP, became less powerful. When the Rump was purged again in October 1659 he threw his lot in with the army, and his political career was over by 1660.

When the monarchy was restored, and the authorities were looking in the capital for the two most influential London opponents of the monarchy, they chose Tichborne and John Ireton, brother of regicide Henry. Royalist pamphleteers, mostly based in the capital and knowing what a boon Tichborne was to the Commonwealth, were overjoyed at his arrest. Remarkably, they spent only four days in prison before being bailed, but the Royalists would eventually catch up with him.

Tichborne was tried at the Old Bailey on 10 October 1660. He was repentant, long-winded and unconvincing. He was not going to go down fighting for a cause that had helped him to prosperity and power: 'It was my unhappiness to be called to so sad a work when I had so few years over my head; a person neither bred up in the laws, nor in parliaments where laws are made [...] Had I known that then which I do now, I would have chosen a red hot oven to have gone into as soon as that meeting.'

He had clearly decided that his lack of a gentry education or a record of being absent from army or Parliament before the execution was his key to survival. He was found guilty of high treason. He had little family property of his own to be confiscated, but a considerable amount of crown and episcopal property. This was taken from him and he was sentenced to death, which was later commuted.

Tichborne is the first of our regicides to have been imprisoned for the rest of his life. Many enjoyed a view of the sea; not for therapeutic or aesthetic reasons, but because a view of the sea meant they were in the middle of nowhere, inaccessible to family and sympathisers, to be forgotten by both friend and enemy. Some gazed out on the Atlantic or the Channel, but Tichborne enjoyed views of the North Sea. In July 1662 he was removed to Holy Island, which was clearly not good for his health. Tichborne's new home had been described as, 'the desolate fortress of Lindisfarne, a tall circular tower perched upon the lofty summit of a rocky pinnacle at the most remote extremity of the island exposed on every side to the bitter winds and storms of the Northern Sea.'[4]

Like many of the regicides, it was a determined and loving wife who petitioned the monarch to make the imprisonment more bearable. In January 1663 Anne Tichborne sent him a servant because he was lame and infirm. This does not seem to have helped. In March 1664 Anne petitioned again, saying that she could not look after her husband because he was too far away. In October 1664 the move south had been agreed but not carried out and Anne feared that her husband could not survive another Northumberland winter.[5]

She was overly pessimistic. Tichborne arrived, alive but not well, at Dover Castle in March of the following year. Anne received permission for her, her two children and a maidservant to live with him; or to be more precise, to be put in prison with him for a crime she did not commit. This was surely loyalty, devotion and efficiency. Thanks to his wife's work, Tichborne, who was nearly dead in 1664, was able to live on until 1682. He was one of the eighteen regicides who died in prison. He was one of the 'luckier' ones, and, like many of his fellow regicides, he needed to thank a woman.

Our third modest militia man is **Owen Rowe**, from the same background and social class as Tichborne and Barkstead. His father was a yeoman farmer from Cheshire. Owen was moved into a London apprenticeship in 1609, which suggests a date of birth of about 1593. He had a middling occupation as a haberdasher (a retailer who sold things smaller than your hand, such as buttons, zips, thread, knives, scissors, caps, necklaces and beads). Rowe seemed to have thrived. He owned property shares in the Massachusetts Bay Company and land in New Haven, New England. He planned to live there and worship in the Congregationalist Church that he hoped to set up.

Rowe was also a member the Independent Puritan congregation of St Stephen's, Coleman Street, which was by far the most radical street in London, and therefore in the country. He was another ambitious and prosperous religious separatist who felt stifled by the religious changes (and to their mind, persecution) of Charles and Archbishop Laud. He was ready to emigrate – the most extreme form of separation from the establishment church – and almost did. Rowe was ready to leave for New England from about 1635, but never did.

Like Barkstead and Tichborne, Rowe was a member of the London Trained Bands (Green regiment), and had been, like Tichborne, a member of the Honourable Artillery Company. During the war he used his skills to find war materiel for the army of the Earl of Essex. In September 1643 Rowe was contracted to find £5000 worth of arms from the gun makers of London. The bad news for the taxpayers of Essex, Kent, Norfolk and Suffolk was that they were to pay for it. The good news is that Rowe was well known for providing weapons that were value for money because they actually worked. Rowe had a reputation for efficient, committed work throughout his business career. He was an expert in quality control in weapons of all sorts. 'He was thus one of those invisible functionaries upon whom the ultimate victory of Parliament depended, and he can claim a major share of the credit for winning the Civil War by making certain that the guns fired properly,' comments a key source on his life.[6]

In 1643 he was commissioned a lieutenant colonel in the militia and given charge of the armoury at the Tower. He would have known and worked with Barkstead and Tichborne. By 1646 he was promoted to colonel, without having to risk life and limb, but Rowe and men like him were vital for the victory of Parliament. In 1655 Cromwell appointed him deputy-governor of the Bermudas, a logical choice as Rowe had maintained his trading links with the area from the 1630s.

In 1659 he supported the army in its struggle with Parliament and did nothing to help General Monck, whose military intervention restored the monarchy in 1660, so he had no allies and no way of evading justice, but he did not try to flee the country.

At his trial he tried to save his life by using his lack of understanding of the law, as did many other regicides, but he also had an extra card up his sleeve, saying, 'I was not brought up a Scholar but was a Tradesman, and was merely ignorant when I went on in that business.'[7] He claimed bewilderment at the whole process, and intimidation by people higher up the social scale, blaming Barkstead and Henry Smith. It was a shame that such a capable man should have to plead weakness and social inferiority, but it did earn him another year of life, albeit in the Tower of London. Rowe died there on Christmas Day 1661 and was buried in Hackney two days later.

Barkstead, Rowe and Tichborne all survived to plead for their lives in 1660, but the fourth metropolitan militia man, **John Venn,** died in 1651, aged about sixty-five. The only place where Venn is remembered is in his home county of Somerset. After the restoration, parishioners in his church at Lydiard St Lawrence were so angry with his memory that they upended the font and carved a new bowl on the top so that newly baptised children would not be tainted by sharing the same space as the regicide. It is still like that today.[8]

Had he lived longer, he would have been as infamous as Barkstead or Pride. He had the same profile as the other modest militia men. The generations before him were yeomen – moderately affluent working farmers – but by the 1630s he was a major player on the London Common Council, and a merchant in linen and silk. Like other regicides, he migrated to the capital for better prospects, was influenced by the type of religious radicalism that he would not have experienced in the West Country. Venn was a member of the radical congregation of All Hallows, Bread Street. He was also a member of the London Trained Bands, in this case the Yellow regiment, the same as Robert Tichborne. He was also involved in the Massachusetts Bay Company at the same time as Owen Rowe.

The Civil War proper would not have happened without the armed political confrontations in London in 1641–1642. Observers like the philosopher Thomas Hobbes noticed, 'But for the city the Parliament never could have made the war, nor the Rump ever have murdered the King.' Venn was a hardened, street-fighting politician who did a lot of damage to the monarch before a cannon was fired in battle. He came to power via the intimidation of the mob, a key indicator that a ruling class was losing control.

Venn was a reminder that you did not need to be a lawyer, politician or soldier to damage the monarchy. The street fighting in London was the precursor to the set battles and the formal declaration of war later in the year. It destabilised the monarchy and John Venn was very much in the middle of it. In June 1641 he consolidated his power by being elected the MP for the City of London, and was able to neutralise the power of the monarch. In November the king had entered London with an intimidating presence, and it was men like Venn who organised the counterforce against him. During the summer of 1642 he was active in the campaign to remove the Royalist Lord Mayor of London, Sir Richard Gurney, and to secure the election of his friend and fellow Puritan, Isaac Pennington. None of this was the result of a calm rational discussion, rather Venn's ability to summon up and manipulate a mob.

There was an army of 2,000 apprentices supporting Parliament by December 1641, but with swords, clubs and halberds rather than argument. Parliament, through men like Venn, encouraged them, despite knowing that it was a dangerous game that could backfire. On one occasion the mob threatened public order to rescue some of their people who had been arrested. Parliament sent Venn to calm them down and he told them untruthfully that their comrades had already been released. He was brave, cruel and a liar.

In early 1642 he told the mob that they 'must go to the Parliament with your swords, for that party which is best for the Commonwealth is like to be outvoted'. An outbreak of the plague had sent many MPs away from London. Charles had sent them an urgent demand to be back by 12 January 1642. Men like Venn realised that, just as organised intimidation had kept the king's bishops away from the Lords, violence could help the Parliament intimidate the more faint-hearted MPs. Another quote attributed to him (by his enemies, but it rings true) was a boast about the political power the mob gave him, 'These are my bandogs. I can let them on, and I can take them off again.'[9]

Without Venn, parliamentary leaders like John Pym would have been unable to operate inside Parliament to oppose the king. Charles acknowledged Venn's importance in turning London against him by declaring him a traitor who would never be pardoned, even before the civil war had started. There were only five other people on the list alongside Venn, which shows that he was as a significant force in the undermining of the monarch.

Venn was present both at the first battle of the civil war (Cropredy Bridge) and the first major pitched battle at Edgehill. Windsor Castle was taken by Parliament in October 1642 when the regicide John Barkstead was a captain under Venn's command. Venn's life became a shuttle between Windsor and Westminster as governor of Windsor Castle, and as one of the regicides who spent most of the war defending a specific town or fortification rather than fighting in major battles.

Windsor Castle was one of the most strategic locations in the country. Despite being a town with a royal palace, Windsor itself supported parliament throughout the war. Venn did a fanatical job, both as soldier and Puritan. As a soldier he resisted a ferocious attack by Prince Rupert and gained a reputation as a parliamentary soldier who was not to be trifled with. As a Puritan he took part in the destruction of religious ornaments and images that reflected 'popish' religious practices.

St George's Chapel in Windsor Castle was very dear to the Stuarts, so much so that they had recently spent over £1,600 on the highest quality plate by the master Dutch silversmith Christian van Vianen. There were nine pieces of triple gilt plate, two large silver candlesticks and two water jugs in the chapel in November 1639. They were not there for long. When the castle was secured by the army these lucrative 'trinkets' were the first target. A Captain Fog demanded the keys from the Dean of Windsor, and when they were not forthcoming, he smashed down the door, took the plate, bar a few basic chalices and flagons, and had the silver sent to be melted down to finance Fairfax's northern army. The castle's coat of mail of Edward the Fourth disappeared, probably because it was encrusted with gold, pearls and rubies. Much melted-down gold and silver would be used to finance the army.

Venn behaved similarly when he arrived at Windsor, though his motives were mixed. It was religion and gain, conscience and venality. In April 1643 the Dean and Chapter, worried about their own well-being and that of their magnificent chapel, petitioned the House of Lords, who later instructed Venn, 'to take care that there be no disorders and disturbances made in the Chapel at Windsor; and that the evidences, registers, monuments there and all things that belong to the Order of the Garter, may be preserved without any defacing.'[10]

He took no notice of the order. John Venn was an iconoclast as well as a Puritan. In May 1643 he oversaw the stripping out of the choir and the selling of anything of value, including fifteen gold embroidered copes. The Dean and Chapter did not need to wear them any more as they had been expelled by Venn. In September the organ was destroyed.

Tombs and personal inscriptions were vandalised and defaced so badly that, after the Restoration, their occupants could not be identified. In the same spirit, Venn forbade what he called 'papistical burials', which included prayers over the coffin. In January 1648 Charles saw for himself his beloved chapel, stripped and vandalised by Puritans, and later the same month the king himself was buried here, in total silence, forbidden to have the Book of Common Prayer.

It's easy to blame Venn, but he was part of a larger movement who believed and behaved the same. On the 20 December 1643 the House ordered him to purify other churches in Windsor and Eton, and strip the famous college of superstitious images. Venn may have been obeying orders, but he was doing so willingly and happily.[11]

There are some mysteries. The Great West Window, created in the early years of the reign of Henry VIII before the Reformation, contains images of twenty-four Popes and ten Saints. It is still there. Some have attributed aesthetic sensibilities to Venn's soldiers, but it is much more likely that the Dean and Chapter secreted it. The 300 carved angels survived. Perhaps they were too high to reach.

Venn was probably corrupt. Like many military governors and committee men, lots of money and valuables passed through his hands. In April 1643 the House of Commons ordered that the gold and silver thread of Sir Peter Ricaut be seized and the money used to pay the Windsor garrison. It was not always the case that all the money ended up in the right place, and Venn was accused – not just by his enemies – of enriching himself with the king's hangings and linen. Mark Noble accused him of pocketing 'the sum of £400 granted to him for supposed loses, which he probably never had.'

Venn was also cruel, a common feature of our metropolitan militia men, with the exception of Owen Rowe. In January 1643 Parliament decided to lodge sixty of the most troublesome captured Royalists at Windsor Castle. When they arrived there was nowhere for them to sleep comfortably and rather than provide beds he asked Parliament for permission, making the prisoners sleep on the cold stone floors until an answer was received. When the Commons suggested the men having beds would be reasonable, Venn made the prisoners pay for them.

Venn resigned his governorship under the Self-denying Ordinance (1645), which forbade him from holding simultaneous military and political posts. At Westminster he became a leading Independent.

He was appointed to the important Militia Committee following the failure of the Presbyterian faction to gain control of the London Militia in 1647. Venn seemed to have been one of those soldiers/politicians who swung against the king and in favour of execution around 1648.

In January 1649 Venn was appointed a commissioner of the High Court of Justice, which conducted the trial of the king, and was one of the signatories of the King's death warrant. After the establishment of the Commonwealth, Venn was active on many parliamentary committees and profited from the sale of church and royalist land. His death, a year later, was a mystery. His daughter reported that he was found dead in his bed on 28 June 1650. Royalists claimed that he committed suicide, but this may have been wishful thinking on their part. We will never know whether Venn would have supported Cromwell – most of our metropolitan militia men did – but had he lived, his fanatical and cruel Puritanism would have made an impact on events.

Chapter 6

Turning Point, 1648

Thomas Waite, Thomas Horton, Thomas Wogan

The roots of the civil war were complex, nuanced and long term. The roots of the regicide, to misquote Thomas Hobbes, were 'nasty, brutish and short'. Regicide was unimaginable in late 1647 to anyone with political power, with the exception of Henry Marten (featured in chapter nine). A year later, the events of 1648 made the execution of the king the only practical way out of the political crisis.

Despite the horrors of the civil war, it had lasted a mere four years. The religious wars in Germany had lasted thirty years and were still ongoing at the beginning of 1648. At least the British Isles were spared that. A decisive victory had come quite early, largely through the ability to break sieges and the mismatch in resources between the two sides. On the whole, people had behaved civilly to each other and obeyed the conventions of war. This was changing by the end, but it did not matter, the war was over.

In 1648 war started again. This was a new war, not a continuation of the old one. Charles I restarted a conflict in which he had clearly been defeated, defying the judgement of the Almighty. It hardened hearts, including those of many regicides. It also hardened the determination of moderate MPs to settle with the king, creating more polarisation and strife. It was the turning point for the way a defeated king would be treated.

It was not just a new rebellion of Royalists. The Scots, former allies of Parliament, had invaded from the north, with the connivance of the king. It was also a mutiny: a revolt of a previously loyal parliamentary army that had not been paid. It spread to areas previously controlled by the Commons, where people revolted in 1648 against killjoy Puritans who were arrogant, aggrandising and, in Parliament, self-perpetuating.

Despite a rebellion in 1643, caused more by war weariness and a desire for peace, Kent had been quiet during the First Civil War but revolted when the Puritan local authorities tried to ban Christmas in 1648. Londoners were also grumbling; and there had always been Royalists in the capital ready take advantage of discontent. So this new civil war was more intense and urgent; there was a need to be in lots of places at the same time. Those who had fought the first war prosecuted the second with less forgiveness and more cruelty, and new men appeared who did the same.

Thomas Waite is presented only as an example. Other regicides and thousands of others were equally guilty of deteriorating behaviour towards their enemies. One of these opponents was Michael Hudson. He had worked and risked his life for his king. He had fought for him at Edgehill, had gone back to Oxford to study divinity, and later helped Charles to escape from Oxford. He had been imprisoned in the Tower of London and escaped, and then written a book with the provocative title (for Parliamentarians anyway) of 'The Divine Right of Government Natural and Politique, more particularly of Monarchy, the onely legitimate and Natural source of Politique Government', adding salt to the wounds by writing it while imprisoned. By June 1648 Hudson was garrison commander of his own home, Woodcroft House, Northamptonshire. When challenged by the Parliamentary army, the result was never in doubt. Thomas Waite's forces were to win easily, though that was not the salient point. It was the new cruelty, which started with the king's chaplain, but did not stop there.

Waite knew about Hudson – 'that rogue' – and went into battle with hatred in his heart for a man who had given Parliament no end of trouble. The brutal treatment of Hudson was no accident. Hudson and a few of his men retreated into a tower, and one of Waite's close companions was killed. Hudson was stuck with nowhere to go. He was pushed out of a window, but ended up clinging to a stone gargoyle. His hands (some reports say just his fingers, but this makes it no less horrific) were hacked off and he fell into the moat. As he tried to swim to the side he was fished out by the Roundheads who smashed his head in with the butt of a musket. Then he drowned, or was drowned, and it was widely reported that his tongue was cut out, and carried about the country as a trophy by 'a low-bred shopkeeper of Stanford'.

This barbarity still seems shocking, but there was worse. It seems that Waite had offered quarter at the heat of battle, but withdrew it when the enemy slackened their effort. This was a perfidious act by Waite; even in the most furious battles of the civil war, a promise of mercy was rarely rescinded.

Waite hated Hudson and people like him. All the rules were gone. After the victory he wrote to the Speaker of the Commons with details of his bloody victory, mentioning Hudson particularly, as one who had previously escaped the justice of Parliament. He told the Commons that no quarter had been given, even to the better sort, and the House in turn thanked him. He didn't mention the way Hudson was killed, but it was not from a sense of shame. Waite was obeying orders. He had been urged to severity by Thomas Grey and Leicester's county committee, who had counselled him, 'We are of Opinion, that this Enemy deserves no other Conditions than to submit to the Parliament's Mercy, and do desire that you will not parley with them upon any terms.'

This was the new barbarity of the restarted civil war. In 1642 the fighting was hesitant and fearful, with most of the Parliamentary army wishing no more than a quick victory and a settlement with a weakened king (although many of our regicides were notable for their slightly more belligerent views). Prisoners were disarmed and freed after battle on their word to give up fighting, captured men were released in exchanges, and losers in sieges were allowed to leave with dignity. Many regicides were captured during the war and benefited from this generous interpretation of the conventions of war. By the Second Civil War this had changed: there were more murders in cold blood, more summary executions, more forced marches, more people sold into semi-slavery in the West Indies and more events such as the one at Woodcroft House.

Waite was in many ways a typical regicide. He was one of the 'better sort' himself; the same class that he joyfully reported on murdering. While unimportant himself, he represented a new attitude to the enemy that would eventually extend to the king. He was not, as Mark Noble claimed, an innkeeper's son; such people are not made Justices of the Peace and later Sherriff of Rutland. Waite is also atypical in some ways. He was not ejected during Pride's Purge, but he seemed very lukewarm about the execution. Perhaps it was because it was Lord Grey of Groby who had drawn up the list of those to be excluded. Grey would have been confident of controlling his protégé. Waite certainly left Westminster, had no part in the plans for a trial, and seemed to have returned to London on the day before the sentence was passed.

He was never very prominent after 1649, which was no surprise as he had not been very prominent before that. He was apathetic about the new regime and went home to consolidate his landowning and exploit his tenants. He bought lands formerly belonging to the Duke of Buckingham in Rutland. In March 1654 his tenants petitioned the authorities at Westminster, complaining about Waite's severe exploitation.

Waite was tried for his life in 1660 and cut an unimpressive figure. He made no attempt to justify what he had done, and claimed he could not remember signing the death warrant. This was one of the procedures that all of the regicides had to go through. They were asked if the signature was theirs, and it was enough to warrant a charge of treason if it was. His sentence was transportation to a prison far from friends, relatives and an indignant establishment that was annoyed that someone so obscure could have caused so much trouble. In his case it was Mont Orgueil Castle, Jersey. He would have had company there: Henry Smith, James Temple, Hardress Waller and Gilbert Millington were sent to the same place in 1661.

Like Ireton and Ewer, **Thomas Horton** was a Cromwellian soldier cut down in his prime. He died fighting for the new Republic soon after the execution, and would have been much more than a footnote in most history books if he had lived longer than forty-six years. Cromwell knew him well and mourned his death. In October 1649 Cromwell wrote to the Commons from Ireland, 'Colonel Horton is lately dead of the country disease [typhus] leaving a son behind him. His former services especially that of the last summer I hope will be had in remembrance.'

Cromwell had reason to thank him. 'Last summer' referred to Horton's destruction of the last Royalist army in Wales, ending the rebellion of the king's forces there. There was a lot of discontent in the army about unpaid wages, and Parliament feared defections both from the soldiery and the officers. One Welsh Parliamentarian who had deserted to the king's side was Rowland Laugharne, who had previously done a brilliant job for Parliament, taking and holding the southern port of Tenby. His soldiers were seen parading with papers in their hats saying 'we long to see our king'.

Horton defeated Laugharne at St Fagan's, near Cardiff, a turning point in the Second Civil War.[1] Horton had 3,000 soldiers and the Royalists had nearly three times that number, though numbers mattered less than training and determination. Nearly all of the Royalist army were taken prisoner or killed, thus ending the king's power in Wales. Horton's victory at St Fagan's was even more important for Parliament because they were not fighting committed Royalist soldiers. These were former parliamentary soldiers who were owed money, and felt that they would soon be disbanded and never receive it. Horton made sure that they never did.

Horton passed the good news in a letter to the Speaker. 'We have taken all their Foot, Arms and Ammunition, which is good Store [...] It pleased God wonderfully to strengthen and raise up the Spirits of our Officers and Soldiers. Our Word was "God is our Strength"; and truly we found Him so to be, and desire the sole Glory may be given to Him, and ourselves looked upon as weak Instruments in His Hand, and amongst whom, as I am, so I desire to be accounted.'

This could have been Oliver Cromwell speaking, and religiously, Horton was of the same mind. He was an Independent who hated the strictures of Presbyterianism and was closely allied to another Leicestershire republican and Puritan, Arthur Hasilrige. Horton was of a modest gentry background, and he joined Hasilrige's Parliamentary cavalry at the lowest commissioned rank of cornet. Before the war, Horton had been Hasilrige's servant, perhaps his falconer, and during the war he was a protégé of another Leicestershire regicide, Thomas Grey of Groby, the same man who urged Thomas Waite to kill every enemy he encountered.

Horton had a track record in the First Civil War. He had been at Naseby, and suffered a horrible sword wound to his side. He took eight months out to recover and then went back to fight. Horton became famous when he was appointed one of the eight commanders of the New Model Army Regiments (and who comprised six of the regicides). His main contribution was in the Second Civil War. It began in Pembroke, where a parliamentary mutiny over pay led to a larger revolt. Cromwell, Ewer and Pride were dispatched to quell it. Pembroke was important, despite its position on the periphery of the country, as it was an excellent base from which Charles could bring in Irish soldiers. Wales could not be allowed to be controlled by Royalists.

Like many a successful army officer (such as Pride), Horton was granted the sequestered land of his enemies as a reward, but unlike Pride, he never lived to enjoy them. Cromwell's wish that Horton be remembered and his family protected was given a lukewarm response by the Rump Parliament. The Commons took two years to grant his family a sum of £900. He had a son and a surviving wife, who the Royalists hunted down in 1660, confiscating all of the family's property.

We can rely on Mark Noble for a tendentious summing up: 'His origin was mean, his rise rapid, his career short, and his memory infamous.' Horton left his best horse to Oliver Cromwell in his will, knowing that his friend would appreciate it. Horton was made by the war, and without war could not have risen so quickly, to the point that this modest soldier's signature was needed on the execution warrant for a king.

Events in the Second Civil War created this new thinking. One of the stubborn defenders of Colchester, Sir Charles Lucas, was summarily executed by Fairfax for breaking his solemn promise not to engage Parliament again after he had been set free following the Battle of Stow in 1646. It was a rehearsal for the regicide. Lucas, dragged to a firing squad, defiantly asked Fairfax why he was being shot. Fairfax replied that he was guilty of high treason. Lucas logically replied that carrying out the wishes of the monarch could never be treason. However, Parliament had changed the law; since June 1648, treason was defined as anybody who opposed the House of Commons.

Parliament now resolved to punish Royalists like Lucas and Hudson who had broken promises, restarted wars and lost them, escaped from custody and made Parliament look like fools. But who else did this sound like? 'No quarter' and cruel treatment was extending to more and more people, and now this logic was being extended to the monarch himself by men like Waite, Horton and Wogan.

Not much is known about **Thomas Wogan**. He was from Pembrokeshire, the only county in Wales with the substantial support of the gentry for Parliament. Wales was not a well-regarded place by the Parliamentarians. When Henry Cromwell, involved in a row with John Hewson over the governance of Ireland, conjured up the biggest sacrifice he was prepared to make to show his loyalty to the regime, he offered to live alone in a cottage in Wales. He could think of nothing worse.

Thomas's father, John Wogan, was opposed to the king, despite being surrounded by Royalists. Thomas was active in Wales during the First Civil War while still in his twenties. He was a lieutenant by 1644, and was elected MP for Cardigan in August 1646. Unlike many recruiters, this was as much to do with his family background as his service as a soldier. His main contribution was in the Second Civil war when rebellion broke out across the country and Parliament was hard pressed. He served under regicide Thomas Horton as a captain and was mentioned in dispatches at the crucial Battle of St Fagan's on 8 May 1648, where he fought from the first to the last with great leadership and resolution.[2]

At this point he was made a colonel, granted lands in Wales, appointed governor of Aberystwyth Castle by Cromwell and became prominent enough to be part of the regicide party. Like Waite and Horton, his rise was sudden and it was due to the urgency of the situation in 1648. Waite, Horton and Wogan played a minor part of the Rump. By defeating Parliament's enemies and signing the execution warrant, their useful political life was over. In 1652 lands belonging to the Republic were settled upon Wogan as compensation for the money he had paid out and he returned to obscurity.

When Cromwell died in 1658, his son proved unable to rule and power slipped back into the hands of the army. In 1659 the army leaders invited the members of the Rump to return and the majority had the sense not to take up the invitation. Wogan, however, did return, suggesting that he may have had a principled dislike of Cromwell and was a genuine republican. Unlike other republicans, he did not sway with the wind and would not have been surprised to be excluded from the king's pardon. He surrendered on 27 June 1660 and was imprisoned, but on 27 July 1664 he escaped from the Tower with other prisoners. It seems that he fled to Holland, and in 1666 he was in Utrecht, possibly with Ludlow. He was still alive in 1669, but little more is known. His true importance lies in the fact that the Second Civil War allowed three provincial soldiers called Thomas to join the ruling elite, if only temporarily.

Chapter 7

The Main Lawyer
John Bradshaw

The first name on the execution warrant was neither a soldier, a religious radical nor an MP. He was **John Bradshaw** of Marple, Cheshire, and he was first on the warrant because he conducted the trial of Charles I as the Lord President of the High Court of Justice.

Bradshaw was the leading lawyer in the process, but not the leading lawyer in the country in 1649 by some considerable distance. Some historians have suggested that he was not even the leading lawyer in Cheshire. After the execution he was well rewarded by the new Republic and he rose very high indeed. The Royalist historian Clarendon said Bradshaw was a gentleman of an ancient family in Cheshire, but of a fortune of 'his own making'. The implication was that he had made his fortune perverting the laws of England to kill his king. This was certainly the view of his enemies.

Despite the religious motivation of most regicides, the actual legal charge at the trial was couched in the secular language of opposition to arbitrary power. Charles had endeavoured to set up 'an unlimited and tyrannical power to rule according to his will, and overthrow the rights and liberties of the people'. Charles was also a danger to the true religion, and this was implicit in the charge, but the route to execution was law, not faith, so lawyers such as Bradshaw were vital to the process.

Bradshaw was near the top of the Royalist hate list; behind Ireton and Cromwell and at the same level as Thomas Pride. Like Cromwell, his baptismal records still exist, with the word 'TRAITOR' added to it. Critics at the time, and later, claimed the role of the nonentity Bradshaw was to provide just enough legal process to justify the wishes of the army. Like Cromwell and Ireton, Bradshaw was humiliated in the grisly post-mortem execution of 1661, his head joining the other two on Westminster Hall, where they had had the temerity to claim legal equality with their monarch.

Bradshaw was born near Stockport in 1602 into a family of lesser gentry, the second son of Henry Bradshaw. They were certainly not an important family in their own county, but they were not low born, as the Royalists, predictably, have tried to suggest. Henry may have worked his own land, a definition of not being a member of the gentry, but this is uncertain. We do know that his family were anti-Episcopalian and weary of the power of kings. His education was similar to many lesser gentry in the seventeenth century: first a tutor, then the local endowed grammar school. He attended the Inns of Court in 1620, but this did not automatically mean that he would become a lawyer. Most gentlemen attended to get a basic knowledge of law and property so that they could run their own estates and family businesses. In order to become a lawyer, work would be required afterwards: difficult, long, and, in the case of Bradshaw, unforgivingly provincial in the eyes of his enemies. After 1627 he became a barrister and served in Cheshire, becoming Mayor of Congleton in 1637 and moving to London around the outbreak of civil war.

He was part of the parliamentary establishment without being particularly eminent or important – even as late as 1647, nobody expected to need legal proceedings to bring an end to the war – but he was regarded highly enough to be given Somerhill House, in Tonbridge, in 1646.

In December 1648, when the trial was definitely going to happen, Cromwell looked, with great difficulty, for people willing to take part. No reading of English law allowed a king to be tried, and many, including Cromwell's Leveller enemy, John Lilburne, regarded the idea as a tyranny worse than anything Charles I had committed himself. Cromwell tried to recruit eminent parliamentary lawyers like Bulstrode Whitelocke and Thomas Widdrington. Both men were supporters of the new regime after the execution, but felt they could not take part in the process that created it. On 1 January the crime was delineated as 'waging war against the people of England', a novel charge that did not resonate well in English law. On 4 January all three readings of an act to create a High Court of Justice was enacted, in a rush, on a single day. It was, at best, highly unorthodox, and at worst clear treason. More eminent lawyers left town, or suffered sudden, diplomatic, illnesses.

On 10 January 1649 the trial commissioners named Bradshaw as the judge in his absence. He was not a convincing choice. By 12 January Bradshaw was present in London to argue for his unfitness, both for the office and title of Lord President, but was overruled on both issues. To be unnecessarily present when others had absented themselves, and to appear in person to be 'persuaded', suggested opportunism to his enemies, and to accept a job that a dozen better qualified men had rejected suggested egotism. The hostile Clarendon claims he had 'all the pride, impudence and superciliousness imaginable', but then he would say that, wouldn't he?

Bradshaw was, in Royalist eyes, a puppet sprung from the army's tyranny, mouthing the legal fictions that tried to disguise the illegality of the trial. This remains a viable opinion to this day, but there is an alternative; that Bradshaw was the spokesperson for a legal argument that he, and others, actually believed in. Bradshaw has usually been portrayed as a man who was seduced into a job beyond his ability by his own arrogance and ambition, and there is some merit in that. Another view is that he was a brave and principled man who made the best of a very bad situation.

Bradshaw constructed a legal argument against the king alongside two other lawyers: John Cook and Isaac Dorislaus. Cook, who read out the charge at the trial, was a farmer's boy from Leicestershire, and he was one of the first to be executed in October 1660. Others who had actually signed the execution warrant were given lesser punishments. Dorislaus, a Dutchmen, was sought out and murdered by vengeful Royalists in May 1649.

Bradshaw may have been ambitious and self-centred, but he was no coward. He came into Westminster Hall on the first day of the trial wearing oversized clothing and a lead-lined, cone-shaped hat designed to save him from a sniper's bullet. This was not paranoia. The trial was very unpopular beyond a small circle of MPs and officers, and there was real fear of armed opposition. Invasions by foreign armies had been expected, and the Puritans themselves were unpopular in the capital. In 1648 they had to enforce their abolition of Christmas at the point of a sword. Royalist printing presses has been confiscated, known dissidents imprisoned, and vaults under the Painted Chamber searched for gunpowder. It was, therefore, perfectly rational for the Chief Justice of the Court to fear for his own safety.

Another line of defence was precedence, which seems a little surprising for a group that were about to do something unprecedented, but it was part of their desire for legitimacy. The College of Heralds had been consulted on the behaviour and dress for all participants. They tried to make it look like any other trial: 'The said Lord President and his said assistants being all three of long robe sate in their gowns the rest of the Commissioners In usual habits as gentlemen and soldiers.'[1]

There was no historical precedent for the lead lining in his hat, or for the killing of a king. There was also no precedent for soldiers of Hewson's regiment lining the walls of Westminster Hall, armed with poleaxes and looking inward rather than outward. They fooled nobody except themselves, and then not all of the time. Despite their grand dress and use of legal arguments, Charles did not recognise them, either socially or constitutionally, although he did recall the faces of those who had beaten him: Cromwell, Ireton, Harrison and Deane, and those turncoats like Danvers and Edwards who used to support him. The other commissioners were dressed in civilian or military uniforms in order to make an apparent distinction between judge and jury, but in reality they were all part of the same prosecuting power.

The court accepted that Charles was the legal monarch, but by waging two civil wars against the people he was responsible for all of the damage caused and therefore was 'tyrant, traitor, and murderer and public enemy of the Commonwealth of England'. It was not a version of constitutional law that Charles recognised, and made even more risible when the High Court claimed that he was 'elected' king. Bradshaw was in a constitutionally weak position. Despite the constant and successful attack on his credibility, he remained dignified and calm, and as authoritative as anybody could be while making a new law that even kings are answerable to law.

Bradshaw has been criticised for his handling of the trial, with the implication that a more learned judge could have done better. Yet nobody of the requisite experience was prepared to go into battle with the king when Charles had law and tradition on his side. This High Court was an illegal power with no authority, and the English monarchy was neither elective nor contractual. No court could try a king, and the House of Commons was not a court of law. It was not even a full Parliament because the House of Lords had been abolished. It is no wonder that Bradshaw struggled.

Charles had a simple strategy. He refused to acknowledge the legality of the court or respond to the charge. He refused to plead between nine and twelve times, depending on how Bradshaw's words are interpreted. A plea of guilty may have led to a lesser punishment. Historians disagree about this, but his actions and demeanour sealed his fate. There was a lot of petty wrangling. When Bradshaw ordered that the 'prisoner' be taken down, Charles retorted, 'The King, you mean.'[2] The reticence of the king also made it difficult to produce witness statements. Day three was devoted to the presentation of evidence without the king's presence.

Bradshaw was mostly unable to establish his authority, except when Charles claimed to be a friend of the people, and Bradshaw could retort, 'How great a friend you have been to the laws and liberties of the people, let all England and the world judge.' Bradshaw was clearly annoyed on many occasions and had only bluster and threat to help him. Even then, no threat worked on a man who was perfectly prepared to die a martyr. The only weapon that Bradshaw had was the ability to have the king dragged away by soldiers if he did not cooperate, which further supported the king's argument that the court was a creature of the army.

Bradshaw also officiated at another, less well known, treason trial. The king was regarded as the chief villain, but there were others who equally deserved 'no quarter'. Bradshaw sentenced to death the Duke of Hamilton, whose invasion from Scotland was brought to an end by Cromwell's victory at Preston, and Lord Capell, who had given Fairfax so much trouble in Colchester before surrendering (and initially being offered quarter for life, which was rescinded). The Earl of Holland was another young Royalist who had caused trouble for Parliament in Essex. He, too, had surrendered on the understanding that he would not be executed and was captured by regicide Adrian Scrope, who had him shackled with irons.

By 1649 Bradshaw was the leading non-military, non-political figure in the government: a government that prosecuted John Lilburne for High Treason in October 1649. In his opening defence, Lilburne claimed that he was acting in the same way as he did in 1635, when he was being prosecuted by Charles I and defended by a 'Mr John Bradshaw'. This was an attempt to portrait Bradshaw as a hypocrite. Judge Jermin tried to defend Bradshaw but made the situation worse: 'Mr. Bradshaw is now Lord President of the Council of State in England and it would become you to style him so.' The Council of State was the new ruling executive body of the Commonwealth, the new establishment. That was Lilburne's point: Bradshaw the poacher had turned gamekeeper.

Bradshaw became a ruthless servant of the Commonwealth, securing its power and greatly enriching himself. However, he did have republican principles, and these seemed to have triumphed over avarice when he fell out with Cromwell after the Rump was expelled. His attitude to Cromwell was so bitter in the First Protectorate Parliament that Cromwell tried to use his major-generals to stop him being elected to the second one. Bradshaw became disillusioned at the time of the dissolution of the Rump, but was still regarded as one of the Commonwealth elite. He died on 31 October 1659, having just being elected to the Council of State of the returned Rump. He was a republican to the end, and dragged himself from his death bed to support the Parliament.

He was interred in Westminster Abbey with the rest of the elite of the new regime, including his wife, Mary, who had predeceased him. In 1660 Mary was dug up and placed in a common pit in the grounds of St Margaret's Church, Westminster, and in 1661 Bradshaw was exhumed with Cromwell and Ireton. Their corpses were taken to Tyburn – then a village on the outskirts of London – and tied to a sled in the manner reserved for traitors. Bradshaw's coffin was propped up and opened. Cromwell, who had been embalmed, was fresh, but Bradshaw was putrid due to a lack of a regal funeral. The corpses were gibbeted until sunset on the Tyburn Tree, a triangular scaffold that could execute three people at a time. At the end of the day, all three were roughly decapitated and their bodies thrown into the common pit. This was in sharp contrast to the post-mortem fate of Charles I, whose head was sewn back on and who was allowed to rest at St George's Chapel, Windsor, by the order of the three men whose heads were stuck on poles on Westminster Abbey.

Chapter 8

Two Regicide Lawyers
William Say, Augustine Garland

There are lawyers' names all over the execution warrant, and this chapter deals with those who were primarily lawyers and nothing else. Miles Corbet was a lawyer but also a witchfinder, while Gilbert Millington preferred inns and adultery to law, and Thomas Scot was an ardent republican first. So we are left with two purely legal regicides.

Sitting on each side of John Bradshaw at the trial were **William Say** and John Lisle. Only Say signed the warrant. This made no difference when the monarchy was restored, with both men being exempted from pardon and escaping execution or imprisonment by fleeing to different parts of Switzerland. Lisle was one of ten non-signatories who were present when the death penalty was announced. He stood up when the sentence of death was given; legally, he was as guilty as those who signed the warrant. Lisle was tracked down and murdered by agents of the king in August 1664. It proved that culpability went far beyond the fifty-nine in the eyes of the Royalists.

To their critics, both Lisle and Say were no more than pseudo-legalistic cloaks who hid an illegal murder, providing advice for a fanatical minority that required an invented piece of law to cover their crime. Say signed the warrant, and had a part in its drafting. That probably makes him the second-most important lawyer in the process, and as responsible as any colonel or politician on the list in the eyes of Royalists.

Say was like Bradshaw, middling gentry, a university graduate (one of the few Oxford graduates) who practised law after Middle Temple. He was recruited to Parliament as an MP for Camelford in Cornwall, despite his background in Sussex. His lesser status can be seen in the fact that he was temporary president of the High Court of

Justice before the pantomime of false modesty that was the selection of John Bradshaw. Say was a republican, like Bradshaw, and part of the same small pool of legal men who were prepared to countenance execution.

He was an active legal bureaucrat for the Commonwealth. While Cromwell was using brute force to destroy the Levellers, Say was using the law to do the same. In May 1649 he was appointed one of the council for the Commonwealth in the trial of John Lilburne and was involved in the prosecution in October 1649. Lilburne was on trial for writing a pamphlet entitled 'England's New Chains Discovered', which clearly shows the nature of transgression. The regicides had framed their actions in January 1649 in terms of liberty, and Lilburne and other Levellers wanted to know where their new liberty had gone (with the strong implication that Cromwell, Ireton and Bradshaw had stolen it). Lilburne also coined the term 'grandees' to identify and condemn those who had organised the trial. It was also clear that the definition of treason had been greatly extended by the Rump. It was no longer a matter of waging war against the nation. In May 1649 the Rump extended the definition to include incitement to mutiny or indeed any criticism at all of the new government.

These laws were England's new chains, but it was treason to say so. Lilburne was objecting to the type of trumped-up charge and kangaroo court that Say had helped to set up in January 1649 to try the king. Lilburne escaped with his life. The Commons had chosen the 'High Commissioners' for the king, but a jury of Londoners was used for the trial of Lilburne, and he was acquitted.

Like many republicans, Say returned to politics when the rule of the two Cromwells ended, and was a friend of Edmund Ludlow. Both tried to bring the army and civilians together to avoid the rule of a single person. In December 1659, in the dying days of the Commonwealth, Say was elected to the Council of State, and like Ludlow, his principled refusal to support the Restoration meant that in 1660 he had to flee the country. He escaped to the continent, and in October 1662 joined Ludlow at Lausanne, afterwards leaving to seek a place of greater safety in Germany. In 1665 he was in Amsterdam, still conspiring against the Stuart monarchy. Ludlow thought highly of him – another sign of a man attached to the 'Good Old Cause' – and they lived together in exile for a brief time. Say continued to plot with the Dutch Republic to overthrow the Stuarts but without Ludlow's support these plots lacked credibility. He died around 1666, spending his final years alone and fearful of the assassin's bullet.

Augustine Garland had a similar career to William Say. He is an obscure regicide, famous for one example of bad behaviour after the trial, but interesting for another reason. It's only a small exaggeration to suggest that the centre of political and religious radicalism in civil war England was Coleman Street in the City of London. Despite the name, it was a set of streets and alleys in one of the twenty-five wards of the city of London. You could not live there and not be imbued with new religious and political ideas. Augustine Garland was born there, the son of a lawyer, in 1602. It's hardly surprisingly that he turned against his king.[1]

Coleman Street was the centre of religious radicalism before and after the execution. In the 1630s John Goodwin's gathered church was in constant dispute with the authorities. He became the vicar there at St Stephens in 1633, taking advantage of the fact that the advowson, or right to nominate a new incumbent, was in the hands of local worshippers. He also preached what the establishment would regard as political and radical subversion. When Charles I tried to arrest the five main troublemaker MPs in January 1642 (none of them were future regicides, as none were important enough so early in the war) it was in Coleman Street where they hid from their king, knowing that they would not be betrayed. Later, there were Fifth Monarchists in Soper Lane, Independent Baptists in Bell Alley, and public houses like the Star Inn or Nags Head, where Cromwell and his allies consulted and plotted. The exact influence on Garland is unknown, but he shared many of the beliefs that were generated there.

Many of Goodwin's followers were members of the Honourable Artillery Company and they made alliances with city radicals such as the regicides Tichborne and Rowe, whom Garland would have known. Goodwin worked with Philip Nye, and the regicide Alured was part of his congregation. Goodwin supported the execution of the king as a righteous working out of God's plans for England. Many regicides agreed with him, but preachers like Goodwin had reached the conclusion first, and it was the regicides who were following him. Garland was also part of another network in the University of

Cambridge, which was more involved in regicide and civil war than Oxford. John Goodwin was there in 1617, and Garland went to the ultra-Puritan Emmanuel College, where he and hundreds of others would hear the sermons of Puritan ministers.

His republican sympathies were similar, if not more intense than Say's. We have some indication of his character through the distorting effect of bad things being recorded and good things being forgotten. He was admitted to Lincoln's Inn on 14 June 1631, a contemporary of the regicide John Dixwell, and Garland seemed to have led a student riot there in 1635.[2] When his father died in 1637 Garland was effectively missed out from his father's will, with the bulk of the estate going to his three sisters and one of them given the usual male duty of proving the will. When he was assessed for tax in November 1644 he pleaded with the Committee for Advance of Money that 'his estate in lands is but for life'.[3] That would have been another of his father's punishments.

In June 1648 he was recruited to the House of Commons. In August his wife died of 'smallpox in childbed', the initial disease being exacerbated by the strains and dangers of giving birth. Her name, tellingly, is unknown; the obscure wife of an obscure man. Her death led to a period of inactivity in the Commons. He may have been devastated by this loss. The belief that people in the seventeenth century mourned only briefly after premature or tragic deaths and then 'moved on' is a myth.

In the crisis month of November 1648 Garland sprung into action, and he did enough work in the background to be regarded as an underrated regicide. Noble said he was chairman of the committee that prepared the bill for the legal proceedings. It was Garland who presented an ordinance in January 1649 'for erecting a High Court of Justice for Trial of the king'. Amendments were asked during the day and Garland must have spent all night preparing them, because they appeared, completed, first thing the next morning. Garland was one of the men who worked hardest in creating and justifying the 'High Court of Justice'. His friends in Parliament were republicans Henry Marten, Thomas Scot and Thomas Chaloner, showing perhaps that the Coleman Street influence had given him more political than religious radicalism.

Garland was a regime man through and through. Perhaps it was lucky that the revengeful Parliament of Charles II had so few MPs who were in the Rump, as they may have remembered Garland's frenetic work for the Republic. The Commons reports contained many comments such as 'Mr Garland reports [...] Mr Garland is to take care of it'. He was a member of over 200 committees during the period 1649 to 1653, more than any other MP then or now.

He continued to be a supporter of Oliver Cromwell after 1653, despite the new regime of the Lord Protector not being very republican. He did seem to have a parting of the ways with Cromwell around 1655, when he became much less politically active.

At his trial in 1660 he was accused of spitting at the king as he left Westminster Hall in 1649. It seemed clear that the event did happen. Despite being on trial for the king's murder, this relatively minor matter was regarded as worth bringing up. Garland denied it, and even Noble suggested that the evidence was not strong. It was mostly the guard of rough, tobacco-chewing soldiers that would have the means, motive and opportunity to spit on the king. The only evidence came from a man called Clench. 'He is an indigent person,' claimed Garland, desperately, and it does seem that Clench was a professional witness looking forward to a pay day. The court was happy to discount his evidence and move on, which was a little surprising. One person's evidence was regularly sufficient to send people to the gallows. It was certainly enough for accusations of regicide, but on this occasion not good enough for loutish behaviour

His mitigation was intimidation and an inability to get away from the trial process without endangering his life. Noble made a valid point on this issue, 'Others were named yet did not act and [were] not injured for declining what their consciences dictated was the highest crime in the law.' He could have simply refused to sign. That remained obvious throughout his trial.

He was sentenced to death. This was later commuted, but in a fit of extra revenge, the Commons tried to kill Augustine Garland (and Hardress Waller) again with a Bill of Attainder in December 1660. An Attainder Act declares somebody guilty of a crime and then punishes them without a trial. The Bill was introduced by Sir Heneage Finch, who had convicted the other regicides two months earlier. The new crime seemed to be barbaric ingratitude. Garland was compared to the Turks, who 'would not eat off any man they meant to betray'. As a former pensioner of the king, he was worse than the heathen in his betrayal. This attack came to nothing. Garland was exiled to Tangier after the Restoration (like George Fleetwood), but it seems that the sentence was not carried before out before his death.

Chapter 9

The Main Republican
Henry Marten

On one level, all of the fifty-nine were republicans. They were prepared to countenance the death of a king and the abolition of the monarchy. For most of the fifty-nine, their first priority was the physical elimination of Charles I. On the morning of the execution it was realised that the Rump had forgotten to abolish the monarchy. The execution was a desperate emergency measure before it was a hardline republican act, but they still did it.

Some regicides had an early opposition to monarchy in principle and enthusiastically endorsed the execution of the king as a good idea in itself. Many fought for the republican Commonwealth of 1649–1653, and had principles so strong that they could not countenance the rule of a single person or the title of king proposed for Cromwell in 1657. The leading republican regicide is Henry Marten. He broke every rule about what a regicide believed and challenged every norm of behaviour at the time. Many MPs in the 1640s and 1650s were labelled 'Friends of Henry Marten', mostly as a term of abuse.

Why was he different? For a start, he was no Puritan; certainly not in his behaviour and, unless politically convenient, not in his world view either. He did not become a republican through his hatred of Charles' religious innovations, or his appalling behaviour during the war, like the vast majority of regicides. He just did not like monarchy, and did not think it could work properly. As early as 1641, when the devastation of war and the perfidy of the monarch were as yet unknown, Marten told Edward Hyde – later the famous Royalist Clarendon – that he believed that no single individual was wise enough to rule a whole nation. Clarendon also said that if Marten's beliefs had been communicated 'they would have been abhorred by the whole nation'. This was true when he said it. What he could not predict in 1641 was that the people in charge of the country would feel differently by 1648.

Marten's enemies knew his views. In August 1642 he was exempt from pardon as the king raised his standard in Nottingham. Charles complained in his declaration of 12 August 1642 that, 'It hath been publicly said by Marten that our office is forfeitable, and that the happiness of the kingdom doth not depend upon us, nor any of the regal branches of that stock.'

Marten broke the mould in religion, politics and everywhere else. Only his family background, the part of his life that was outside his control, was traditional. Marten attended university in his home town of Oxford and then trained as a lawyer at the Inns of Court. He had neither a dutiful Puritan background nor a family with a tradition of opposing the king.

Marten behaved so badly that we know much more about his personality than most others. He was married to a stranger, a widow called Margaret Staunton, but he refused to settle for a marriage of convenience and continued to behave like a single man. He was known to be a wastrel, spending thousands of pounds of his father's money annually on nothing in particular. Much of the money was spent forgetting about his unhappy marriage. 'He was a great lover of pretty girls, to whom he was so liberal that he spent the greatest part of his estate,' said the unshockable John Aubrey.[1]

He united Charles I and Oliver Cromwell in their disgust for him. Charles had him ejected from a race meeting and Cromwell called him a 'whoremaster' (in 1640 and 1653 respectively). At the beginning of the civil war he raised a regiment of horse, which was probably an improvement on his improvident lifestyle, although that too may have been paid for with his father's money.

The war started with the fiction that Parliament was fighting against the king's evil advisers, and that the army of 23,000, which was formed by the Earl of Essex, was designed to defeat the king once, weaken his power and redistribute power amongst those who already had it. Marten, like the other Republicans in the next chapter rejected these ideas. The history of Britain would have been different, and Marten forgotten, if one side had unambiguously won the first pitched battle at Edgehill in 1642.

Bradshaw the lawyer regicide.

Ludlow the republican regicide.

Corbet the bureaucrat regicide.

Okey the soldier regicide.

Edward Earl of CLARENDON Lord High CHANCELLOR of England and Chancellor of the University of Oxford An.º Dom 1667.

Above left: Edward Hyde / Earl Clarendon.

Above right: Lucy Hutchinson.

Left: General George Monck.

Cromwell pypeth unto Fairfax.

Huson the Cobler entring London.

Above left: Fairfax dances to Cromwell's tune.

Above right: Hewson the Cobbler.

Right: Matthew Hopkins.

MATTHEW HOPKINS,
OF MANNINGTREE, ESSEX,
THE CELEBRATED WITCH-FINDER.

Pride the drayman.

Marten the assassin.

Pride's Purge, Victorian view.

The Seal of the
Commonwealth.

Expulsion of the Rump.

ROASTING THE RUMPS IN FLEET STREET (FROM AN OLD PRINT) (*see page* 95).

Roasting of the Rump, 1660.

Cromwell the war hero.

Cromwell the ally of Satan.

THE JUDGES' CAVE. Page 194.

Hiding Place for Whalley and Goffe – Judges' Rock.

A. THE OLDE HOVSE. B. THE NEW. C. THE TOWER THAT IS HALFE BATTERED DOVNE. D. THE KINGES BREAST WORKS. E. THE PARLIAMENTS BREAST WORKS.

HOLLAR'S VIEW OF BASING HOUSE c. 1644

Basing House – where the civil war became uncivil.

The LORD PROTECTOR lying in State at Sommerset House.

Engraved by J.ʳ Caldwall, from the original print in the Collection of JOHN TOWNELEY E.SQ.ʳ

A 'king' rests in state. (Wellcome, London)

1. *Cromwels haupt.*   2. *Bratſhew.*   3. *Ireton.*

Three dead usurpers are executed – Cromwell, Ireton and Pride.

In 1643 Parliament developed a 'peace party' and a 'war party', and Marten was a member of the latter. The extreme war party was small, but held an influence far beyond its numbers. It did so by drawing people's attention to the worrying side of the king's behaviour. This did not turn the other MPs into republicans, but it did make a peaceful settlement much less likely. War was not popular, and a string of parliamentary defeats in 1643 made it less so, but fanatics like Marten made sure that the Commons could not retrace its steps into a negotiated peace. In that respect only, Marten's behaviour was similar to the king in that there was no desire for peace in 1643 from the monarch's side either.

Marten was adept at the mad-cap, anti-monarchical publicity stunt. On 30 March 1643 he broke into Queen Henrietta Maria's private chapel, assisted in the destruction of a Reuben's masterpiece depicting the crucifixion, and smashed other images of the Virgin Mary. His partner in crime was John Clotworthy, MP and opponent of all things Catholic with a passion verging on the psychotic. Clotworthy was described by Veronica Wedgwood as 'a heartless, dour and repellent man who throughout his life showed a consistent inhumanity towards his fellow men.' To Clotworthy, this vandalism was a religious act, but for Marten it was different: it was a necessary attack on Henrietta Maria. She was being very troublesome to the men in Parliament. In 1643 she had risked her life arriving on the east coast and had delivered much war materiel to her husband's army. Marten believed she was as guilty as any commoner who provided the king with assistance. He stoked up fear against Henrietta Maria, and provided a proxy target for those too faint-hearted to condemn the king himself.

Marten also got himself into trouble in the same year when he broke into Westminster Hall with 300 soldiers, looking for the crown jewels so they could be sold. 'Why should lesser delinquents be sequestered and the greatest one allowed to go unpunished?' was his cry. In the end, he found nothing but coronation garments, and one of his friends paraded around in them. 'With a scorn, greater than his lusts and the rest of his vices, he openly declared that there should be no further use of these toys and trifles,' said an enemy.[2] After the break-in the lock and key to the Treasury were changed, but a few months later Marten was locked up himself.

He took a step too far when, on 16 August 1643, he told the Commons that the destruction of one family (the royal family) was preferable to the destruction of many families. When asked to clarify, he exacerbated the insult by claiming that he only meant the king and his children. He was expelled from Parliament for his pains, and did not return until January 1646, after spending a short time in the Tower of London.

His sojourn in prison saved him from another problem. The war was not going well for Parliament, and the Scottish army's price for its assistance was that the MPs subscribe to the Solemn League and Covenant, which bound the signatories to work for a Presbyterian Church in England. It would have been a minor problem though. Marten could have signed it without believing it; his conscience would not have been troubled. He was not a Puritan, nor indeed a Presbyterian. In fact, he seemed not to be religious at all. In the Commons he mocked those members of the public who had flocked around the king to receive his touch against scrofula. He mocked the idea of a divinely inspired king as childishly irrational.

Most of the regicides were socially very conservative. Few wanted to upset the social order or bring democracy. Marten was quite close to being a democrat in the way we would understand it today. He was a friend and supporter of John Lilburne and supported his ideas. He detested and mocked the unelected House of Lords. When some enemies of the Lords declared them useless and dangerous, he disagreed with the second part on the basis that they were too useless to be dangerous.

His enemies called him an atheist, but it was a little more sophisticated than merely being a disbeliever. He was sceptical, not of the existence of a supreme being, but of the ability of humans to fully comprehend the subject. He would have stood out from his fellow rebels and regicides by failing to see the hand of the Almighty in all events. His religious position became one of ultra-toleration, but a toleration borne out of a kind of apathy rather than fervent Puritan principle. His views seem very similar to his close friend, William Walwyn, who argued that Jesus didn't need force or compulsion, therefore his contemporary followers had no right to use it. Both men were very radical in their views, evidenced by the fact that they included Roman Catholics in their formulation.

He was an active part of the Commonwealth, but went quiet during the Cromwell years. His skills and background were legal and political, and he was far better at creating ideological turbulence than achieving anything practical. There was nothing he could offer the Protectorate, and nothing that he would be prepared to contribute to a regime that looked even more monarchical than that of Charles I. From 1655 to 1659 he was imprisoned for debt, having gone back the free-spending days before the war without the income to sustain it.

He made no attempt to flee at the Restoration and was imprisoned for the rest of his life. This moderate punishment took many by surprise, especially considering the insouciance he had showed at his trial. His first line of defence was a misspelling on the list of exemptions to the Act of Indemnity. A Henry *Martin* had been exempted from justice, and he was Henry *Marten*. This may sound a little weak today, but legal cases have been thrown out due to such technicalities. For arraignments as serious as these, details had to be correct. As Marten said at his trial, 'I humbly conceive all penal statutes ought to be understood literally.'

He survived the Restoration with his life, and spent the next twelve years locked up in Chepstow Castle after some time at Berwick, and then Windsor Castle, until Charles II decided that it was too close for him to bear. This was not only royal distaste, but may also have been fear of his republican ideas. Marten's wife continued to live in Berkshire, and Marten himself shared his semi-confinement (he was allowed out on walking trips in the village of St Pierre) with his mistress, Mary Ward, and their three daughters. The public were shocked, not just by this adultery, but Marten's complete lack of secrecy about their thirty-year relationship. He died, aged seventy-eight, in 1680, while eating his supper too quickly and choking to death, although it may well have been as a result of a stroke.

He was a witty, friendly and incisive man, a good friend but a formidable enemy. Even his enemy, Antony Wood, noticed his good features, but he would drink too much too quickly and the wit and mirth would stop. Towards the end of his life, he wrote a poem about himself, with the first letter of each line spelling out his name. The last line was, '[It's] Not how you end, but how you spend your days.'

Chapter 10

The Hardcore Republicans
Thomas Chaloner, Thomas Scot, Valentine Walton

Veronica Wedgwood, who condemned many of the regicides out of hand, was probably wrong when she suggested that **Thomas Chaloner** was an opportunist driven only by spite.[1] Many of the gentry class were alienated from the monarchy by the Stuart's desperate attempts to raise money to fill the gaps in taxation caused by the failure to call Parliament. In this case, Chaloner's father had set up Britain's first alum manufacturer in North Yorkshire. This was a great aid to the British textile industry, but the Chaloner family property was claimed as Royal mines. At first the family were mollified by promises of compensation; instead the mines were sold off for the profit of the king's courtiers.

Both Thomas and his brother, James, became enemies of the king at this point. Wedgwood's point was that this was Chaloner's only principle, but that is unfair. His alum mines were returned by the Long Parliament during the civil war, but his republicanism did not diminish. In any case, he passes the main republican test: he was extremely active for the Republic for the three years of its existence, but disappeared from public life in 1653 when the rule of a single person was re-imposed by Cromwell.

Chaloner, like his friend, political ally and drinking buddy Henry Marten, was a convinced and early-adopter republican. Many of the apparent republican regicides had their views created by events in 1648, and would have been happy to accept a weakened monarchy and strengthened Commons until the Second Civil War changed opinions. Chaloner wanted a Republic like Venice or the Netherlands from the very beginning.

Marten and Chaloner were similar in many other ways, including religion. Anthony Wood, talking about Thomas May, the librarian of the

Parliament, made a link to Chaloner. 'He [May] became,' says Wood, 'a debauchee, *ad omnia*, entertained ill principles as to religion, spoke often very slightly of the Holy Trinity and kept beastly and atheistical company, of whom Thomas Chaloner the regicide was one.'[2] Wood continued, 'He was as far from being a Puritan or a Presbyterian as the east is from the west.' A ploughman who uttered Marten's or Chaloner's words would soon find himself hauled up before the Justice of the Peace, but as a member of the establishment, Chaloner was safe.

Chaloner was born in Steeple Claydon, Buckinghamshire. The county's reputation for religious opposition to the king did not extend to him, or his family. Thomas was the son of the courtier Thomas Chaloner, who was an ally of the court and no Puritan or radical. Like Marten, Chaloner junior spent time on the early version of the Grand Tour, like Marten, he didn't finish his university education, and, like Marten, this did not matter.

Mark Noble has particular scorn for Chaloner; both low and high born regicides were a puzzle to him. Low-status regicides were, in his opinion, unnatural and stupid: 'Chaloner's crime was not Puritanism or republicanism, but ingratitude.' This seems unfair, as his principles were real. Chaloner had fled the country in 1637 when Archbishop Laud was after him. He clearly had principles irksome enough to annoy the Archbishop of Canterbury.

Just like Marten, Chaloner had an early track record in opposing the monarchy. In October 1646, when the Commons was manoeuvring to negotiate with the king, Chaloner (a recruiter MP for Richmond after 1645) was objecting to the idea of monarchy being the first consideration for any state. Parliament was 'not bound to preserve his person further than they found his person the defence of the true Religion the liberties of the People and privilege of Parliament.'

The opposite was true. The Commons would protect the king if he was an asset, and punish him (or anybody) if they were a danger to the Commonwealth. As Chaloner said, 'are they not plainly by the same Covenant to bring to condign punishment as of all delinquents?' His example of the delinquents were Strafford and Laud, both executed by Parliament, with Chaloner playing his grubby part, especially against Laud.

By 1648 he was 'King Cudgelling Tom Chaloner', whose bloody-mindedness towards monarchy had become much more fashionable, partly due to the king's own bloody-mindedness in restarting the war. Chaloner, Harrison and others did not need to appeal to God's providence or blood guilt. They had been potential regicides for half a decade, and now Charles I obliged them.

After the execution Chaloner was a member of the Council of State and took a keen interest in Commonwealth trade and foreign policy. He regarded the Dutch as England's main rivals rather than the Catholic powers of Europe, and supported the War with Holland in 1652–54. In 1651 he was made councillor of state and master of the mint. In 1653, at the violent dissolution of the Rump, Cromwell called Chaloner a drunkard.

When Cromwell died in 1658, Chaloner continued to struggle against Richard Cromwell, not only as 'a single person', but as the beginning of a new hereditary dynasty. Chaloner returned to Westminster in 1659 when he was elected MP for Scarborough in the Third Protectorate Parliament. He joined the republicans in working for the overthrow of Richard Cromwell, and supported attempts to re-establish the Commonwealth. With the Restoration of the monarchy in 1660, Chaloner was excluded from pardon and fled abroad. He died in Middleburg, Netherlands in 1661, not daring to put his real name on the gravestone in case the Royalists came looking for him and dug him up.

The republican **Thomas Scot,** the fifty-seventh name of the fifty-nine, has also been forgotten. Like Chaloner, he never served in the Parliamentary army, nor had battles or sieges to his name. He was far from obscure at the time, however. Scot was one of the first regicides to be singled out for immediate and savage punishment by the Royalists because he developed his republicanism very early and never compromised or changed his mind.

Many of the regicide lawyers tended towards republicanism, and Thomas Scot was no exception. He was a lawyer in Buckinghamshire and grew to prominence as the treasurer of the region's County Committee between 1644 and 1646. He worked with Henry Marten, and was made governor of Aylesbury after Marten's expulsion from Parliament and imprisonment in the Tower. Like many of the more radical men who were not really part of the political establishment at the beginning of the war, he did not become an MP until later; in his case the recruiter MP for Aylesbury in 1645, a logical choice as it was part of his power base.

He replaced Sir Ralph Verney, the famous Royalist, who had died for his king at the battle of Edgehill.

Both Scot and Marten were political animals rather than soldiers; men who could use charm or intimidation when necessary, and had the knack of making deals. One Royalist described Scot as 'a man who crept into the House of Commons, whispers treason into many of the members' ears, animating the war [...] and studying aggravations thereunto.' He eloquently opposed negotiations with the king in 1648, when the Presbyterian majority in Parliament were trying to settle with the king as if the Second Civil War had never happened, declaring, 'that there could be no time seasonable for such a treaty, or for a peace with so perfidious and implacable a prince.'

Scot was an assiduous organiser of the execution, being one of the four chosen (with Waller, Tichborne and Harrison) to select an open street in which to execute the king. After the execution, Scot loyally served the new Republic as a member of the Council of State (1649–1651) and more importantly, as Britain's first spymaster (and the only Head of British Intelligence ever executed for treason). The Commons was looking for somebody committed, intelligent and ruthless, and they found that Scot fitted the bill. He was the first to use proactive methods to monitor and infiltrate enemy groups. The most famous spymaster is, rightly, John Thurloe, but he did not take on the task until 1653, and he would have found the job impossible without the network of spies, codebreakers and *agents provocateur* that Scot had built up. The records were so rigorous that they were used by the restored Stuart monarchy in the 1660s to establish their own spying service. It was Thurloe who, by briefing the incoming government, was allowed to fade into obscurity rather than face justice in 1660, saved by his own work and that of Scot.

With the fall of the Republic in 1653, Scot became one of the Protectorate's most vocal opponents, organising anti-Cromwell opposition inside the Parliament as MP for Aylesbury instead of retiring to the country in bitterness and sulking, which was an option that Cromwell would have preferred.

Scot returned to politics in February 1659 in Richard Cromwell's Parliament and did everything he could to undermine it, because it was part of a constitution that he could not abide. Alongside non-regicide republican Arthur Hasilrige, he filibustered debates, attacked the House of Lords, and tried to make overtures to the army officers, who were also dissatisfied with their own treatment and position in the constitution. With perhaps thirty republicans in the Commons, they were strong enough to sap the confidence of Richard Cromwell's government, but not strong enough to destroy it and replace it with something more effective.

When the army officers ejected Richard Cromwell and brought back the Rump in April 1659, Scot became a major player in the government. He reprised his role as spymaster when John Thurloe was rejected for being too 'Cromwellian' a figure for the Rumpers to suffer. Even in November 1659 he was supporting the Rump, and in 1660, when the tide had turned in favour of the return of the monarchy, he never stopped trying. When the Rump was removed for the second time, he and his ally, John Okey, tried to take the Tower of London, on 12 December 1659. They fled to join the Parliamentarian navy the next day when they failed.

On 2 January 1660 the Rump, restored for the third time, reached a nadir. Its attendance hovered just about the quorum of forty. Monck was moving southwards with his army and, while people were unsure about his motives, it was clear that he was not planning to help them as he had promised in October. A desperate oath was organised, renouncing monarchical government, but only thirteen MPs signed it. The powerless, discredited and hated Parliament then sent out Thomas Scot to intercept and welcome Monck and his army. Scot's attempt to influence Monck failed. It was now clear where the real power was.

His support for the Commonwealth shifted from the principled to the utterly reckless. On the last day of the Rump, 16 March 1660, with the Restoration imminent and a new, more Royalist Parliament to be elected, MPs decided it was time for a little *mea culpa*. This was not the Rump speaking. Monck had returned seventy-three members purged by Thomas Pride on 20 February and Scot was now outnumbered and more than little peeved. One MP, a Mr Crew, thought it best to end the session by showing his personal loyalty to the regime that was to come. He proposed that, 'before they separated they should bear their witness against the horrid murder of the king.'

Scot then put his life and estate in great danger with an intemperate rail against the inevitable: The House of Commons Journal recorded it for posterity: 'Mr Scot rose in his place and replied, "I desire no greater honour in this world than that the following inscription may be engraven on my tomb here lieth ONE WHO HAD A HAND AND A HEART IN THE EXECUTION OF CHARLES STUART late King of England" and then left the house, followed by all those attached to his principles.'

Scot was a marked man, and was easy to find. He and his family lived in non-republican splendour in one wing of Lambeth palace, which had been purchased cheaply from the estates of the late (and executed) Archbishop of Canterbury. Scot was a little ambiguous about what to do next. He was thirty-three years old, a young regicide, and his inclination was to resist rather than martyr himself. He fled to Brussels, but later returned on the basis of the king's royal proclamation with the hope of pardon. He was one of many who claimed that he had come back to England to take advantage of the king's mercy. He was in the Tower of London by July 1660, and it was there that he was told that he had already been excluded from the pardon.

Thomas Scot was brought to trial on 12 October 1660 and was the first of the regicides to defend himself. He chose a legal defence with no illusion that it would be successful (in the opinion of Edmund Ludlow, the outcome was a foregone conclusion).[3] Unlike some of the others who cut a poor figure in an attempt to avoid a grisly punishment, Scot was unrepentant, 'I bless His name that He engaged me in a cause not repented of.'

The prosecution's legal defence was the same for all regicides. It used Treason Act of Edward III to condemn as traitors anybody who 'encompassed or imagined' the death of a king. Scot was charged with sitting in the High Court of Justice at the trial of King Charles I and with signing one warrant for summoning that court, and another for the execution. He was further accused of wanting 'Here lies Thomas Scot, who adjudged the late King to die' on his gravestone. Essentially, the charge was not just that he did it, but that he was proud of it. Both accusations were true.

When the regicides came to plead, they were given the normal, binary choice of 'guilty' or 'not guilty'. This did not suit some of the defendants. They wanted to make a comment, either in mitigation or justification, and defend a different version of the law; one that they believed in sincerely, but that their enemies insisted that they had made up.

Scot's defence was elaborate. He claimed parliamentary privilege, saying, 'Whatever had been spoken in the House ought not to be given in evidence against him, not falling under the cognisance of any inferior court, as all men knew.' He had acted under the protection of that legal Parliament, which was a higher authority than that which he was facing now.

When he claimed that the king was executed as a legal act of Parliament passed by the 'authority of the Keepers of the Liberties of England', the judge shouted him down: 'Sir, if you speak to this purpose again, I profess for my part I dare not hear any more: 'tis a doctrine so poisonous and blasphemous, that if you proceed upon this point, I shall (and I hope my lords will be the same opinion) desire that the jury may be immediately directed.'

Scot liked to make long speeches, much to the distress of the parliaments of which he had been a member. However, this time nobody was listening. Almost nobody else had been as vocal as Scot against the monarchy, and witnesses against him were easy to find. The jury was directed to find him guilty.

At his execution some of his last words were, 'I say again; to the praise of the Free Grace of God; I bless His name He hath engaged me in a cause, not to be repented of, I say, not to be repented of.'

There was a split between those regicides who thought that Charles had broken the law of God and those who thought he had broken the law of man as well. Scot was one of the latter. Religious motivations have lost their meaning through centuries of secularisation, but Scot's ideas still resonate. He died, in his mind, as an elected politician with a mandate from the highest authority in the land rather than as a member of God's elect. He feels like a very 'modern' regicide.

Valentine Walton is remembered most for being a member of Oliver Cromwell's extended family. He married Margaret Cromwell, daughter of Robert Cromwell and sister to Oliver, in June 1617. Earlier in the same month, Robert Cromwell had died when the Cromwell family was at a low ebb. Neither family would have any inkling of their rise to power in the future. Like Cromwell, Walton was a Huntingdonshire man, and was elected to the Commons in 1640 despite the opposition of Sir Oliver Cromwell, Oliver's uncle. Walton started the war early and tried to intercept the silver plate of the University of Cambridge that was being transported to the king to help him finance his war. He tried unsuccessfully on his own at first, with the inefficient Trained Bands of his county, but succeeded in alliance with Cromwell. This was the beginning of the war, and it was naively believed that it could be financed on the proceeds of melted-down precious metal worth £20,000 rather the mass appropriations and ruinous levels of taxation that were required later on.

Walton was captured at Edgehill and imprisoned in Oxford Castle for nearly ten months until exchanged with a Royalist prisoner in July 1643. In September 1643 he was appointed governor of King's Lynn in Norfolk after its capture by the Parliamentarians. The town became a place of refuge for those of independent religious views, according to the hostile contemporary commentator Clement Walker.

Valentine's eldest son, also Valentine, served under Cromwell and died at Marston Moor in July 1644. It was Cromwell, who had lost his own son Oliver earlier the same year, who passed the message on to him in a letter.[4] It is a mixture of the empathetic and the religiously fanatical: 'Sir, God hath taken away your eldest son by a cannon shot. It broke his leg. We were necessitated to have it cut off, whereof he died.' The letter also showed Cromwell's ability to understand Walton's grieving with a reference to the death of his own son: 'Sir, you know my own trials this way; but the Lord has supported me with this.' And he went on to provide consolation, 'There is your precious child full of glory, never to know sin or sorrow any more', before adding, 'A little after [the amputation] he said, one thing lay upon his spirit. He told me that it was, that God had not suffered him any more to be the executioner of His enemies.'

Cromwell went on to say that God, not man, is the creator of all successes and setbacks: 'An absolute victory obtained by the Lord's blessing upon the godly party principally God made them as stubble to our swords.' This shows the insight into suffering that happened thousands of times during the civil war and it tells us much about the two men. This is what Cromwell wanted to say, and what he believed his brother-in-law wanted to hear.

Despite a record of working hard and effectively during the war, and signing the death warrant in 1649, Walton was not a major figure in the Republic. He was regularly voted onto the Council of State, and was appointed governor of King's Lynn and Croyland. His main contribution was as a member of the Navy Committee, alongside regicides Corbett and Clement, who had the important job of expanding the new Republic's navy and purging it of any opposition elements. The navy doubled in size in the three years after 1649, and although the successes of the army are well known, they would have been impossible without the supplies and logistical support of the navy.

Like the vast majority of all republican regicides, his principles did not preclude profiting from his powerful position. In 1653 he purchased Somersham House, the former property of Queen Henrietta Maria in the Isle of Ely, for a sum that was later called a 'small matter' by his enemies. Walton was a 'real' republican, who wished to change the form of government entirely, and refused honours under Cromwell's protectorate, but he was an unswerving follower of Cromwell before 1649. Noble believed that Cromwell distrusted him and had him monitored. Walton was certainly inactive while the Lord Protector ruled.

Walton played his part in the chaos after the death of Oliver Cromwell. Like Okey, Ludlow and Scot, he wanted to be returned to Richard Cromwell's Parliament in order to cause trouble but was opposed by spymaster Thurloe, who was now working as assiduously for the son as he did for the father. Like Ludlow and Scot, he put his faith in the return of the Rump Parliament, and when it failed and was replaced by an army committee of safety, he was one of the men who seized Portsmouth in December 1659 as an active protest and a way of getting the Rump returned. When the Rump *was* returned again in late December, Walton (and Okey) accidently showed its precarious position by riding for two days to Westminster and rushing into the Commons without even changing their clothes. It did not matter how much they stank, people had to be on seats to make sure that it was not purged again. In late February 1660, as soon as it was politically possible, George Monck removed Walton from his army command.

Walton made the trip to Hanau, like Okey and Barkstead, but did not stay there long. He seemed to have been protected but not anonymous there, and his fear of a Royalist assassin made him give up his identity. He died in obscurity and poverty in Flanders. He would have feared the peripatetic Royalist killers and freelance bounty hunters all his life. The Royalist revenge was very effective. It was rigorous enough to create fear in the hearts of the regicides, but never intensive enough to incur great cost for the new government.

Chapter 11

Well Documented Men?

Edmund Ludlow, John Hutchinson

The quantity and quality of historical sources about each regicide varies, as would be expected. Those at the very centre of the action – Cromwell, Ireton, and Bradshaw – are well documented and there are other, less significant regicides who have left a large amount of correspondence which allows us to examine their personalities and motivation.

We have two near-contemporary narrative life stories of significant length for the republican regicides John Hutchinson and Edmund Ludlow. One is a biography and the other – seemingly – is an autobiography. This would appear be everything that a historian would want – we are not feeding on scraps and inferences as with some regicides – but this is an example of being careful what you wish for, as both sources have problems.

Edmund Ludlow's work looks like an autobiography – problematical in itself as a historical source – but it is tainted a little by the fact that somebody seems to have taken the original and altered it extensively, to the extent that historian Blair Worden called it 'a forgery'. Ludlow's autobiography was originally entitled *A Voyce from the Watch Tower*, but was edited and altered, probably by the republican John Toland, and published as *The Memoirs of Edmund Ludlow* in 1698–9. The new version removed all the Puritanism and enhanced the republicanism for an age more interested in the distribution of political power than religious disputation. It was generally regarded as authentic until 1970, when part of Ludlow's original manuscript was discovered at Warwick Castle, and a comparison made with John Toland's version.

Ludlow was certainly a republican. His doctored memoirs make that clear, and that indeed was the point of them. His father was an MP for Wiltshire who became an extreme critic of the king, the only example of a regicide's father, rather than the regicide himself, who made it to Charles's 1642 list of traitors for saying that he was not fit to be king. This was a sentiment too far for MPs who were merely planning (very reluctantly) to battle with him to bring him to heel. In the last year of his life, 1643, Ludlow's father declared that the king's power came from Parliament and not the other way around. Edmund followed in his father's footsteps, becoming an ally of Henry Marten after Marten's release from prison.

This alliance of two republicans working together made sense, but this is where the reliance on his doctored memoirs causes problems. There two men were different. The memoirs strip out all of the fanaticism and reliance on the biblical interpretation. Ludlow's opposition to the king had a deep religious base; something that nobody wanted to hear when the memoirs came out. For all regicides, apart from Marten, religion was their main motivation, and politics was how they reacted when Satan threatened God's church.

So, Ludlow was certainly a Puritan and republican of the 'extreme' sort, and, like so many regicides, came from a traditional country family, and had university and legal training. Ludlow opposed the king from the outset, and opposed the king militarily before becoming a full-time politician. Ludlow joined the gentlemen of the Earl of Essex's lifeguard, who were recruited from the Inns of Court. Fellow regicide Thomas Harrison was also a member. They played an important role in the avoidance of defeat at the battle of Edgehill in October 1642.

Ludlow spent most of the war in Wiltshire, rising to be colonel of a cavalry regiment. His defence of Wardour Castle in Wiltshire in 1643, when the Parliament was at its lowest ebb, brought him to national prominence. He lost the castle in 1644, but his tenacity made his name. He was briefly held prisoner at Oxford but was exchanged. Ludlow fought at the second battle of Newbury in October 1644, and the third, successful, siege of Basing House, which was led by Cromwell and featured great cruelty to the defenders, many of whom were Catholics. Not only were hundreds of civilians put to the sword, but ten priests were executed, six after the battle and four after being paraded in triumph in the capital.

Ludlow was also appointed Sheriff of Wiltshire, and was active on the county committee. On the formation of the New Model Army in 1645, he was one of the godly commanders who were being considered for a leading position, but it seems that pressure was applied by the locals to keep him in Wiltshire. Ludlow was a keen enabler of both Pride's Purge and the execution of the king, with some Leveller inclinations. He failed to support Cromwell after the Putney debates when a Leveller rebellion was suppressed at Ware, in Hertfordshire.

He was influential both in politics and in the army. He was not only on the Council of State after the execution, but also drew up the instructions for its election and processes. Ludlow was clearly the third military man of the republic. Its most pressing problem was the conquest of Ireland, the 'back door' that its foreign enemies could use as a base. Cromwell spent nine months there, and the command passed to Ireton and then to Ludlow when Ireton died in November 1651. Ludlow returned to Ireland as one of the civil commissioners and became commander-in-chief, appointed by his fellow commissioners. Ireland was the best place to exploit his passions and keep him away from Westminster, and he used his energy to provide the civil support necessary for military occupation of the country and the violent mistreatment of its defeated population.[1]

Cromwell is blamed for most of the events in Ireland, causing much resentment in the nine months he was present there. Cromwell, however, was part of a system, represented equally well by men like Ireton, Hewson and Ludlow. It was Ludlow who carried out the new regime's policy in Ireland, insisting on the complete surrender of the Irish and pursuing the policy of mass transportation of Catholics – on pain of death – to the less fertile parts of the country, which had been devastated by plague and war and was not desired by the conquerors. 'To Hell or Connaught' was Ludlow's cry as well as Cromwell's.

Men were executed merely for fighting against the new Republic. Those who refused to relocate would be starved by their harvests and food being confiscated. Laws were passed forbidding the poor Irish to be fed, others were sent to the Caribbean as indentured servants; one tiny step up from slaves. Many of the dispossessed became tenants working for the former parliamentary soldiers who settled there.

After Cromwell made himself Lord Protector in 1653, Ludlow went into opposition, claiming that Cromwell had betrayed their republican principles. It was at this point, around 1654, that Ludlow joined a Baptist congregation in Dublin. Cromwell was reluctant to act against Ludlow, but he prevented him leaving Ireland for a year, on the principle that he could cause less trouble there than in Westminster. Pointedly, Ludlow refused to resign from his position as lieutenant general because he was appointed by Parliament, and it maintained his influence in the army. In revenge, the regiment he commanded was disbanded. When he did return he was arrested and spent six weeks imprisoned in Beaumaris Castle.

When he met Cromwell in August 1656, Ludlow refused to give any promises about his behaviour. According to his own memoirs, a clearly exasperated Cromwell asked him a simple, open question, 'What is it that you would have?' Cromwell thought that his relatively stable rule should have been enough, but the reply was uncompromising. 'That which we fought for,' answered Ludlow, 'that the nation might be governed by its own consent.' Cromwell allowed him to retire quietly to relatives in Essex, not trusting him to go back to Wiltshire and blocking his election to any of the Protector's parliaments.

When Oliver Cromwell died in 1658 Ludlow returned to politics. His plan was to undermine the government of Richard Cromwell, which he regarded as equally unconstitutional and considerably weaker than his father's. He was returned to the Parliament of January 1659 for the Wiltshire constituency of Hindon. At first he would not take his seat as he objected to the oath of allegiance to the new Protector, but had to be present in order to fulfil his task, so he just ignored the oath and hoped nobody would notice. It was noticed, but nothing was done to stop him sitting. He would not have been so leniently treated by Oliver Cromwell, a sign that this was a weak regime.

Ludlow also worked outside of Westminster. He collaborated with John Okey in a propaganda blitz of republican pamphleteering as early as February 1659. Their central aim was the return of the Rump Parliament that had executed the king, then the abolition of the single ruler with his executive power and 'negative voice' (veto) in law making. He believed, rightly, that Richard Cromwell's main parliamentary allies were the same people who tried to press kingship on Oliver. For Ludlow, this was a chance to bring back the republican commonwealth with significantly more chance of success. This was the 'Good Old Cause': go back to the Rump, they thought, and all would be well. It wasn't personal. Richard Cromwell was not the right man to rule, but the same lack of leadership qualities made him a difficult man to dislike. In May 1659 Okey and

Ludlow got their wish; the 1653 Parliament was returned and Richard Cromwell forced to resign. But everything turned out far from well, despite a promising start.

Ludlow was the first republican called on when the army officers decided to replace Richard and his Parliament with a returned Rump. It was Ludlow who provided the list of the previous members. Ludlow then regained the power than he possessed a decade earlier. He was back on the Council of State, coming third in the election, was given the command of an English regiment, and in July was chosen as commander-in-chief of the Irish army, with the rank of lieutenant general. He returned to Ireland and reformed the army on strict republican principles. With the help of fellow regicide Colonel John Jones, he expelled the Cromwellian officers and replaced them, said his enemies, with sectaries, Baptists and other fanatics. Eight hundred were purged in three months.

The restored Rump was good for Ludlow but was not a magic formula for the settlement of the nation's problems. It was less popular that Richard Cromwell's Parliament. It was revived because the army did not want Richard Cromwell and they could think of nothing else to take its place. This wasn't constitutional legitimacy, but power of the pike and gun. It looked like the last five years had never happened, but it was an illusion. Ludlow and his allies were better at undermining Richard Cromwell than working out what action to take next, a recurring problem for politicians after the execution of the king. The republicans also seemed not to understand that more change in a republican direction was the exact opposite of what the nation wanted.

In October 1659 the Rump was removed once more by the army, with faults on both sides, but partly due to the provocations of regicide republicans like Okey, Walton and Scot. Ludlow returned to England and left the regicide Colonel John Jones in charge of Ireland. It was at this point that Monck started to consider using his military force to return a free Parliament. Republicans thought he meant the Rump, and Monck gained some political leverage by being unclear about his aims, but as the political anarchy continued, it became clear that Monck was not going to rescue this discredited Parliament. Ludlow's position became untenable. His aim was to reconcile the republicans and the army and secure the recall of the Parliament. The first aim was impossible and the second was highly unpopular. Less principled men were now reconciling themselves with the Royalists, or at the very least distancing themselves from the present regime.

Ludlow tried to return to Ireland in December 1659 when the Rump was returned for the third time, but Jones had taken Dublin Castle on behalf of the Parliament, and he and Hardress Waller forbade Ludlow from returning on pain of impeachment. Ludlow returned to London in January 1660 to the news that the Parliament now wanted to impeach him. His firm belief in conciliation, albeit between two forces that were equally inept and unpopular, had led him into the political wilderness.

Ludlow's own fate was sealed when it became clear that there was no prospect of a constitutional settlement without the monarchy returning, and that Monck would be the instrument of this return. He was now in great danger: he had neither changed his mind about the desirability of monarchy, nor made any moves to placate his enemies and build up favours to face an uncertain future. In April 1660 he was ready to join the last-gasp republican revolt led by John Lambert, and did not do so only because it collapsed so quickly.

Like John Hutchinson later in this chapter, Ludlow's greatest support was from his wife, Elizabeth Ludlow. When Charles II issued his proclamation calling on all the king's judges to surrender themselves, Ludlow records in his memoirs that his wife, Elizabeth, took advice from her own circle of influential people, 'from knowing friends, what they would advise me to do in this case.' She also visited the new Speaker of the Commons, to negotiate her husband's surrender in a dignified way.

The other regicides' wives did consult and network.[2] There is no name for the wife of William Cawley, apart from a single source that she was living in hiding in 1660: 'Mrs Cawley, whose husband was one of the King's judges, and is not yet discovered, lodges at her brother's in Red Cross Street, London, and is intimate with the wives of Ludlow, Goffe, and Whalley.'

The decision to flee must have been made by the very beginning of May. The Stuart monarchy had been restored by others, yet without the restrictions that could have been imposed. The desire for revenge, and the political power to inflict it, was increasing. The new Convention Parliament (April 1660), so called because it had not actually been called by the king, was full of new politicians, mostly eager Presbyterians who wished to be *plus royaliste que le roi*. Ludlow and Thomas Scot were only two republican regicides who had secured a seat, but they were both soon ejected on spurious technicalities. On 8 May Charles II was declared king.

When the couple made the joint decision to hide, Elizabeth went with him to a safe house in Southwark, where they did the necessary preparation for Ludlow to flee the country alone. Progress was slow. Ludlow was still in London when Charles II arrived in triumph in late May. It was late August before he escaped. He was waiting in the forlorn hope that the Stuart dynasty might yet be overthrown, and partly to maximise his cashflow. He tried to collect the rents from his poor farmers in Ireland. He may have been a devout Puritan and republican but, like nearly all the regicides, he was not in any sense an egalitarian or early socialist. He soon had enough money. His wife had arranged letters of credit to be delivered at various stops throughout France, and a bill of exchange was waiting him when he arrived at Geneva.

Life in exile was mixed. Unlike most regicides, he was united with his wife when she joined him in 1663, but, though they would have another twenty years of married life together, it was lived in fear of assassination. To his dying day he wore a concealed sword and a breast plate under his clothes, and was right to do so. Heneage Finch, who proceeded over the trial of those who did not flee, said Ludlow was condemned to 'perpetual trembling, lest every eye that sees, and every hand that meets them, should fall upon them.' Ludlow's friend, Lisle, was ripped apart with three bullets to the torso a mere twenty miles from Ludlow's home, and Ludlow knew that he was the Stuart monarchy's bogeyman, higher up the list than Lisle and considered more of a present danger.

He was fortunate that he lived long enough to see the expulsion of Charles II's brother, James II, from the throne, but painful experience taught him that the 'good old cause' was not returning. His life in exile was a bubble, corresponding and engaging only with people who agreed with him, which is probably understandable when you are unsure if people are intent on discussion or murder. He was sensible enough, though, not to get involved in foolish republican schemes of revolt and rebellion that could not succeed.

In 1689 Ludlow came back to England, but not in triumph. He was expecting to be welcomed by the new Protestant King William III and be asked for his advice about Ireland, but he was not welcome. His house became full of old adherents of the good old cause who were mostly reminiscing. Parliament was reminded of his actions in 1649, so he took the hint and left the country. Ludlow died in his bed at home in 1692 with his wife at his side, outliving the other regicides and the dynasty he had fought against all his life. He was one of the lucky ones.

John Hutchinson was similar to Ludlow in many ways. Both came from the higher echelons of the county gentry, both had the same education at about the same time as they were born eighteen months apart (Cambridge and Lincoln's Inn/Oxford and Inner Temple) and both had fathers who were MPs. Both men renounced their loyalty to Cromwell when he became Lord Protector in December 1653. At this point their life experiences diverged as Ludlow took a more active part in events than Hutchinson.

Our insight into John Hutchinson comes from his wife, Lucy. Her *Memoirs of the Life of Colonel Hutchinson* (written c.1670) is a key source for the whole civil war. It also made her famous. In many general history books she appears in the index more often than her husband. It is a useful source once it is recognised that Lucy was both an unrelenting Puritan and a social snob who had deep reservations about her husband's allies, contempt for his enemies, and no interest at all in the lower classes. Her memoirs were not meant to be a public defence of her husband, but designed as a document of record for her children and the close family. It was not seen in public until it was published in 1806 by a later descendent, Julius Hutchinson.

Lucy was born in the Tower of London, not as the offspring of a prisoner, but the daughter of Sir Allen Apsley, who had been appointed Lord Lieutenant of the Tower three years earlier. Both Sir Allen and his wife, Lucy, wanted their daughter to practise 'female accomplishments' *and* be academically educated. As it turned out, Lucy liked Latin, reading, and theology more than music, dancing and needlework, and she seemed to have managed to get her own way. She seemed quite dour and intellectual. She reported that when an hour was allotted for play and recreation, she smuggled herself away to read more books.[3] In later life she became an author, poet and translator in her own right. She had many intellectual achievements, as she said so herself, and she was right.

Lucy was a stern, unrelenting Puritan with a monochrome attitude to Roman Catholicism. She loathed it, and saw conspiracy everywhere. She wrote a brief history of England. This was her version of the Reformation under Henry VIII:

> When the dawn of the gospel began to break upon this isle after the dark midnight of papacy, the morning was more cloudy here than in other places by reason of the state interest [...] King Henry the Eighth who by his royal authority cast out the pope did not intend the people of the land should have any ease of oppression but only changed their foreign yoke for home bred fetters dividing the pope's spoils between himself and his bishops.

As far as Lucy and similar Puritans were concerned, the reformation of the church was unfinished, and the present church had been corrupted by an untrustworthy monarch.

Lucy met John through a shared intellectualism. John, who was studying law at the time, was attracted by her accomplishments and was impressed that she owned books in Latin.[4] John had first met Lucy after learning to play the lute with her sister, Barbara, and became infatuated with the older sister. They married in July 1638, with Lucy still bearing the scars of smallpox, and instead of following tradition and moving to the husband's house in Nottingham, they stayed in London for two years. It seemed that she was more devout than he, and Mr Hutchinson had his religious views thrust upon him. The Puritanism of John Hutchinson was a creation of Lucy, so his wife says, and she was right again.

Under her good influence, we are confidently told that he became an honest, principled and hard-working individual whose physical appearance and moral stature made him a giant amongst men. Lucy loved her husband, and admired Henry Ireton, but more or less loathed everybody else, including Cromwell, whom she hated for his apparent hypocrisy and ambition.

When the war started, Hutchinson believed that it was his duty to defend his county. This was the primary loyalty in the seventeenth century, and the peripatetic Parliamentarians who fought all over the country were very much the novelty. Hutchinson's main contribution to the First Civil War was being the military governor of Nottingham

Castle from July 1643. During the civil war he held the strategic town and castle for Parliament despite some setbacks. He clearly wasn't perfect. His constant quarrels with the Nottinghamshire parliamentary committee suggest that he was strong willed to the point of military inefficiency. Lucy provides us with a detailed description of his role and the inadequacies of everyone he worked with. Nottingham was vital for the Parliamentarians, but not quite as important as Lucy suggested since the important sea and river port of Hull had been secured early in the war. This would not have been Lucy's view.

John was not a major part of the Rump Parliament after replacing his father as MP in the Commons in 1646, or a key figure in the execution and events afterwards. He was the thirteenth signature on the execution warrant, and he went through the process with some reluctance, according to his wife. Lucy reports that John pondered the facts and examined his conscience before taking part in the trial and execution. Just like his initial involvement in the civil war, he came to the conclusion that he was acting in obedience to God. He was not the only regicide who agonised about the execution, just one of the few for which we have evidence. His general importance is overrated. Hutchinson would be a regicide on a par with Dixwell, Scrope or Robert Lilburne if not for his wife's hagiography. 'His fame rests on his wife's commemoration of his character, not on his own achievements.'[5]

In 1646 the Hutchinsons decided not to baptise their new baby. It was a controversial decision. Godparents and holy water at baptism had already been forbidden by a Puritan Parliament, which caused considerable distress for people brought up with the belief that child baptism was vital. The decision, taken jointly, was initiated by Lucy and confirmed by John, and is an example of the kind of decision-making processes in other Puritan marriages that have been lost to history. John had been protecting Baptists in Nottingham for a few years, so these actions were a logical culmination of his beliefs. Lucy did not believe in telling her husband what to do, and she was not really a proponent of women's rights, but she claimed the right to be involved in such decisions. Many Puritan women claimed a spiritual equality with their husbands, and therefore the right to be involved in matters of conscience. Some Puritans believed that a righteous wife could not be constrained by an unworthy husband in matters of faith, but this was not the case here, as John Hutchinson was a paragon amongst men.

If women crossed Lucy's red lines, then her judgement was severe. She hated Queen Henrietta Maria for manipulating King Charles with her wit and beauty. When Thomas Fairfax refused to move towards regicide, she blamed his wife, Anne, who was another forceful woman and a Presbyterian, which were two reasons to dislike her. As a snob, Lucy also disliked Elizabeth Cromwell, wife of the regicide, for her ordinariness. To the Royalists, she was 'Joan', a name that implied commonness and vulgarity, and Lucy would have agreed.

After one year in the Rump's Council of State, John Hutchinson retired to Nottinghamshire, not being able to stomach the pretentions of Oliver Cromwell.[6] Hutchinson counts as a republican as he ceased to support the government after Cromwell became Lord Protector in December 1653, but does not really make the cut as a republican opponent of Cromwell. He went home to Nottinghamshire and seemed to turn into a dabbler and dilettante. In exile in Owthorpe, he spent his time gardening, landscaping, planting woodland and making fishponds and terraces, as if there had been no civil war at all. His wife worked on her translations of poetry.

He made an attempt to get back into Parliament during Cromwell's protectorate, and there is some evidence that Cromwell, through Major-General Whalley, dissuaded his neighbours from putting his name forward. Lucy believed that it was only his death in September 1658 that prevented Cromwell arresting her gallant husband, but though the Protector had form with some other opponents, there is no proof of this. He might well have been obscure enough to be left alone, a sentiment that Lucy would not have been able to accept. Hutchinson's retirement was interrupted in the winter of 1659 when sixty 'insolent troopers' invaded their house at Owthorpe and six others demanded money for taxes to pay the army. By threatening violence to the six and offering wine and wise words to the sixty, Hutchinson apparently defused the situation. He warned one of the more belligerent soldiers that behaviour like this would be the end of the Commonwealth, 'these carriages will bring back the Stuarts'.

Hutchinson returned to politics in May 1659 when the army forced the resignation of Richard Cromwell. At this point he would have met Ludlow again, but whereas Ludlow was a central figure who had helped plot the return of the Parliament with the army, Hutchinson did not appear in the first tranche of returners that was organised by the army.

His view of the army was less sanguine than Ludlow's, seeing them as 'encroaching slaves' and part of the problem.

Hutchinson was a demoralised member of the Rump in January 1660. Like many others, he feared Monck's intentions but did not know how to stop him. The Rump's actions against the Stuarts were seen as the pointless posturing of those who were now powerless but lacked the humility to see it. Lucy reported John's reaction: 'The colonel thinking it a ridiculous thing [to] swear out a man when they had no power to defend themselves against them.'

Claims that he provided some help to General Monck in January 1660 when the general was proceeding towards London are hard to prove, and were only made after the Restoration. He certainly did nothing to prevent the return of the monarch, so when the monarchy was restored his position was reasonably strong. He had no friends in the new regime, but few enemies either. His family knew some Royalists, including Lucy's elder brother, Sir Allen Apsley, and more importantly, he had his wife on his side.

In May 1660 Hutchinson apologised to the House of Commons using the soon-to-be common argument of youthful ignorance, and the fact that he was a Royalist deep down. This seemed to work. He was largely regarded as harmless and obscure, and this was effective because it was largely true. There was a worry though. Monck, whose intercession could save lives, was silent throughout Hutchinson's peroration. Clearly, Hutchinson was short in the ledger of positive action. Was the 'lack of malice' argument going to be enough?

By the beginning of June calls for punishment were becoming more strident and extensive, and a letter was sent to the Commons claiming to be from Hutchinson, modifying his insouciant comments in May into something a little more grovelling. In his last apology 'he did not speak in the House with a sufficient sense of his guilt'. Lucy's love transcended their long-held and firm principles, and it seems that she forged this letter of recantation in his name and mobilised her social contacts to get him off the hook (which is not merely a metaphor considering the grisly end he was threatened with).

It worked. On 9 June 1660 the House of Commons agreed that his punishment should be the relatively mild one of being discharged from Parliament (he was one of the few regicides who were elected to the Convention Parliament) and prohibited from holding public office, but that he should be allowed to retain his liberty and estates. Other minor regicides had the same mild punishment offered to them, only for it to be overturned in the Lords. The Lords upheld the Commons' vote on this occasion, and Hutchinson's name was struck from the list of regicides to be executed by Act of Attainder. One of the people who spoke warmly in his defence was Heneage Finch, later to be the judges at the trials of those who were less fortunate than Hutchinson.

He was not free for very long. In 1663, he was implicated in a poorly organised attempt to overthrow the monarchy in a republican uprising based around York, but with simultaneous risings around the country, with Hutchinson (supposedly) leading the Nottingham contingent. Ludlow, despite being in Switzerland and opposed to foolhardy schemes like this, was supposed to be gathering troops in the west of England. The plot was riddled with spies and failed dismally, and Hutchinson was brought in for questioning. His guilt is unproven and almost certainly unlikely. The aims of the rebellion – to destroy the Church of England, kill the bishops, abolish the Book of Common Prayer and bring in religious toleration – seem too rich for his tastes. Decisive action and risk-taking were not in his character. He was arrested on 11 October 1663, while he was giving religious instruction to his servants.

It seemed that the authorities wanted him out of the way. The trials and executions of the other conspirators came and went. By this time Hutchinson was in the Tower of London being kept in solitary confinement in an airless cell, the same one, according to Lucy, where a previous tyrannical monarch had killed the princes. Mr Hutchinson was the new Prince in the Tower.

He was there twenty-four weeks without charge, on a dubious arrest warrant, and was harassed by jailors who wanted fees while still mistreating him. John had never experienced anything like it, said his angry wife. Perhaps this was because he had not been imprisoned with the other regicides in 1660. When Lucy re-recruited Sir Allen Apsley to the fray, John insisted that he didn't want to be saved this time, and she relented a little, remembering how much 'she displeased him by saving him before'.

Hutchinson's initial place of exile was planned to be the Isle of Man, but it seemed that Lucy managed to negotiate a change to Sandown Castle in Kent, much more accessible by boat from London or Gravesend. When he was transported there in May 1664 Lucy took up lodgings in nearby Deal. John Hutchinson's new home was at least as bad as the other regicide prisons. Lucy noticed this when she came to visit him. She found it, 'a lamentable old ruined place, almost a mile distant from the town, the rooms all of it repair, not weather proof, no form of accommodation for either lodgings or diet, or any convenience of life.'

From her base in Deal she fed her husband and through her efforts he was allowed to walk occasionally on the beach. His accommodation was still dank and damp, and John died of a fever four months later, on 11 September 1664. Lucy was certain of the cause, 'for that chamber had killed him'. His wife obtained permission to bury him at the parish church at Owthorpe, rather than in the prison grounds. She was buried with him fifteen years later.

Chapter 12

The Main Fanatic

Thomas Harrison

It is hard to believe that a subset of the regicides could be labelled 'religious fanatics', given the already revolutionary actions of the fifty-nine, and the intense religious convictions of nearly all of them. Many people today would regard the ordinary seventeenth-century Puritan as fanatical, or executing the king in public as a revolutionary act, but some regicides went beyond even this level of commitment. Their religious views led them to social and political opinions that terrified Royalists, Parliamentarians and even other regicides. These are the radical millenarians, known after 1651 as the 'Fifth Monarchists', and sometimes, wrongly, as the 'Fifth Monarchy Men'.[1] Our radical millenarian regicides were Thomas Harrison, John Carew, John Jones and Thomas Grey.[2]

Millenarianism implied the end of temporal kings, and the start of the thousand-year reign of Jesus on earth. The Fifth Monarchists, like many US millenarians today, were exceptionalists, with an exaggerated belief in the spiritual significance of their own country. The millenarianism of men like Harrison, Carew, Jones and Grey was an extreme example of English exceptionalism. None of these fanatics doubted that God's purposes for the whole universe would be expressed by events in a relatively obscure and poor group of islands on the periphery of Europe, whose best days were still in front of them. When Christ returned to earth to rule over the saintly, it would commence in England and then would spread around the world as kings were destroyed everywhere.

It was common for Christians to believe that the end of the world would happen at some time in the future as the level of sinfulness on earth was unsustainable. Unlike most millenarians, the Fifth Monarchists believed that that moment was imminent. The four kingdoms (Babylonian,

Persian, Greek and Roman), had been destroyed by the Almighty and the reign of Charles would be destroyed by God and his instrument, the army. Then the rule of the saints would begin.

Most of the regicides believed that God had witnessed against Charles; but for them the execution had been the end of the revolution. Fifth Monarchists went beyond most of the new men and women who wanted religious toleration and moderate republicanism. They wanted the rule of the Kingdom of God on earth, government by divine law and the spread of the faith, in preparation for the arrival of King Jesus. In twenty-first century terms they sound like fanatical jihadists wishing to export religious revolution.

The consequences of the rule of the saints were to be revolutionary. There would be no place in this earthly paradise for churches and priests, and certainly no role for lawyers and landlords and the owners of property. This also challenged the rigid social structure on earth, but it was not democratic: God's elect were all equal, but not everyone was a member of the elect, so not everybody would be saved. They were much more radical than the 'average' regicides, and it is hardly a surprise that their enemies labelled them 'Anabaptists' as there was some crossover between the Fifth Monarchists and the more radical Baptists.

Thomas Harrison was the most notable of these men and the third most influential regicide after Cromwell and Ireton. His father was a butcher and grazier, a substantial citizen of Newcastle-Under-Lyme who had been mayor of the town, like his own father. Royalists tended to emphasise the word 'butcher' as if he owned a shop, but Harrison was one of the middling sort who would have been a big wheel in this small Staffordshire town if war had not turned the world on its head.

He rose through the ranks, like many regicides. He was a member of the Earl of Essex's bodyguard recruited from the Inns of Court, and fought in his army. Clarendon detested him, but admitted that he was competent, diligent and sober. In 1644 he was a major at the Battle of Marston Moor, where he earned the enmity of the Scots Presbyterians by downplaying their contribution to the battle. By 1645 he had risen to the rank of major-general and was a noted friend and supporter of Oliver Cromwell. He was one of the religious zealots who were singled out as an Anabaptist by the Earl of Manchester, which would not have bothered Cromwell one bit and did not affect their friendship.

Harrison was present at the third siege of Basing House in 1645. Quarter was neither requested nor offered during the battle, but Harrison's interpretation was without any sense of mercy at all. A Major Robinson, who was about to surrender, was killed on the spot by Harrison, with the words 'cursed be he who does the Lord's work negligently'. Harrison would have known the next line from Jeremiah, 'and cursed be the one who restrains his sword from blood.'

Like many of the New Model Army officers, he was elected to the Long Parliament in 1646, and his own regiment was one of the most radical and fractious during the crises of 1646 and 1647. Up to this point Harrison seems like a pro-army, religiously independent military man-turned-politician, like many others. There were crucial differences, however. Harrison's republican views were not created by the Second Civil War, they had always been part of him. He invented the most famous condemnation of the king as early as 11 November 1647, a year before the idea became commonplace in the army. 'Charles Stuart, Man of Blood' was his own invention, though strictly speaking the origin was the Almighty, as expressed in the Book of Numbers: 'The land cannot be cleansed by the blood that is shed herein, but by the blood of him that shed it.' His desire to bring the king to justice predated that of Cromwell and Ireton. While men like Ireton and movements like the Levellers looked to new political constitutions and settlements, Harrison looked to heaven and his reading of the Bible.

Charles I was living in fear by 1648. It was a reasonable concern. Charles knew his history; kings had been killed before, so his mind must have gone through a grim list of possibilities: poisoned food, a bribed barber to cut his throat, shot 'while trying to escape', or a convenient accident. Every scuffle outside his door while imprisoned at Hampton Court was construed as an assassin sent by the army to solve the political impasse with murder.

Charles feared few of the future regicides on a personal level and believed that he could charm or bamboozle them for much longer than seems logical to us today, but he was afraid that Harrison, or a man like him, would be his assassin. He knew of Harrison's reputation, and when Charles fell into the hands of the army rather than Parliament in June 1647, his anxiety increased.

In December 1648 Charles was moved from the Isle of Wight to London by Parliament. After a three-hour crossing in choppy waters he was kept on the mainland at Hurst Castle, a bleak fortification built by Henry VIII on the spit of a shingle beach surrounded by freezing malarial-ridden tidal swamps. Sir Phillip Warwick described it as containing 'only a few dog lodgings for soldiers being chiefly designed for a platform to command the ships.'[3] It was no place to accommodate a king.

The lodgings were poor but the treatment was regal. Fairfax allowed the king a court of sixteen servants, and on the night before his removal to London he was served his meal by servants on bended knee, as tradition required. But in the gloom and damp of a castle where candles were needed at midday, Charles fretted about his well-being. When Harrison arrived with unknown orders Charles was worried. Even his supporters felt that he was discomposed. 'I perceive that your Majesty is so much troubled,' said Thomas Herbert. His killer had arrived. Charles relayed his fears to his servants; 'To my knowledge I never saw the Major, though I have heard oft of him, nor ever did him injury.'

This last sentence showed a profound lack of self-awareness. To Charles, everything was personal, in the sense that everything could be understood with reference to him. Harrison was actually at Hurst Castle to organise the king's movement and there was no need for Harrison to meet him. There was a political process at play, in which the king was now a pawn, a position that he never really understood until he was dragged away by soldiers at the last moment of his trial two months later.

When the king finally met Harrison on the journey to London, he was reassured. Harrison was flamboyantly dressed, 'gallantly mounted and armed, a velvet monteir was on his head, a new buff coat upon his back and a crimson silk scarf about his waist richly fringed.'[4] The slightly portly Harrison liked his clothes, especially military ones. Lucy Hutchinson thought him a hypocrite for claiming to be godly while being both vain and greedy.

The king liked the look of him; this was clearly no monster. He told his servants that he was a good judge of faces. Later, the king glimpsed him again in a crowded house in Farnham and beckoned him over with a finger and asked did he want to kill him? The law was equally obliging to great and small, and justice had no respect of persons, said Harrison. The king (according to accounts) went away merrily from this conversation, but it is hard to see why. A fortnight earlier Harrison's own regiment, with those of five other regicides, had asserted that 'neither birth nor place might exempt from the hands of justice,' which is more or less what he said to Charles, who did not understand the implications at all.

The king's self-proclaimed excellent judgement about superficialities did not help him. Harrison's extravagant, unpuritan attire and his surface politeness meant nothing. He was dressed well because that was one of the things about war that he loved; combat could be a crusade for the Almighty and a chance to show off. He could address the king on bended knee but still frame a law to execute him.

Bishop Burnett, a hostile commentator, believed that Harrison favoured summary execution: 'He was a fierce and bloody enthusiast. And it was believed, that, while the army was in doubt, whether it was fitter to kill the king privately, or to bring him to an open trial, that he offered, if a private way was settled on, to be the man that should do it.'[5] Burnett's comments were made in 1660, after the event. Even then, he did not understand the radical nature of Harrison's beliefs.

Harrison was a key part of the Commonwealth from the beginning, until December 1653, despite not being elected to the Council of State in 1649. Like Henry Ireton, he was regarded as an extremist by a Parliament that edged its way to regicide with some reluctance, and both men were rejected. Of the fifty-nine regicides, only twenty-two were elected to the first council; the other eighteen were non-regicides. It is a reminder that the execution warrant was a moment in time. Many who did not sign it would matter in the future, and many who did sign it would become insignificant.

Despite his own personal vanity and expenditure on clothes, Harrison wanted a moral reformation, and took part in an attempt to improve the clergy in Wales. Success was modest but this did not halt Harrison's career. He was promoted to the rank of major-general in 1651 and fought at the battle of Worcester in September 1651 against the Royalist/ Scottish army put together by Charles II.

The pinnacle of cooperation between Cromwell and Harrison was in 1653. The Rump had failed in its attempts to make the necessary godly reforms, and the defeat of its external enemies now concentrated criticism on its own failures. When, in April 1653, the Rump organised its own replacement and postponed its dissolution, Cromwell ran out of patience, dispersing the MPs by force. Harrison pulled the Speaker out of his chair by a tugging on his cloak. This was mostly symbolic, but did represent the violence that would had been offered in response to any resistance.

The Rump was not mourned, but what would come next? Calling another elected Parliament would be constitutionally difficult. Cromwell had no authority to do so, and another Parliament would reignite the legitimacy of dissolving the old one. Cromwell, in his extended rant against the Rump, told them that the Lord had chosen 'honester and worthier instruments for carrying out his work.'

However, it was Cromwell and his allies, not God, that organised the next step: an assembly of godly men, with a time-limited remit to reform the nation. The civil war and its aftermath had produced a backlog, and the law needed reforming to make it accessible. Prisoners, poverty and education needed improvement and decisions had to be made about tithes, and with them the future of any national church that they financed.

Harrison and Cromwell worked in tandem on these arrangements, but the unity was an illusion. Harrison suggested an assembly of seventy, based on the Jewish *Sanhedrin*. Cromwell, who maintained control of nominations, doubled this number to 140, diluting its possible radicalism and making it look more like a Parliament. Harrison himself was initially excluded by a Self-denying Ordinance of English officers, which also excluded Cromwell himself. Both were later added *ex-officio*.

Harrison was one of about twenty-five Fifth Monarchist and religious radicals who hoped for great things from this assembly. Cromwell opened the assembly at Whitehall and sounded like one of them, 'Truly, you are called by God to rule with Him, and for Him,' but he wasn't. Cromwell, like most Puritans, was a millenarian in principle, but did not see the arrival of King Jesus as imminent or something to make laws about. The Parliament became fractious. Changes in the law were suggested, but none of them came close to the millenarian desire to create a new Mosaic Law inspired by the Bible. Many MPs (they voted very early to style themselves as a Parliament) wanted reform of tithes. Many tithes were held by laymen, while others were unevenly distributed among the clergy and were a burden on the poor, but only men like Harrison wanted them abolished and the financial support for a national church cut off.

When the moderate members of the Parliament resigned their power to Cromwell in December 1653, Harrison and a viable quorum of forty stayed together until they were dispersed by force by William Goffe. He and Harrison had prayed together regularly and had fought with devastating effect on numerous key occasions, but now the split between republicans like Harrison and Cromwellians like Goffe had been created forever. A few days later, Harrison was summoned and asked whether he could accept the new government and was stripped of his military commission when he said he could not.

The Fifth Monarchist and Baptist churches were outraged. Cromwell, previously Moses, was now Satan. They denounced the new single rule of Cromwell as Lord Protector, inaugurated on 16 December 1653. King Jesus had not arrived, but King Cromwell seems to have done so. Cromwell even blasphemed in his new title, said his enemies, in that only the Almighty could be styled 'Lord Protector'.

Harrison was to spend much of the next four years in prison by order of the Lord Protector, with some tinge of regret from Cromwell, who remembered better times between them. There was a Fifth Monarchist uprising in London in 1657 in which Harrison was accused of involvement. As it was an attempt to speed up the second coming of Christ, his participation is plausible but unproven. He and John Carew were sent briefly to the Tower of London. Harrison also declined to flee abroad and was arrested in May 1660 while waiting patiently for the authorities at his home in Stafford. He knew that he would be excluded from the general pardon. His impressive stable of horses was taken to London and handed over to the king.

Harrison then endured six months of 'close confinement' in the Tower. This was not merely being watched closely; his movements would be limited by being manacled and he was not allowed legal advice. The first time Harrison was offered a pen and paper was at the commencement of the trial, when it was too late to make any difference. However, Harrison got his revenge.

He was the new regime's star prisoner, with top billing. The Solicitor-General, Heneage Finch, more or less said so: 'The first that is brought is the prisoner at the bar and be deserves to be the first, for if any person now left alive ought to be styled the conductor, leader and captain of all this work, that is the man.' He regretted the death of the other ringleaders, but consoled himself with the thought of their eternal damnation, 'They are in their own place.'

When Harrison was asked to plead, he was initially reluctant. He was then reminded that the punishment for silence was *peine forte et dure*; being crushed to death – and possibly starved – under heavy stones and iron, with the punishment contrived to take as long as possible. He relented, but not because he was afraid of death; he was a man who knew about pain and bravery, and whose impetuous behaviour in war showed that he was unafraid of physical injury. He knew that a painful death would be the inevitable consequence of the trial, but also knew that refusing to plead would mean that he would be taken down from the bar and his words would never be heard.

Throughout the whole process Harrison waged a guerrilla war against a superior power, and strived to achieve as many small victories as possible. When told to hold up his hand when his name was announced, he shouted 'I am here' instead. Harrison, Scope, Carew, Clement, Jones and Scot were on trial and the initial plan was to have one jury, but it was soon realised that this would not be possible as each defendant objected to different members. Harrison and Scot took turns to object to different people, which meant that each defendant would have to be tried separately.

Harrison was first. Each juror was presented to him, and he rejected most of them. 'I do not do this to keep you off from your businesses,' he lied. Told he could reject thirty-five of them, Harrison asked the court to keep count for him. The court was annoyed but worse was to come. Unlike many other regicides, Harrison made no attempt to apologise for his actions.

Harrison was to be executed first, on 13 October, a mere thirty-six hours after the guilty verdict. Not only was he considered the worst of the surviving regicides, he was regarded as a current threat as a Fifth Monarchist. When, in 1661, there was a desperate Fifth Monarchist uprising in London, their slogan was 'King Jesus, and the heads above the gates'. They were grieving for Thomas Harrison, a man who would never grieve for himself. The day after his execution there was a pause in the schedule. Harrison was being compared by some to the Protestant martyrs who had defied 'Bloody' Mary. That is what he would have wanted.

Chapter 13

Three Religious Fanatics

John Jones, John Carew, Thomas Grey

Our trio of Fifth Monarchists begins with the one who was most like Thomas Harrison. John Jones Maesygarnedd – normally referred to as **John Jones** as the last part of his name is the place of his birth – was the only Welsh speaker amongst the regicides, and one of two Welshmen amongst the fifty-nine (the regicide William Goffe was also born in Wales but does not seem to have been regarded as Welsh; although when he visited Haverfordwest, the town of his birth, in 1648, the local dignitaries took the precaution of wining and dining him extravagantly). Despite a modern reputation for radicalism, industrialisation and free churches, Wales was Anglican, Royalist and relatively poor in the seventeenth century.

Jones seems to have come from a modest gentry family – he was born in a single-storey farmhouse[1] – in a country where all social groups were already poorer than those in England. He was a prominent opponent of the existing monarchy – rather than one particular king – in a county that was overwhelmingly Royalist. During the war he was known by his enemies as the 'most universally hated man in North Wales'.[2] Jones, like many future regicides on the periphery of the country, seems to have moved to London in the 1630s. In 1633 he was a Freeman of the Grocers' Company.

A large collection of Jones's and Harrison's letters survive, including many to each other, showing the closeness of the two men, and providing quotations which the enemies of Puritanism believed summed them up (they refer to each other as 'my most endeared brother'). This quotation comes from 1651, when the Rump Parliament was trying to improve the morals of people, despite their clear reluctance to be improved: 'I had rather do a people good, though against their wills, than please them in show only, to the hazarding of their peace and well being.' At the same time, Jones conceded that the Royalists and their lax morals were probably more popular in the country. To their enemies, men like Jones and Harrison were a religious vanguard, working against public sentiment and glorifying coercion.

The failure of King Jesus to arrive in 1649 was a concern to men like Jones. Some looked forward to 1666, significant as the 'number of the beast' in the Book of Revelation. In the meantime, morals on earth could be improved, whether this was welcome or not. An Adultery Act was passed that made this moral transgression into a capital crime. Its unintended consequence was that the act managed to abolish adultery in the sense that juries became extremely reluctant to convict even when presented with convincing evidence of guilt.

In 1650 an act was passed to improve the morality of Wales by spreading the word of the gospel more efficiently, but in reality it was an attempt to remove those accused of 'Delinquency, Scandal, Malignancy, or non Residency'. Harrison headed the commission at first, with Jones being the third name on the list of commissioners. In the end, 278 clergy were removed from their livings, but as an attempt to puritanise Wales it was no more than a beginning. Amongst the twenty-five Approvers who advised the commissioners on the suitability of clergy to replace those ejected was the Fifth Monarchist and former Welsh itinerant preacher Vavasour Powell. There were Fifth Monarchists in positions of influence outside the Commons, which made them even more dangerous in the eyes of their enemies.

Jones was unable to serve as the Commonwealth sent him to Ireland to be one of the four civil commissioners for Ireland, a challenging job for which a high degree of commitment was required. While in Ireland, Jones still fretted. What would become of poor Merionethshire if that country was denied gospel mercies?[3]

Jones opposed the establishment of Cromwell's Protectorate in December 1653. To Fifth Monarchists like him, the arrival of 'King' Cromwell was in no way a precursor to the rule of King Jesus, but he was much more ambiguous in his opposition than Harrison. He assisted in the rule of the major-generals, and in 1656 he married Cromwell's widowed sister, Catherine. Jones was elected to the Second Protectorate Parliament as MP for Merioneth and was appointed to

Cromwell's Upper House in 1657. Cromwell knew his beliefs, but seemed to take a pragmatic response; Jones was doing a good job, and that was enough.

Jones did not extend his loyalty to the son. When Oliver Cromwell died, he reverted to his position as a republican opponent and made no attempt to hedge his bets as the monarchy was restored. While based in Ireland, he resisted Charles II to a point of no return for his life and estates.

He did not put up the kind of guerrilla resistance attempted by Harrison at his trial. He did not go through the pantomime of challenging the jury or questioning the witnesses. He used the same argument as Harrison, Scrope and others – that his actions had been made legal by the sovereign power of Parliament. The argument had gone down exceedingly badly when Harrison used it, and merely suggesting it was declared by the judge as a form of treason on its own. There was some truth in that. The House of Commons without monarch or House of Lords has never been a court of law.

Jones seemed to face the prospect of being hanged drawn and quartered with equanimity. He had some support in the crowd. The newspaper *Mercurius Publicus* reported that he lifted up his hands as he was drawn upon the hurdle and at the place of execution to gain the people's prayers. He was also looking forward to meeting honest Harrison and fellow regicide John Carew in heaven.

He might have been worried about the organised cruelty and pain that was about to be inflicted on him, but he was sustained by faith. It was good for true believers to suffer. It added to their glory about to come in heaven. In the words of Jones, 'The more the Saints are tried, the more their lustre will appear.' Jones even made some light-hearted comments on his way to being executed: the sled taking him to die was like Elijah's Flying Chariot, except that it went through Fleet Street. He consoled Adrian Scrope's children with promises of their father's dispatch to heaven. He worried about those who had fled and whether they had done the right thing. From his incarceration in chains at Newgate he said 'in what a sad condition are our dear friends beyond the seas, where they may be hunted from place to place and never be in safety [...] how much have we gotten the start of them for we are at a point and now going to heaven.'[4]

It was carnage before it was heaven. John Evelyn, the diarist, saw the aftermath: 'The traitors executed were Scrope, Cook and Jones. I did not see their execution, but met their quarters mangled and cut and reeking as they were brought from the gallows in baskets.'

The next millenarian radical was **John Carew**. Carew was a Cornishman and, like Jones, an active and brave Parliamentarian in a county full of powerful Royalists. Carew was never a soldier, unlike the other two, and would be listed amongst the committee men if it were not for his extreme religious and political views.

After 1654 Carew took to pen and protest, agitating for the release of Fifth Monarchist prisoners, refusing to acknowledge the legitimacy of the new Cromwell government. Carew was summoned before the Council of State in 1655, and imprisoned in St Mawes Castle on the grounds that he would not pledge to abstain from taking part against Cromwell and his government. He took no active part in politics during the Protectorate. During the dying days of the Republic he refused to turn up when the Rump Parliament was returned.

When the monarchy was restored Carew knew that his life was in danger. The most common strategies were running away, belatedly cooperating, or asking for mercy, but our 'saint' did none of these things, being neither repentant nor afraid of death. Carew's name was on the list of the forty-four who had to give themselves up within fourteen days, so he left Cornwall and was arrested in the capital, though the legal officer initially refused to detain him as a result of an error in the official description. He almost had to insist.

There was no point in defending himself to gain an acquittal. God's impending kingdom played a strong part in his defence. When asked to plead guilty or not guilty, he replied, 'Saving to our Lord Jesus Christ his right to government of these kingdoms I say I am not guilty.' When found guilty and asked for a comment, Scot, Jones and Clement made ritualised pleas for mercy from the king. Carew was different, saying, 'I commit my cause unto the Lord.' The court's audience started humming to drown him out.

Like his fellow believers, Carew was able to die in the steadfast manner that unassailable views could provide. 'Mr John Carew suffered there also, even their enemies confessing that more steadiness of mind,

more contempt of death, and more magnanimity could not be expressed,'
said Edmund Ludlow.

One republican religious fanatic who stands out as different from the
rest is **Thomas Grey**, who inherited the title of Lord Grey of Groby,
Leicestershire, when his father was created the Earl of Stamford in 1628.
Grey never entered the House of Lords because his father outlived him,
or more accurately, the son died prematurely at the age of thirty-four in
1657 and never inherited his father's earldom. This was, perhaps, a good
thing, as the father became completely alienated by the son's outrageous
behaviour. His father was a supporter of Parliament, both politically and
militarily, but his son became an Independent, an enthusiastic regicide
and a Fifth Monarchist.

Father and son started off on the same side in 1640. The earl had
fought for the king against the Scots in 1639–40, but he admired the
Scottish Presbyterians to the point where he could no longer work with
Charles, and the king felt the same way when the earl crossed the battle
lines to have an evening meal with them.

In November 1641 father and son were members of what would,
in retrospect, be called the 'Long Parliament'. The son was one of
the youngest regicides, born in 1623, and exceedingly precocious. He
was an active supporter of John Pym and was one of twelve MPs who
presented the king with the 'Grand Remonstrance' in November 1641,
listing Charles's failings and weaknesses, especially in the areas of
'Oppressions in Religion, Church Government and Discipline'. He was
an active soldier for the Parliament before his twentieth birthday.

When the war started, both men went to Parliament's aid. The father
did his best, but deep down he was a monarchist; the type of soldier who
claimed to be fighting for 'King and Parliament', and without whom
the initial prosecution of the war would have been impossible. Like
many of the early rebels, his father fought the war for the same reason
as commanders like Essex and Manchester: to weaken the monarch
so that Parliament could rule. His father's military career fizzled out
with claims of incompetence and cowardice in May 1643, but the son's
reputation went from strength to strength.

The dynamic young aristocrat helped the Parliamentary cause
immensely. His presence refuted the Royalist propaganda that the

Parliamentary officers were 'dirty men with no faces'. Mark Noble detected this; 'Parliament was proud of a young nobleman that could assist in their cause.' The attention, said Noble, went to his head; a slur that Noble tended to use for low-born regicides rather than the aristocracy. Clarendon refers to him in 1642 as being 'a young man of no eminent parts, and only backed by the credit and the authority of Parliament', although such comments from enemies may be expected, and were not borne out by events.

Grey started the war as a protégé of the Earl of Essex, a Presbyterian aristocrat like his father (and about as competent as a soldier). Grey, like many Parliamentarian rebels, thought of the protection of their own county first, their region second, and their country third. This was common amongst combatants on both sides, and even amongst the key regicides who became national figures. In the spring of 1643 Grey failed to turn up at a rendezvous with Colonel Cromwell and Colonel Hutchinson at Newark because he felt that his own county and family property would be jeopardised.

Lucy Hutchinson did not like him very much, noting that he lacked experience and had a credulous good nature. The latter comment was not meant to be a compliment and was later proved to be false. None of this stopped Grey's military career from flourishing. Perhaps Lucy was being a little harsh. Grey's work at the siege of Gloucester and the Battle of Newbury earned him the recorded thanks of the Commons, and though he was criticised by Lucy Hutchinson for his failure to tackle Queen Henrietta Maria's army when it passed through the region in the summer of 1643, that was because Lucy disliked the Queen a little more than she hated Grey.

Grey's focus on Leicestershire meant working with the County Committees, and he did not get on well with many of them. Some were gentry, a step below him in social status (like many of the bureaucratic regicides in chapter sixteen), but the war had brought the lower class of tradesmen and artisans into positions of power, and it seems that Grey could not cope with this apparent levelling. In the spring of 1644, Richard Ludlam, an active local committee man, was placed under house arrest at Burley House, Loughborough, 'for an affront done to the Lord Grey; and [...] since his return he hath humbled himself to his lordship; which may prove a good example to others, to refrain themselves from the like offences, and teach them better manners.'

He was a young, dashing aristocrat, feted by the authorities, a nobleman with friends and supporters in the aristocracy, and a man who was conscious of a social snub and who was prepared to humiliate people to get revenge. He sounded like a Royalist. Yet he was a hard line supporter of the Fifth Monarchist and Levellers. Just like Lucy Hutchison, he held radical political and religious views while still having a dim view of the plebs.

In 1646 his Presbyterian mentor, the Earl of Essex, died in a hunting accident, and Grey became more even radical. He fell out with his father and fell in with the extreme Independents in Parliament. This was entirely his own doing. Most people had to flatter and obey the leading family of their county. Thomas Grey did not have to do anything that he did not want to.

Like many who became regicides, his heart was hardened by the Second Civil War, and he was a major player in the trial of the king. Grey was present at Pride's Purge; indeed he was the man behind it, literally. He stood behind Colonel Pride and had the final say in who was to be excluded as he knew everybody by sight, and Pride did not. One historian of the Grey family has suggested that the events be renamed 'Grey of Groby's Purge', which would be less alliterative but far more accurate.

Grey was the most socially prestigious of all of the fifty-nine. His name appears on the document in second place, after Bradshaw, for that reason. Thomas Grey was the only aristocratic regicide, the only one who would have been entitled to sit in the House of Lords had it not been abolished by men like himself. Religiously and politically, Grey travelled further and faster than anybody else, and richly deserves the title of 'fanatic'.

The House of Lords stood in the way of the trial and execution. There were only about twelve regular attendees by late 1648, and none of them had any reason to be loyal to their king, but they baulked at what Grey, Cromwell and Ireton were trying to do. Grey, a man who had earlier stood on his dignity when affronted by the lack of deference of the lower orders, colluded in abolishing both monarchy and the House of Lords (despite the latter being his own birthright). It was a contradiction that was noticed at the time. The eighteenth-century historian John Throsby, writing about Leicestershire in the civil war, recounted this anecdote from his great-grandfather, 'This good old man was in Bradgate Park conversing with Lord Grey when his son arrived from London immediately after the condemnation of Charles I and received the unwelcome news, like that nobleman, with horror. "Well, Thomas," says the father to the son, "king or no king?" "No king, my lord," replied the son. "Then no Lord Grey," rejoined the father and left him in disgust.'[5]

The elder man's retort worked on three levels. The young man was rejecting the institution, his father, and himself as the future lord. After the execution, Grey was a vital member of the republican government, elected to the Council of State every year, and was a key member of the new regime to the point of being a serious rival to Cromwell.

Despite Grey's belief that the Kingdom of Jesus was at hand, he was still enthusiastic about buying the property of distressed loyalists and taking gifts from a grateful Parliament. Mark Noble noted that after the war he became very greedy, while during the civil war he was merely greedy. After the Battle of Worcester in 1651 he received £1,000 per year for his services, but money and power was clearly not enough. Despite the grasping and cruel nature of a man called the 'grinning dwarf', he had principles that were the undoing of him.

He was far too republican by 1653 to accept the single rule of Oliver Cromwell and was moving towards an extreme Leveller position. He was a friend of Henry Marten, and by 1654 he was an enemy of the regime. Grey was elected MP for Leicester in the First Protectorate Parliament (1654), but was arrested on suspicion of taking part in the former Leveller John Wildman's plot against Cromwell in early 1655. Grey, like Harrison and Carew, was implicated and Grey was imprisoned at Windsor Castle until July 1655 when he was released after making an appeal to Cromwell. He was imprisoned again when associated with the Fifth Monarchist Shoreditch Plot (1657), a violent attempt to take London by force as a prelude to the arrival of Jesus as king on earth. Grey died in the same year, probably of the gout that also badly affected his father. Gout was, and is, caused by a malfunction of the kidney, not by rich living, although Grey managed to experience that as well. He crammed a lot into his thirty-four years.

Men like Harrison, Jones, Carew and Grey have been judged harshly by history. Charles Simpkinson, the early twentieth-century biographer of Harrison, commented, 'The Fifth Monarchy Men whom

Major-general Harrison represents have generally been judged to stand as hopeless defaulters at the bar of commonsense.' This largely stands. Unlike the Levellers, who clearly had a point that is accepted today, or the Baptists and Quakers who morphed into respectability, the Fifth Monarchists still look a little strange, and in our age of religious extremism, they look dangerous too. But they were brave, committed, and never changed their minds; characteristics shared by some of the best (and worst) people in history.

Chapter 14

The Main Cromwellians
Edward Whalley and William Goffe

Only two regicides come as a pair, their names linked together in the history of this period. These are William Goffe and Edward Whalley, and, generally speaking, the linking of their names is justified. For a start, they were related. Whalley was Goffe's father-in-law. Their religious beliefs were similar, though Goffe was more intense than Whalley (he was known as 'praying William', a significant epithet in an age that was already intensely religious). They escaped revenge together in the New World, lived out the last years of their life as fearful fugitives, and still have roads named after them in Massachusetts.

By about 1655 most of the 1649 regicides were either opposed to Cromwell, apathetic, or already dead. Whalley and Goffe belong to a small group who were constant supporters of Oliver Cromwell. 'He rose to great honour under the Cromwells [and] was one of the few who remained true to their interest throughout', commented Mark Noble on Goffe, not meaning it as a compliment.

Cromwell's power increased dramatically in 1653. He closed the Rump by force and became the single ruler of the new Protectorate in December 1653. Those who had died before that date were spared the decision about whether they approved. Some relatively insignificant regicides retired to their counties, and their opinion did not matter. Those with republican views took against Cromwell, with various degrees of success. Whalley and Goffe supported Cromwell, with some reservation (Goffe could just about live with the proposed title of king in 1657, Whalley could not), but they still deserve the title of being the 'Main Cromwellians'.

William Goffe was a relatively low-status regicide. His father, Stephen, had been a Sussex Puritan vicar who was deprived of his living. Goffe senior was a marked man because, as early as 1603, he was petitioning

James I for the abolition of the bishops. Historians have attributed Goffe's position to the rigid Puritanism of his father, but this does not explain why two of Goffe's brothers were active for the king; another example of the many divided families in the civil war.

Goffe, like many younger brothers, ended up in trade in the capital. Anthony Wood claimed that Goffe was averse to learning, which is why he was apprenticed. That's an opinion from a hostile source, but he was definitely a dry-salter who worked himself into a respectable position as a Freeman of the Grocers' Company in the year that war started. Goffe chose war rather than business and volunteered for the Southern Army when new regiments were added after Edgehill, possibly as a quartermaster to use his skills handling food.

He served the parliamentary cause faithfully during the First Civil War but made his biggest mark at Dunbar (1650) and Worcester (1651). He became politically influential in 1647 at the same time as other regicides such as Pride, Okey, Ewer and Harrison.

Goffe's pious nickname was deserved. He was always praying, and always the first to suggest that God's guidance be sought and that individuals gave witness to any revelation of the Almighty. It was Goffe who suggested the four-hour prayer morning at the Putney Debates when no compromise was possible between the Levellers and the Army 'Grandees' (as John Lilburne had named them). Goffe's intense, mystic and often violent prophesying and exhortations to the Lord made him a Fifth Monarchist in the eyes of many contemporary commentators.

In November 1647 Goffe was asking for God's guidance on minor civil matters, and it is reported that even Cromwell, a man whose life was ruled by God's intention for him, thought it was too much. In April 1648, in the midst of the civil war, Goffe was present at a prayer meeting of army officers at Windsor Castle. These Puritan soldiers, who interpreted their earlier military success as God's approbation, now had to consider the meaning of the Second Civil War and the Royalist rebellions all around them. Some moderately reliable reports state that it was Goffe who had the soldiers first in tears, then in a fury of determination to defeat the enemy of God with a sermon based on Proverbs 1:23: 'If you Turn now to my reproof, behold I will pour my spirit into you.' Goffe himself reported that he had a message from heaven, 'we have sinned against the Lord in tampering with His enemies.' He was taken seriously by key people: Ireton said that Goffe always touched his heart when he spoke; and Cromwell made it clear that he, too, waited for the Lord to speak to him in this way.

Edward Whalley (born 1607) was the fourth name on the execution warrant. He was the son of Nottingham gentry rather than a Sussex vicar, and never quite managed Goffe's religious intensity. He was a man in the mould of fellow Nottinghamshire regicide Henry Ireton. Noble called him honest, loyal, and with 'his religious instincts wild and enthusiastic' (meaning 'intense' rather than merely 'keen').

Whalley also deserves to be in the chapter on war-winning soldiers. He is recorded, very early in the war, as a cornet of the 60th regiment of horse. He was keen, but socially modest. He needed the influence of regicide James Temple to start his military career. He was present at the Battle of Gainsborough in 1643, where he would have witnessed the first collaboration of Fairfax and Cromwell, and also present at the big three battles of the First Civil War: Edgehill (1642) Marston Moor (1644) and Naseby (1645). Like Goffe, he fought at the crucial battles of Dunbar and Worcester. The only main gap in this impressive record is the lack of service in Ireland.

After the first civil war his cavalry regiment was one of the most militant. When the army secured King Charles, Whalley's regiment was given the responsibility of guarding him during his imprisonment at Hampton Court, from 24 August to 11 November 1647, when the king escaped. Whalley refused to take the blame for this when he was obliged to report to the Speaker of the Commons four days after the escape. He had followed Cromwell's instruction to the letter. Charles had been afraid of assassination, and Cromwell gave Whalley instructions to prevent this 'horrid act' under all circumstances, while still giving the king the freedom to roam the palace. Whalley had already pointed out the difficulty of guarding a man who was allowed to what he liked in a palace with over 1,500 rooms. On the day of the escape Whalley had been forbidden to go into the king's room after not seeing him for a few hours, and was reduced to peeking through the keyhole to see if the king could be glimpsed.

When Charles escaped he left Whalley a graceful note thanking him for his consideration, but it was Cromwell's wishes that he was fulfilling. There was no desire for the king to die, quite the opposite, but Charles's fears were reasonable. A letter given to him by Whalley said as much. Clearly, the king's correspondence was not even being read. When he regularly boasted that he was 'no ordinary prisoner', it can be seen where he got this idea from. Whalley distanced himself from being part of such a plot, saying that he would have died in defence of the king. Fourteen months later, his was name number fourteen on the death warrant, but much had changed. Whalley spent the Second Civil War in Kent, he was present at the Siege of Colchester, and had his determination strengthened by events in the same way as the other military regicides.

Goffe and Whalley were two of the ten major-generals who were involved in the eighteen-month experiment (starting in August 1655) which, to their enemies, summed up all that was wrong with Puritanism enforced by a standing army. The country was broken up into military districts for the purpose of national security, the stamping out of rebellion, and the reformation of manners. Their tasks also included the collection of taxes from papists and other opponents, removing the ungodly from positions of influence and overseeing their replacement with godly ministers, looking after the deserving poor, and chastising idlers.

The major-generals were given the right to override the local power base, and so were able to make themselves unpopular with everybody. To be a major-general was to be a Cromwell loyalist. Being a regicide was not a qualification for the post; all of the major-generals were successful Puritan soldiers from the 1640s. Goffe was major-general for Berkshire, Hampshire and his own county of Sussex. Whalley administered the Midlands counties, including Nottinghamshire.

As major-generals, Goffe and Whalley were similar. They had both earned the trust of the Protector by 1655, and both did the job as required. They both suppressed theatres, bear-baiting, cock fights and horse racing. This was not an animal rights issue, though, but a matter of morality and national security. Any large public gathering was regarded suspiciously as a cover for conspiracy. Whalley was a little more lenient, allowing the Lincolnshire races – Lady Grantham's Cup – to take place to allow the gentry to have some diversion, ignoring the fear that a crowded racecourse was an ideal cover for Royalists.

Whalley seemed a little more pragmatic than the average major-general. He was concerned with helping the deserving poor, monitoring enclosures so they did not increase poverty, and making sure the poor were not cheated at markets. All major-generals chased up papists and delinquents to collect money from them. Neither man had any sympathy for Quakers.

Both men were opposed to Christmas, which was regarded as a popish creation with no scriptural justification behind it. This was a common view amongst all Puritans, not just regicides, and we know that both men tried to extirpate this annual celebration. Like many traditional believers, the diarist John Evelyn was celebrating Christmas in secret in 1657 when the chapel was surrounded by soldiers. He was detained, and after lunch was interrogated by Whalley and Goffe about his infraction of the ordinance against observing 'the superstitious time of the nativity' (which predated the execution of the king by half a decade and was not the work of Oliver Cromwell). Had they toasted the health of Charles Stuart? Had they used the Book of Common Prayer ('which they told me was but the mass in English'). Evelyn was contemptuous – 'they spoke spiteful things of our Lord's nativity.' He regarded them as men who were above the law, yet at the same time unable to get their own way. Finally, though, he was freed, 'they dismissed me with much pity of my ignorance'.[1]

In 1657 Cromwell was offered the title of king by a Parliament desperate for the return to the form of government that had an element of hereditary monarchy about it. This tested the loyalty of both Whalley and Goffe. Both men were against the idea, but not in an intimating way such as the non-regicide army grandees, Charles Fleetwood and John Lambert. Whalley was ready to accept if the consequence was a settled country and both men accepted lordships in Cromwell's 'Other House'.

Both men supported the new regime when Cromwell died. Goffe signed the order proclaiming Richard the Protector. As late as April 1659, with Richard Cromwell's support draining away, he still had the support of the two men; so much so that Goffe was relieved of his command when the army removed Richard Cromwell in May 1659. Their identification with the Cromwell regime was so strong that there was no chance of escaping the most severe form of justice in 1660.

Whalley and Goffe left Gravesend on the *Prudent Mary* on 14 May 1660, just eleven days before the arrival of Charles II at Dover, and four days before the House of Lords had decreed the seizure of the regicides. They fled with over a hundred Puritans, and the son of the regicide John Jones as another fugitive passenger. Goffe was disappointed with the turn of events, but remained defiant and unreconciled. They saw the popular jubilation that was the immediate – but short-lived – reaction to the return of the king. Goffe wrote in his dairy, 'There was much rejoicing among the people, but God's people lamented over the great profaneness with which that joy was expressed.' Goffe still believed in signs from the Almighty, 'it was observed that many dogs did that day run mad: and died suddenly in the town.'

Both men arrived in Boston, making no attempt to hide their identity. At this point they were celebrated visitors rather than fugitives from justice. On the very same day as they arrived in Massachusetts, the Parliament in London was so full of revenge that the king himself had to tell them to scale down their bloodlust a little. Whalley and Goffe had made the right decision.

Their exile ended miserably, but began quite joyously. They were more popular in Puritan New England than Stuart Britain. They justified their actions in front of enthusiastic crowds. Whalley was quoted as saying that he had no regrets about the execution and would do it again. They may not have been so brave at the bar of the Old Bailey. Charles II was furious. His curt proclamation of 27 July 1660 put a bounty of £100 on their heads and decreed that assisting the two men was a traitorous act that could imperil both the people who helped them and the autonomy of the colony.

By February 1661 they were on the move again, to New Haven. Another impatient and vaguely threatening decree was issued by Charles II in March 1661. The manhunt had failed so far, but it must have given the king some satisfaction to know that they would now live out their days looking over their shoulders. Towards the end of their lives they were probably in little practical danger as the political imperative to catch them fell away, but they did not really know that. Noble was sorry for Goffe and Whalley for living in a cave 'for three years', but it seems that they spent far less time than that actually hiding at West Rock in New Haven: in reality it was about a month, from 15 May to 11 June. The location is now part of the local tourist trail.

Whalley was in failing health by 1674 and probably died the next year. There are no more reports of Goffe's whereabouts after 1679. It is not easy to ascertain their feelings, even in the early days when they were still being feted in Boston. Should they have witnessed the strength of their beliefs by staying and suffering? Had they achieved a minor, dishonorable triumph by escaping? Did they think the new Stuart regime would fail and they could return? They are at least as famous in Britain as those who stayed and martyred themselves, and more famous in the USA, where they have been held up as beacons of liberty and precursors of religious freedom.

Chapter 15

Cromwellians

John Dixwell, Robert Lilburne, William Constable,
Anthony Stapley

No other regicides showed the same commitment to Cromwell as Whalley and Goffe, but some came close. It wasn't always an easy decision, but nearly all accepted Cromwell taking on the mantle of a single ruler in 1653, and most showed their loyalty by swallowing their doubts about Cromwell being offered the title of king in 1657. Some even supported Richard Cromwell and therefore admitted to the *de facto* creation of a hereditary Cromwell family monarchy.

John Dixwell (1607–1689) is often linked with Whalley and Goffe, but he was a lesser figure. Whalley and Goffe had national reputations, while Dixwell was another 'regional regicide'. He was from Kentish gentry and his influence was in his own county rather than the major battles of the civil war or the political battles of Westminster. His role was similar to that of John Hutchinson, but Dixwell is less well known because he did not have an adoring wife to write up his every action and laud his every good intention.

In the first six years of the civil war he was a member of the Kent county committee and a captain in the local county militia. He first came to prominence as the recruiter MP for Dover in August 1646, but was never very active in Parliament, rising to the rank of colonel mainly due to his loyalty. After the execution, Dixwell's friendship and close cooperation with Marten and Ludlow marks him out as republican, but it does not seem that he was morally suspect as a 'friend of Henry Marten'. He was a mainstream Puritan who wanted to make the Commonwealth a success, and, unlike Marten, Harrison, Okey and Ludlow, his republicanism did not prevent him from supporting Cromwell when he became the single ruler in December 1653.

Like Hutchinson, Dixwell was a regional military governor. Hutchinson's Nottingham was an important location before the execution, but Dixwell's Dover was far more important afterwards. Kent was relatively secure for Parliament in the First Civil War and experienced little fighting. Rebellions broke out in the county in the Second Civil War, however, and the retention of Dover was crucial in the defeat of the rebels.

In January 1652 he was appointed governor of the town's great castle, a place of vital importance in both war and peace. Dover Castle was a strategic location for controlling trade and monitoring its greatest commercial rivals. He was elected to the Council of State in 1651–52, and took a particular interest in naval affairs, especially in relations with the Dutch Republic. This Protestant republic seemed at first sight an obvious ally of the Commonwealth, but trade and profit came first. In October 1651 the Rump Parliament passed a Navigation Act, which reserved English international and coastal trade for English ships. It was aimed at the Dutch because of their pre-eminence in that area, and in order to enforce the law, the English needed to control the English Channel.

The conflict with the Dutch started in 1652 with a dispute between the two countries about the requirement for foreign ships to dip their flags in English waters. Dixwell coordinated the local militia and administered the castle during the war. When peace arrived in 1654, Parliament imposed a tax on the coastal counties of Sussex and Kent to finance the navy, which was exactly the same expedient that Charles I had used, controversially, in the 1630s. The counter response of men like Dixwell may well have been that the extra taxation was actually being used to establish an effective English navy for the first time.

On 25 May 1660 Charles II stepped ashore at Dover and the monarchy was restored. Dixwell had no intention of waiting on events or pleading for his life. A week earlier, on 17 May 1660, an order was issued to seize Dixwell and sequestrate his estates. Three days later the Speaker informed the House of Commons that he had received a petition from a relative of Dixwell's. This stated that the regicide was ill and begged for benefit under the act if he came forward within a fixed time. Parliament extended the time and Dixwell seems to have used this to his advantage.[1]

His obscurity probably meant that there was not too much urgency about apprehending him, and his name seemed to have been omitted from some of the early legal paperwork. He also benefitted from a lack of certainty about where he fled to. He was certainly in Hanau, Germany, with Okey and Barkstead, and then perhaps in Switzerland. His obscurity led to the belief that he had died quite soon after the Restoration. There were no resources or political pressure applied to find him.

He fled to the New World, meeting Whalley and Goffe in February 1665, but because he had not arrived in New England in a blaze of publicity, he was far less easy to track down. Dixwell lived on until 1682, earning his living as a merchant in New Haven. Unlike Whalley and Goffe, who spent most of their time looking anxiously over their shoulders, Dixwell survived and thrived.

He had never married in England, but did so twice in his new home. His first wife, Johanna Ling – who was the daughter of the couple with whom he lodged – died a month after their marriage. In 1770, aged seventy, he married thirty-two-year-old Bathsheba How. Ezra Stiles, the president of Harvard in the late eighteenth century and an extreme republican, wrote a glowing biography of Dixwell, and had one of Dixwell's books in his possession, Walter Raleigh's *History of the World*. It had been banned by Charles I because of the veiled but obvious criticism of the Stuart monarchy. It was a favourite book of Oliver Cromwell, who advised his son to read it. One quotation from the book is famous: 'Whosoever commands the sea commands the trade; whosoever commands the trade of the world commands the riches of the world, and consequently the world itself.' That is exactly what Dixwell was trying to do in Dover.[2]

John and Bathsheba Dixwell had two children, John and Mary, who survived into adulthood and produced offspring that generations of Americans were proud to claim as their relatives. Like all the regicides who escaped after 1660, he was fully expecting the Stuarts to be overthrown, and seemed to have confidence in the future. He made a will leaving all of his property in Kent to his wife, so he must have been expecting a pardon. He was right. An ally in England wrote to him in September 1689, telling him that the Stuarts had been overthrown and a pardon was waiting for him. He should return via Amsterdam, said his friend, clearly not knowing the direction in which he would return home. Dixwell never received this message. He had died in March 1689, aged about eighty-two, and definite news that the Stuarts had been overthrown did not arrive until a month later.[3] His tombstone was anonymous, inscribed with the letters 'J.D.' for John Davids, the name by which he was known. He did this, according to Stiles, 'Lest his enemies dishonour his ashes.'[4]

Dixwell's identity was revealed later, but his remains were protected. This was a country that still believed, 'Rebellion to tyrants is obedience to God'. Like Goffe and Whalley, he had a road named after him in New Haven, Connecticut, which is also the location of Ezra Stiles College, named after the man who made sure that his legacy lived on.

Robert Lilburne is overshadowed by his more famous younger brother, John, but they came to different conclusions about the major issues of their day.[5] Robert concluded that the execution of the king was necessary, while John believed it was as great an injustice as Charles had inflicted on his people. John had spurned Cromwell by 1647, while Robert remained loyal. Another brother, Henry Lilburne, who turned his coat in August 1648 and was subsequently killed by Parliamentary forces at Tynemouth Castle, was denounced by both brothers.

Lilburne was very much a 'northern' regicide, in the same way as men like Bourchier, Constable, and Mauleverer. Lilburne was from Durham, so he was recruited into the Northern Army of the Earl of Manchester in 1642, and did most of his fighting in the north. He was never an MP during the Rump, although he held powerful positions as governor of Newcastle and York and was major-general of Durham and Yorkshire. Like so many regicides, he became famous during the unrest of the army in 1647. He was with Ireton, Okey and Pride in March when they took on the MPs who had come to Saffron Walden to neutralise them politically in March 1647. In his actions he always supported the regime, and his military record was second to none. He defeated Parliament's enemies in the north east and Lancashire during the Second Civil War, earning Cromwell's commendation in the House of Commons.

His own regiment was much more radical in the crises of 1647 and 1648 than those of more famous regicides. When they supported the Leveller revolt at Corkbush Field in November 1647, and had to be constrained by Cromwell, Lilburne was not there, but it did not affect his own promotion prospects. He opposed the attempts – both by the Presbyterian-dominated Parliament of 1646–48, and the Cromwellian

Commons of 1649 – to restart the war in Ireland, which was a key policy of Cromwell. His loyalty to the Commonwealth survived when his brother, John, was put on trial for treason (and therefore his life) in October 1649.

In early 1652 he was sent to govern Scotland as a replacement for Richard Deane. Lilburne failed to suppress some key rebellions, while at the same time maintaining his reputation for supporting religious separatists. He was recalled by Cromwell, partly over a disagreement about the level of resourcing needed for the Scottish occupation, but it seems that a reasonable relationship continued. His replacement, George Monck, immediately restricted the Baptists there, in contradiction to the policy that Lilburne had pursued.

As well as being an acknowledged Baptist, Lilburne was influenced by the Quakers, and perhaps was a Quaker himself by the time of his death. Quakers in the civil war were not the thoughtful and peaceable Christian group that we recognise today. They called themselves the Society of Friends – it was their enemies who called them 'Quakers' – and they were created out of the chaos of the civil war. They rejected social hierarchy, took off their hats for no man and called everybody 'thou'. Their worship was inspired by the 'inner light' of their members and women took an equal part. They refused to take oaths of loyalty to the new regime, and therefore seemed dangerous. Their leader, George Fox, consolidated this reputation with his famous outburst, 'Oh ye great men of the earth, weep and howl for the misery that is coming'.

Lilburne (like Whalley and Goffe in Chapter 14) showed his Cromwellian credentials by being appointed a major-general in 1655, and his time in this role reveals much about him. Despite being nominally John Lambert's deputy in the north, Lilburne had full executive powers in Yorkshire and Durham. He could do as he wished, and he spent his time vigorously following his joint brief of punishing delinquents and improving the morals of the people. He worked actively against Royalists and other delinquents with a genuine hatred (after an insurrection in York in 1656, he called them 'such kind of cattle'), making sure that they paid their decimation tax and ensuring that none got into positions of power.

He corresponded with Cromwell regularly, and in one letter cautioned against the appointment of Richard Robinson as High Sheriff of Yorkshire as he considered him, 'one somewhat of a loose conversation, and one that is too much addicted to tippling, and that which is called "good-fellowship".' The last phrase was in speech marks because it actually meant 'sinful behaviour'.[6] Lilburne's desire to improve people also included building new educational establishments, an unusual ambition during a civil war, and in an era when the duopoly of the English universities was taken for granted. His plan for a place of learning serving the north at Durham had to wait until 1832.

Lilburne maintained his reputation as a sectary by defending Baptists and Quakers.[7] As governor of York in 1654 he was known to be sympathetic to the latter, and their leader, Thomas Aldram, thought so. Cromwellians like Goffe and Whalley had no time for them. Lilburne was clearly different and Cromwell probably shared some of his sympathies. In October 1656, when Lilburne was defending Quakers in Yorkshire, the Quaker James Nayler passed through Bristol on a donkey in a deliberate attempt to replicate Christ's entry into Jerusalem. Nayler already looked like the typical image of Christ at the time, and he arranged his hair and clothes to make the comparison more obvious. There was outrage, especially amongst those MPs who feared that religious toleration was becoming an excuse for blasphemy. For the Presbyterians in Cromwell's Parliament, this case was a chance to put a limit to religious toleration by making a huge fuss, and to neutralise the Quaker movement.

Nayler did not help himself with his defence. He had not been impersonating Christ, he said, but argued that Christ was in him. He had seen a vision and was under instruction from the Almighty, and in any case, was there not a portion of Christ in all of us? The answer given by most Presbyterian MPs was an emphatic 'no'. Goffe demanded the death penalty. William Boteler, a fellow Cromwellian major-general, suggested stoning. The parliamentary motion for Nayler's execution was lost by a mere fourteen votes. Instead he was whipped 310 times, pilloried, branded, and his tongue mutilated, and then given a period of unlimited imprisonment with solitary confinement and hard labour.

There is a chance that Lilburne knew Nayler personally.[8] Nayler was a cornet and Lilburne was a captain when they attacked Pontefract Castle together in December 1644. Lilburne did not speak up for Nayler in the Commons. This made sense. It was not a quiet attempt to protect tender consciences in Yorkshire, but a national case where a deluded individual, who did not even have the support of the Quaker's leader, was used as a pretext by Westminster politicians.

Cromwell felt differently. This was clearly Parliament acting above its power, but he allowed it to continue to rant and rave so his point became obvious. 'By the proceedings of this parliament, you see that they stand in need of a check or balancing power, for the case of James Nayler may happen to be your case,' said Cromwell, advancing the argument both for his proposed 'check' on the Commons (his new 'Other House') and for a degree of religious toleration.

Lilburne's loyalty to Cromwell did not extend to Richard. Given his sympathy for the Levellers, and his clear republicanism, the real mystery is not why he rejected Richard but why he was so steadfast for Oliver. He was just about able to live with the hint of a returned monarchy when Oliver Cromwell rejected it, but saw that those who were around the new Protector wanted the same thing. And it was clear that the protectorate of Richard would reduce the power of the army, while Lilburne's whole life was testament to the importance of the army in creating the Commonwealth.

He fought against the return of Charles II until January 1660, when, as governor of York, he surrendered to Fairfax. He then fell into the hands of Monck, who was marching down to London to restore the Rump and then the king, and was implicated in Lambert's last-ditch attempt to prevent the Restoration in April 1660. He was sentenced to be hanged, drawn and quartered on 16 October, later commuted to internal exile in the Isle of St Nicholas in Plymouth. His father, Richard, was still alive, so Robert never inherited anything that he could forfeit to the Crown. He died in 1665.

Lilburne was a friend and comrade of **William Constable,** another Yorkshire regicide. Constable deserves to be better known. He was a regicide with a chequered history and many and varied motivations that serve as a reminder about how complex the issues were. Constable was an older regicide, born in 1590, so was active in his county of Yorkshire in the 1620s. His political patron was Thomas Wentworth, the future Earl of Strafford, who became one of the two most hated on the king's advisers, and Constable became a county MP and deputy lieutenant of the county.

Constable looked much more like a man who would support the king than Parliament in any future war, but his suspicion of bishops and of the king's power made him oppose the Forced Loan of 1626–27. Charles could dispense with Parliament if these money-raising strategies worked and were repeated. Due to the fact he was married to Dorothy Fairfax, the sister of Fernando Fairfax, his response to the demand for the Forced Loan has been recorded in the family correspondence. When challenged to respond to the king's demands he 'returned answer by one of his servants that he was not at leisure, or had other business.' He ignored the threats of retribution and was arrested and threatened with prison. He spent the winter of 1627–28 incarcerated in the Fleet Prison with John Hotham. One hundred other members of the gentry were eventually imprisoned for non-payment. This puts Constable at the forefront of opposition to the king's policies.

Constable's entry in the official records of Members of Parliament is a tangle of legal disputes about debts and property; what might be called today a 'chaotic lifestyle'.[9] Constable seemed to have financial problems in the 1630s when he sold off property in Yorkshire and decided to emigrate to either New England or the Protestant Netherlands. Like many Puritans, he decided on the shorter, much less perilous journey. In April 1637 he received the king's permission to leave the country for three years and crossed the English Channel to religious freedom.

While in the Netherlands he was a member of the English congregation of Philip Nye at Arnhem.[10] Another member of this rich and influential group was Henry Lawrence, a religious refugee from East Anglia who had emigrated, and rented his land in St Ives to a tenant farmer called Oliver Cromwell. Nye was also an influence on John Alured in the 1640s, as Nye returned to England via Hull and Yorkshire and preached there.

Constable himself returned from exile in 1641. This time it was not Thomas Wentworth who influenced him (he was languishing in the Tower of London by order of Parliament) but Ferdinando Fairfax, father of Thomas Fairfax, his brother-in-law, who would have facilitated his election as MP for Knaresborough. He had lost the original vote by thirty-three to thirteen, a reminder of the narrow base of the electorate, but was eventually elected through the power of the Fairfax family, an insight into how elections worked in the seventeenth century.

Constable raised an infantry against the Royalist faction in Yorkshire in 1642 and fought at Edgehill, where his regiment came out with credit. Constable stands out as the only regicide who was listed as an important member of Essex's army in 1642 (the other was Thomas Grey of Groby, a member of the House of Lords). So, by 1642, Constable did look like a Parliamentarian, but did not seem to be the type of person who would turn to regicide in the later part of the war.

After the Self-denying Ordinance in April 1645 he resigned his commission following a very successful campaign in Yorkshire. The previous year the Commons had rewarded Constable with the rents from the manors of Holme and Bubwith, the property of Royalist Marmaduke Langdale. Rewarding loyal Parliamentary officers with the property of the defeated was common, but there was a twist in this case. Constable had, in 1633, sold his interest in the manor to Langdale, who was at that point his friend and fellow troublemaker against the king. By 1644 Langdale was an enemy and Constable used his power to extract the profits from property which he had already sold. The counter-argument was that Constable had paid out his own money to equip his soldiers, but it was still an audacious move, and was remembered by his enemies many years later. In 1650 he went further and persuaded Parliament to give him the manor back in its entirety. The property reverted to the Langdales in 1660, and perhaps in this case justice was served.

He was an active pro-army Independent in the crisis of 1646–47, and was prominent enough to escape to the army in 1647 when he felt threatened by the Presbyterians. Constable was one of the officers who Fairfax tasked to guard the king when he was 'imprisoned' at Carisbrooke Castle, on the Isle of Wight, from January 1648. Charles had arrived there in November of the previous year. He started off as a guest, but by February he was a prisoner of Parliament. Fairfax sent out Constable (and William Goffe) as men he trusted to provide the necessary security. Charles was restricted to the walls of the castle, but a bowling green was specially built for him (no surprise, then, that he still thought he held all the cards). Constable was given the power to remove the king's courtiers at will in January 1648, but within a few days all of that power was deputed to Colonel Hammond, kinsman of Oliver Cromwell.

From 1648 Constable was a member of the Army Council in the events leading up to the king's treason trial, and sat as a commissioner of the High Court of Justice during the trial itself, signing the king's death warrant. After the execution at the Banqueting House, Whitehall, he sat on the Council of State and attended many parliamentary committees, mostly concerned with military matters.

He continued to act in Yorkshire and was appointed High Sheriff in 1653. He lived long enough to accommodate and accept the increasing power of Oliver Cromwell. Whether it was Fairfax, the army, the Parliament or Cromwell, he never seemed to have any problem accommodating himself to those in power. He served the new state when other local gentry would not, and had similar views to Cromwell himself (religiously radical but socially conservative). He had done much to win the civil war and establish a new regime and he was treated like a national hero when he died in 1655. He prepared for death like a true Puritan, stipulating a simple funeral without excessive grief in his will of December 1654. Like other Puritans of the new establishment, however, this was not what he got.

He became one of the twenty-one major figures from the Cromwell regime buried in the Henry VII Chapel at Westminster Abbey. Constable and Deane were the only two regicides, but it also included Bradshaw's wife, Mary, and Cromwell's mother, Elizabeth. Constable's inclusion could have been the result of his death at the right time, and his constant support of Cromwell, but the fact remains that he was important enough to be part of the new elite.

After the Restoration of the Monarchy in 1660, his body was exhumed from Westminster Abbey and reinterred in a communal burial pit in the grounds of St Margaret's, the church across the road. 'Reinterred' is too probably too generous a term. When the vault was re-examined in Victorian times, the bits of coffin mixed with mixed bone fragments rather suggested that the remains were scooped out in one pile without any reverence at all. The Commonwealth had created a new ruling elite, and the restored Stuarts felt the need to destroy all traces of it and punish it for its presumption.

Anthony Stapley was one of the seven Sussex regicides and was old enough to serve as member of the parliaments of 1624–25 and 1628, without having much impact. He showed his Puritanism in two ways. In 1639 he refused to finance the war with Scotland, not due to any concern for the Scots, but rather a fear that Charles's success would give more religious power to bishops in England. His puritan leanings were reported to William Laud in 1640. In another reminder about how narrow the electorate was, and how murky the process, Stapley managed to gain election for two constituencies in Sussex in the aborted 1640 'Short Parliament'. His house, Patcham Place, still survives and is apparently haunted, although Stapley lived such a charmed life it is hard to believe that the ghost is him.[11]

Stapley was fifty-two when the war broke out and was never going to be an active soldier, despite holding the nominal rank of colonel. Mark Noble, a man who was always ready to impute an unflattering motive, suggested that the civil war turned his head a little, and he threw himself into the new politics because it gave him an enhanced sense of his own importance. Noble tended to divide the regicides into categories: those who had nothing to lose, grander men from better families who had nothing to gain, and insubstantial men who enjoyed their new political status.

Like many of the obscure regicides, he made little impact outside his county. He was present at the Siege of Chichester in December 1642 under William Waller, alongside regicides Cawley and Livesey, and was governor of Chichester between 1643 and 1645. His main struggles seemed to be about resources and avoiding the blame for the brief Royalist capture of Chichester.

During the new Republic, Stapley was mostly a man of minor contributions. The new Commonwealth did not wish Royalist versions of the king's trial to circulate. In November 1649 it appointed a committee to investigate, and Stapley was working with the spymaster Thomas Scot and the judge John Bradshaw. He was a junior member, but clearly a man who could be trusted.

Stapley supported Cromwell all his life and was member of the Council of State from 1649 to 1652. He was a constant Cromwellian of no great significance, but he did defeat obscurity on one occasion. When the Rump Parliament was removed in April 1653, the country was administered by a Council of State. This was a very powerful executive and administrative body, essentially an interim government, and Stapley was a member. This was not to be his path to greatness, though; he was there as an administrator, somebody with useful regional experience of the military. Stapley was a personal friend of Cromwell, and that must have helped as well. This temporary fame tilts Stapley into the Cromwellian camp rather than the bureaucrats. He was appointed to the Nominated Assembly (or 'Barebones' Parliament) in 1653, for which the only real qualification was being godly, reliable and acceptable to Oliver Cromwell.

Stapley was elected to Cromwell's First Protectorate Parliament in September 1654. About one hundred successful candidates were purged, or more accurately pre-purged, by Cromwell, and Stapley was not one them. Noble did not know when he died, and did not care much about a man whom he saw as insubstantial. He did speculate that Stapley 'was too much a republican to have been satisfied with Oliver's assumption of the government which I presume he did but just see'. Noble was probably wrong: Stapley was more Cromwellian than republican.

He actually died in January 1665 and was buried at a church in Patcham, Sussex. There was no room for this peripheral regicide in the great tomb of the new Commonwealth in the Henry VII Chapel of Westminster Abbey, unlike Ireton, Constable and Deane.

Chapter 16

The Committee Men

William Purefoy, Miles Corbet, Vincent Potter

There are a handful of regicides who were more active in committee meetings than glamorous battles, and so have been forgotten by history, but this is unfair, for a few reasons. Firstly, even the bureaucrats sometimes went into battle and risked their lives, often holding a commission in the local militia; secondly, wars cannot be won without the efficient administration of resources; and thirdly, many of our regicide bureaucrats took decisive actions that were as significant as many military ones. The civil war took a lot of organisation, centrally and locally. As Lucy Hutchinson commented, 'every county had the civil war, more or less within itself'.

William Purefoy is a regicide who deserves more recognition. He was mostly an administrator, but was also ready to take military action. In the year of his death, 1659, he took to arms in his native Warwickshire against the uprising of Royalists in Cheshire, securing Coventry for the Commonwealth when other men were wavering and starting to hedge their bets with the Royalists. Ludlow noticed, 'old Colonel Purefoy who had one foot in the grave, was obliged to undertake the command of the forces in the county of Warwick in place of Colonel Fotherby, who declined to act.'

Purefoy was the oldest of the regicides, born c.1580. His first year at the ultra-Puritan Emmanuel College, Cambridge was the same year in which Oliver Cromwell was born. His Protestantism and republicanism seemed to have been engendered by visits to Geneva as a young man rather than any family influence. Throughout his life, he seemed attached to the privileges of Parliament, and that was his main principle. He refused to pay Charles I's Forced Loan of 1627, and like other regicides, declined to attend the coronation and pay to be knighted.

Like many of the bureaucrat regicides, he split his time between his county and Westminster, although this was no longer necessary as no parliaments were called for a decade after 1630. As sheriff of Warwickshire in 1631, his main interest seemed to be the reformation of manners, dealing severely with disorderly characters and alehouses.

In 1641 Purefoy was a key ally of John Pym in the struggle to wrest power from the king. When Pym published the Grand Remonstrance, listing their religious and political objections to the rule of Charles I, it was Purefoy who manipulated the Commons to pass a resolution to have the Remonstrance published and publically distributed. This was seen by many at the time as an appalling breach of etiquette, bringing the ordinary people closer to politics. It was the first step to civil war, and Purefoy was at the heart of it.

Purefoy was a marked man within a week of war being declared, and was one of the first victims of the conflict. Charles had already omitted Purefoy from the Commission of Array, an order to the loyal gentry to raise soldiers for the king, and when the king's nephews, Rupert and Maurice, found themselves in Purefoy's Warwickshire in the first week of the war, the urge for revenge was too strong. They besieged Purefoy's home at Caldecote Hall, near Nuneaton. It was defended by his wife, Joan, his son-in-law and his eleven servants. Tradition suggests that William himself was hiding in the hop garden, another hint that his civil war was not going to be a martial one. In his defence, he was sixty-two years old and later proved that he could do his bit on the battlefield.

The events at Caldecote Hall were a taste of what was to come; it was the civil war writ small. The 500 Royalist soldiers were ineffective and ill disciplined. In order to defend the house the Purefoy family had to sacrifice the contents by melting down pewter goblets and cutlery to make bullets for their muskets, just as the nation had to do for four years, spending blood and treasure on defending itself from fellow Englishmen. Like most of the civil war, it was a nasty skirmish rather than a glamorous pitched battle, and when the Royalists could not take the house, they gained the victory by burning down large parts of the outhouses. It was a battle against 'bad' individuals rather than ideas, and there was a degree of civility that was not going to endure. The defenders had their lives spared by Prince Rupert as a reward for their gallant defence.[1] The manor has long gone, but the original door survives, and still bears the bullet holes from this early siege of the civil war.

During the war Purefoy was an active iconoclast. In June 1643 he ordered his soldiers to demolish Warwick Market Cross and deface the monuments at St Mary's church. Apart from cleansing Warwickshire of popish superstition, his main administrative work was the same as most parliamentary committee men; collecting money. In the 1640s he was one of the men in charge of assessing the wealth of the locals to work out their contribution to the war effort.

His active service was impressive. In 1643 he was commissioned with his own regiment of horse, and fellow regicide Vincent Potter was one of his captains.[2] Purefoy's crest bore a very apt motto for such a committed Puritan: *'Pure Foi, ma Joie'* ('My pure faith is my joy'). He was at the siege of Gloucester and performed well at this vital victory for Parliament, although some sources suggest that he was prickly and not easy to work with, perhaps due to be being considerably older than most other officers.[3]

When the war finished Purefoy becomes more of an enigma. He seems to have been neither an Independent nor a strong political supporter of the army, although he served with Miles Corbet on a committee designed to grant indemnity to soldiers. He seemed to want a tight Presbyterian settlement that would normally have put him on Ireton and Thomas Harrison's list of those to be purged in 1648, but he not only did he survive that, he also played a voluntary part in the trial and execution.

Purefoy may have come to the conclusion that maintaining a Parliament was more important than worrying about the fate of a bad king, and he was one of the few regicides who opposed the abolition of the House of Lords when it raised objections to the trial. In 1653 he once again supported the Rump Parliament when Cromwell dissolved it and in 1657 opposed the title of 'king' for the Lord Protector.

His contribution after 1649 was modest but not unimportant. He was always voted onto the Council of State, was president for a month in 1652 (its rapidly rotating presidency meant that it was not that much of an honour), worked on various committees, and remained an MP for all three of Cromwell's parliaments. He worked on all the committees that could guarantee kickbacks and cheap bargains of land from bishops and Royalists, but was not linked with corruption. Indeed, he had spent his own money at times in the defence of Coventry. In 1651 he was present after the Battle of Worcester, interviewing prisoners and dispatching the most displeasing of them into semi-slavery in the West Indies. He was a solid, hard-working republican and Puritan. He died in September 1659, still committed to a country without a monarch, and his estates were confiscated the following year.

Our second bureaucrat-regicide is **Miles Corbet** (born 1595). Like Purefoy, he was a local bureaucrat and indispensable part of the parliamentary war machine. The civil war would not have been won without their vital contributions: liaising with the military, rooting out rebels and punishing them, maintaining supplies and collecting the weekly assessment from local property owners. Parliament decided the weekly payment of each county and the local committee decided how much each person was to pay. The personal power, and the scope to do injustices, was huge. Some bureaucrats were famous for corruption, but Corbet was different. Rather than chase power and money, he used his position to hunt out, try and execute 'witches'. He is as well-known for this as for his execution of the king.

Both sides in the civil war believed in the existence of evil and of the active involvement of the devil in people's lives. Both sides called the other the 'anti-Christ' and both sides believed they were fighting the power of Satan. The Royalists noted 1 Samuel 15:23, 'rebellion is as the sin of witchcraft'. Cromwell was an obvious Satan figure. When Charles II received the news of Cromwell's death in 1658, his tennis match was interrupted by his courtiers shouting 'the devil is dead', and the king knew to whom they were referring. The message was reputed to have been given by Stephen Goffe, brother of the regicide William Goffe, who was also fighting against Satan from the other side of the argument.

Puritans certainly believed in the power of evil. Prince Rupert's dog (a bitch called Boy) was reputed to have devilish powers of catching bullets in its mouth and being invisible at will. It was killed at Marston Moor by the godly Cromwellian soldiers who believed it to be satanic.

Witchcraft was a recognised phenomenon. James I (as James VI of Scotland) wrote a book about it, and the laws were tightened in 1604 to make it a capital offence, even if nobody had died. There were a limited number of prosecutions for witchcraft before the civil war, each of them a tragedy, but until the social and economic dislocations of war, accusations of witchcraft were very likely to fail, and other explanations sought, including fraud, lack of evidence, a previous medical condition, or simply the malice of fearful or aggressive neighbours.

The increase in the number of witchcraft accusations was caused by the calamitous events of war. At the time, the rise of evil was regarded as one of the consequences of the civil war. There was an upsurge of prosecutions against so-called witches around the time of the Battle of Naseby (1645), when life was at its most desperate, and scapegoats were required by a bewildered and panicked population facing illness, harvest failure, the deaths of animals and the dislocation of society. 'Witches' were a convenient target. They proved that evil was active in the world, so that the horrors of life could not be blamed on God, or, even worse, lead to the conclusion that God didn't care or didn't exist. Part of this 1645 spike in prosecutions was the work of Corbet himself.

The two most famous witchfinders were Matthew Hopkins and John Stearne. Men like Corbet provided the administrative back-up, which sounds facetious, but is not. These famous witchfinders could not operate without it. Concerned locals would pass complaints about behaviour to influential locals like Corbet. He could have sent people home with a proverbial flea in their ear and tell them to find less superstitious reason for their misfortune, but because of the strains of war and the influence of Puritanism in the justice system, he didn't. He passed them on to men like Hopkins and his assistant.

Hopkins started his persecution in his home town of Manningtree, but he needed agents in the localities to spread his net wider. The discovery of 'witches' was limited mostly to the Puritan counties of Norfolk, Suffolk and Essex. When Royalists taunted the Puritans about the number of witchcraft cases in those parts of the country dominated by them, their reply was that 'the devil is bound to put his chapel where the godly put their churches'. A more rational view would be that it was the existence of Puritans and their stranglehold on local government in that area that created the persecution.

Corbet was the Recorder for his home town of Great Yarmouth, an important magistrate and chairman of the Committee of Examinations, which actively sought out people accused as witches. He was a fearsome man, and hated by the Royalists as a hardline Puritan. They also hated him for his efficient administration of the army of the Eastern Association, and for his vicious extraction of money to win the war. Corbet was, it seems, a melancholic and ill-favoured man, ultra-serious, brooding and physically a little repellent: 'bull faced, splay footed and bacon faced Corbet', was the comment of one enemy. Abraham Kicke, who met him in the last years of his life, called him a dwarf. To others, more mindful of his power, called him England's 'grand inquisitor'.

Corbet had arrested several 'witches' in 1645 and enthusiastically pursued them. His literal reading of the Bible gave him encouragement; 'thou shalt not suffer a witch to live'. Elizabeth Bradwell, an old, poor, iterant begging women, and therefore a witch suspect straight from central casting, was accused of putting an evil spirit on the son of a local alderman. You did not need to be a proven consort of Satan to be accused; any use of bad supernatural powers – *maleficium* – would be enough. After a strenuous but flawed collection of evidence, Corbet presided over judgement of Elizabeth and others. One of the grand jurors was Henry Moulton, son of Bradwell's alleged victim. In December six women were sentenced to be hanged with Corbet presiding. He was the 'prologue to the hangman that looks more like the hangman than the hangman himself'.[4]

Great Yarmouth was a town that looked isolated and safe in terms of land-based attack, but vulnerable from the sea. It was a commercial town, based on shipbuilding and trade in herring and coal, and like many similar places, its local ruling elite was Puritan. The extreme eastern location made them both outward-looking and conscious of their own security. They worried about pirates and sea rovers disrupting their trade, and when the civil war came, they worried about foreign invasion and tried to spend money on fortifications to repel the Dutch enemy. This was 1645, the same year as the Corbet-inspired witchcraft accusations. Corbet was fighting both the enemy within and without.

Corbet had a history of opposing the king as well as Satan. He was the centre of opposition to Charles's attempt to extract forced loans as early as 1627, and he was a Member of Parliament continuously from 1640 to 1653. He was identified as one of the hardline war party as early as 1643, always a good signifier of those who later supported regicide. During the crisis of 1647–49 he was condemned by the Presbyterian part of the House of Commons and the implication was that much of his busy committee work was for his own benefit. His greatest political moment was in January 1649, when he was selected by the Rump to tell the king that the 135 commissioners had been appointed and his trial would proceed. So, Corbet was probably present when Charles came to the realisation that his next act would be to die as a martyr.

On 4 October 1650 he was appointed one of the Commonwealth's four civil commissioners in Ireland; two of the others being the regicides Ludlow and Jones. Despite the benign-sounding name, their main responsibility was to establish and maintain the armed occupation of Ireland and redistribute its land, and in 1655 he became Chief Baron of the Exchequer in Ireland, a senior legal position. He lived in Malahide Castle, just outside Dublin, granted to him by Cromwell as his share of the confiscation of Royalist and Catholic lands. Corbet escaped to the Netherlands at the Restoration but was betrayed by the English ambassador, Sir George Downing, and returned to England for execution. He was hanged, drawn and quartered in April 1662, claiming purity for his motives to his last breath.

Vincent Potter was an administrator of national importance during the war. He was one of the men who kept the army running and was admired for this by Oliver Cromwell. He has been forgotten by history because his specialism was finance and logistics, and the passage of time has not made these subjects any more interesting. (Though neither has it made them any less vital. When Napoleon said that an army marched on its stomach, it was not an original thought.)

Potter, like many Puritan regicides, had links with New England, but unlike most, he actually spent some time there in the 1630s. Potter left England for Boston (via Holland) on the *Elizabeth and Ann*, a ship full of Puritans destined for work with the Massachusetts Bay Company. Most of them had no plan to return, given the state of religion and trade in England. When circumstances changed in 1639, many did return. Potter (and William Constable) were the only regicides who did so, as far as we know. Potter had been a competent military man; indeed, he had been a soldier for much of his time in the New World and also a trader, taking on an apprentice as late as 1639.

He was a Warwickshire man, like William Purefoy, with only an approximate date of birth and unknown parents. His relative social status can be seen in the fact that he was a captain in William Purefoy's regiment of horse, and most of his fighting was in his own county. After July 1645 Potter gave up active military service and became parliamentary commissioner residing in the army, a job previously done by his brother, John, who had died at Naseby. His job was to supply the army, and by doing this effectively he helped win the war.

His claim to fame was that he was good at this crucial job. Many of his account book records survive from his time in the Warwickshire militia, which may have over-stated his reputation a little. Potter stands out as a man who was worried about the dramatic effect of war on civilians. He was severe in his condemnation of plunder and free quarter, which he recognised as a major cause of hostility from local people. He recognised the civilians as 'poor oppressed people', which was not a common view at the time.

One poor Oxfordshire peasant, who had all his belongings stolen, made a list: '7 pair of sheets, 3 brass kettles, 2 brass pots, 5 pewter dishes, 4 shirts, 4 smocks, two coats, one clock, 1 waistcoat, seven dozen candles, one frying pan, 1 spit, 2 pair of pot hooks', and all of his food supplies (wheat, eggs, oatmeal, salt and everything that his family would need to prepare their food). The rich were no better off. If you had ready cash, it would be taken from you. The historian Peter Gaunt suggests that 200 hoards of coins from the civil war have been located by archaeologists and detectorists.

Soldiers on neither side were paid on time, and even when they had money, they rarely paid out for a roof over their heads at night, as the home-owners were issued with semi-worthless IOUs for any accommodation they supplied. Marches and battles could not be conducted on diets of cheese and biscuits. Plunder included food and drink, and under the guise of military imperative, horses and their hay. Most soldiers had stolen a horse, and it was no surprise that indemnity from charges of theft was high up on soldier's demands after the war. Plunder was also having an environmental impact; 1648 was the third bad harvest in a row, when statistically there was a bad harvest every six years on average. Plunder meant crops were stolen or destroyed to deny them to the enemy; animals were killed, new crops were not planted, and farm buildings and tools destroyed.

Potter actively tried to buy horses and provisions for the New Model Army rather than allow people to steal them. He would follow the armies and fill in any gaps, buying locally, which was much more efficient than buying them and then hoping to get them to where they were needed. Horses were bought from those already riding them, given back, but now owned by the state. It was politically important to do so. Most people would have already been squeezed for a local assessment. If your property was stolen or hungry soldiers foisted on your household, you would be paying twice for the same army, which would not engender loyalty.

Both armies were ruthless robbers of both rich and poor. The Parliamentary army, with the help of professional procurement experts like Potter, were able to alienate the locals just a little less than the Royalists. In the crucial campaign in the south west in 1645, the Parliament's more efficient bureaucratic methods, slightly more disciplined army and lack of desperation caused by impending defeat ensured that the armed neutrals ('Clubmen') could be persuaded that Royalists were more of a problem. These primitively armed neutrals could sometimes be persuaded to focus their firepower on the king's forces. Lord Goring, the Royalist commander, was in a semi-permanent drunken stupor, which got worse with each setback. That was not the case with the Puritan Fairfax and his bureaucrats such as Potter.

Despite the best efforts of men like Potter – he was said to keep lists of unpaid wages in the army – the problem of irregular payment never disappeared, and by February 1647 the infantry were five months in arrears and the cavalry nearly eleven months. Both wanted their pay, and indemnity from the horses that they had stolen when none had been provided. Had army pay been up-to-date in 1647, it would have been much easier to disband it, and then the history of the period would have been very different.

Many of our regicides were at one time appointed by Parliament to administer the estates of delinquents, and Potter was no exception. In 1648, after the rebellion orchestrated by Rowland Laugharne was crushed by fellow regicide Thomas Horton, Potter was one of several commissioners whose job it was to seek out all of the delinquents' property, seize it and sell it at the best price available. The scope for corruption was obvious, but we don't know if Potter succumbed (though this doesn't sound like him). Potter was promoted to colonel in June 1649, and was responsible for provisioning Cromwell's campaigns in Ireland and Scotland. This was another absolutely crucial post and a sure sign of Cromwell's trust in the man's talents.

Potter was arrested in 1660 and brought to trial as a regicide. He was found guilty of treason and condemned to death, but died in prison before the sentence could be carried out. The trial record reported that he was having a fit of the stone, so he would have been experiencing a fever, intestinal pain, and a desire to urinate despite being in agony. He was allowed to sit, but refused permission to pass water. John Lilburne was also denied permission to do the same in his treason trial in 1649. Lilburne reached for a pot and peed in it, but Potter suffered in silence.

He was, like all the regicides, in chains and irons during the court proceedings, and felt it more acutely than others because of his size, 'I hope I may be freed from irons, I am in pain, and a man of bulk.' He cried a lot during the process, through pain rather than fear. He was never able to speak in his defence. We know nothing about the spouse of Vincent Potter. We only know that he was married because there are sources that mention his brother-in-law. He is undeservedly obscure, a victim of the paucity of historical sources about the importance of supplying and feeding an army.

Chapter 17

Unprincipled, Choleric Malcontents?

Thomas Mauleverer, John Bourchier

Dame Veronica Wedgwood, the great historian of the civil war, believed that out of the fifty-nine, 'there were about thirty to forty who gave character, solidarity and strength to the High Court of Justice.' Those are the regicides who performed the deed for a well-considered reason, be it political or religious, who worked with others and not just for themselves, and who persevered when the going got tough.

This leaves us with between nineteen and twenty-nine unworthy regicides, which is not only a large range but also a large number. Her worst offenders were **Thomas Mauleverer** and **John Bourchier**, described by Wedgewood as 'unprincipled, choleric malcontents'. This is an unhelpful and difficult concept. All the regicides were malcontents, based on the premise that the king's actions gave them something significant to be unhappy about. Many were driven to anger and frustration by the events of 1647–48. They saw their anger as righteous.

The idea of regicide being an unprincipled act is also difficult to accept. They signed the warrant, and there was some sort of principle there, but it might not be seen as a 'good principle' (but is there any acceptable principle that justifies execution?). If they killed out of 'principle' does that redeem them? Who decides what 'principled' means? Is it just shorthand for people that you agree with?

Mauleverer and Bourchier were both Yorkshire landowning gentry. John Bourchier went down the route of Cambridge and Inns of Court, like many of the regicides (and, of course, thousands who were not). His family were only distantly related to the Bourchier family who married into the Cromwell family when Oliver married Elizabeth Bourchier in 1622. The regicide Bourchier was socially much grander.

The early career of these two men explains why some people have doubted their motives. Like many of the older regicides, Bourchier (born 1595) had a track record of working with the Stuart administration, to a limited extent anyway. He was knighted in 1619 by James I and made a Justice of the Peace by Charles I in 1625. Mauleverer had the regular roles of the gentry in Yorkshire in the 1630s. He was knighted by King Charles in August 1641, just before the constitutional struggle, which suggests that he was not regarded as an enemy at that time.

However, both men were so definite about their allegiances when war broke out that it seems that the judgment of Wedgwood may be too severe. Like many older regicides, Bourchier opposed the king's attempts to raise money with a Forced Loan in 1627, and when King Charles summoned the Yorkshire gentry to attend him in June 1642, Bourchier argued violently with the king's supporters. On the outbreak of civil war, he was arrested and imprisoned at York until June 1643.

Thomas Mauleverer became an enemy of the king just as quickly. Just over a year after his knighthood, in late 1642, he was cited in a list of people whose actions put them beyond pardon. He had made a negative impression by enthusiastically raising a regiment of foot and a troop of horse for Parliament. He later claimed back the money – £15,000 – which his enemies interpreted as cynical, but there is a clear difference between reimbursement of expenses and enriching yourself.

Neither man, therefore, could be accused of being lazy or uncommitted. Mauleverer was an active iconoclast; a noted Puritan principle. His troops became notorious for pillaging and defiling churches (or cleansing them, depending on your point of view). In March 1643 Mauleverer's regiment broke into Ripon Cathedral and the soldiers damaged the Great East Window, defaced the tombs, destroyed the organ (Puritans did not like the idea of music in a religious context) and melted lead pipe to make cups and plates.[1] There is no doubt this event happened and that Mauleverer received criticism for it, but it was similar to other events and not restricted to regicides. The Presbyterian Earl of Essex oversaw similar damage to Worcester Cathedral the year before.

Some modern historians have suggested that his soldiers were using the cathedral as their headquarters rather than 'breaking in'. This was common practice. Mauleverer is also accused of 'exercising many cruelties towards the inhabitants', which was also common. The occupation of

Ripon was short-lived, thanks to the governor of Skipton Castle, Sir John Mallory. He commented that there was an attack by the Royalists 'upon the rebels by surprise in the Market Place where they had kept their main guard […] [and] made them feel the sharpness of their swords.'[2]

Mauleverer was part of the Parliamentary defeat – rout might be a better word – at the Battle of Adwalton Moor on 30 June 1643. This Royalist victory meant that most of Yorkshire was in the hands of Mauleverer's enemies, leading indirectly to the plundering of his own ancestral estate at Allerton in January 1644, while Mauleverer was campaigning in Cheshire. He may have been choleric, but he does sound like a man of principle, sufficiently committed to see his own estates sacrificed when he fought for Parliament in another county.

Only Hull was left supporting Parliament in Yorkshire after Adwalton Moor. When the Royalists marched to besiege the town, Fairfax commissioned Mauleverer to seek out spies and traitors. Mauleverer seemed to have the confidence of the most senior soldier in the Parliamentary army. Sir John Hotham, one of the early parliamentary heroes in Hull, was one of his victims. Mauleverer was appointed a commissioner of the High Court of Justice in January 1649, and was a signatory of the king's death warrant.

During the Commonwealth, Mauleverer was active as a Justice of the Peace in Yorkshire. He died in June 1655. He is another example of the painful split in families caused by the civil war. His son, Richard, was an active Royalist, for which he was cut off by his father both socially and financially. This act ensured that, when Mauleverer died in 1655, his estate was not taken by the Crown in 1660 but restored to his son. Mauleverer seems to have been not much different to lots of the other regicides. Wedgwood's verdict may seem a little harsh, though there seems to be evidence that he was not a very nice man, but history tends not to be made by people with pleasing personalities.

John Bourchier had harboured resentment against the Stuart monarchy since the 1630s. He may have been discontented and angry, but he had his reasons. As the Stuart monarchy ran out of money, it resorted to desperate measures, including excessive felling of trees in forests. The Forest of Galtres, near York, which had provided a managed a sustainable supply for centuries, had more of less completely disappeared by 1630.

It was often the local gentry who organised this, rather than the monarch. The Bourchier family certainly initiated deforestation for their own profit. In 1633 one of the king's advisors, Thomas Wentworth, bought the forest as a park and put up fences, partly to stop the Bourchiers, who owned land in the former forest, but the Bourchiers had the fences pulled down. There were similar disputes all over the country. This affected the prosperity of many of the gentry and they resented it. Furthermore, each new tax or revenue meant that Charles could survive longer without Parliament.

It was the Star Chamber, one of the king's prerogative courts, which put Bourchier in prison and fined him heavily. Bourchier clearly resented this, and the implication that his actions were caused by his incipient madness. It was a low blow, made by Wentworth in the full knowledge that Bourchiers's life had been turned upside down when his father, William, was declared insane when he was three years old. In 1641, when Wentworth was under attack as an evil adviser of the king, Bourchier was not in the forefront of the attempt to execute him. The image of the bitter and angry man is largely unproved.

Bourchier was present at the king's summons of the Yorkshire gentry on Heworth Moor, near York, in June 1642. It was meant to rally the local gentry around the cause. It was impressive, with 150 knights in complete armour, and was attended by 800 infantry among a mostly supportive crowd of 70,000. A petition from Parliament was presented to the king by Thomas Fairfax, asking Charles to cease his armed preparation for war and talk to Parliament. This would have been Bourchier's aim as well, but the arrogant attitude of one of the king's courtiers pushed him towards war. Bourchier was attacked and abused by Lord Savil, who attempted to pull him off his horse and told him that 'he came to sow sedition'.[3]

Bourchier's response is unknown, but he spent a year in prison for his pains. There was no strong Parliamentary force in York that could protect him from the king's wrath, and he knew it. Some may call this choleric, but an alternative would be 'very brave'.

After being released from York Castle in 1643 Bourchier made his way to Hull, the only stronghold of the Parliamentary cause in that low point of the civil war, and was involved in the hunt against John Hotham, along with fellow Yorkshire regicides Alured, Pelham and Mauleverer. Bourchier did not risk his life in battle. He was the High Sheriff of Yorkshire and entered the battle of the House of Commons as a recruiter MP for Ripon at the comparatively late date of 1647.

He continued to be a committee man, and in 1654 he became a Trier and Ejector, which suggests an interest in Puritan reformation of manners. The Triers were a centralised group who set standards for preachers and school masters, and Bourchier would have been a local Ejector who hunted out those who failed to reach the necessary standard of morality and efficiency. Like most regicides, he did the deed to make people better behaved, not to improve their social and political rights.

Bourchier died without apology for what he had done. His own son, Barrington, was a member of the Convention Parliament called by General Monck in 1660, and was a Royalist who had taken part in Booth's uprising. Luckily, Barrington was absent abroad and was not present in the Parliament that decided his father's fate. By the Restoration of the Stuarts, Bouchier was sixty-five and dying, a relatively advanced age for the seventeenth century. He was too ill even for a trial to take place, and Ludlow suggested that his family were pressurising him to recant to save their inheritance. He reportedly sat up from the chair that he had been bound to for days, reaffirmed his belief that the regicide was the correct thing to do, and died a few days later. As it turned out, Barrington was able to hold on the family house at Beningbrough Hall, and Bourchier was able to die with his principles intact.

Chapter 18

Mostly About the Money

Humphrey Edwards, Gregory Norton, John Downes,
Daniel Blagrave, William Cawley

The Bible, much quoted by Puritans and believed without reservation, is absolutely clear on the subject. Timothy, verse six, chapter ten: 'the love of money is the root of all evil: which while some coveted after, they have erred from the faith, and pierced themselves through with many sorrows.' Puritans would read these words (or a version of them if they were not using the official Church of England translation of 1604–10), and accept it absolutely.

How many of the regicides were unworthy men, whose main, or sole, principle was financial gain? Such people clearly existed in the eyes of contemporaries. As the regicide Miles Corbet was about to be horribly executed along with Barkstead and Okey at Tyburn on 19 April 1662, he claimed exemption from this category. Corbet wanted to be seen as a man of principle: 'When I was first called to serve in Parliament I had an estate; I spent it in the service of the parliament. I never bought any king's or bishop's lands; I thought I had enough, at least I was content with it; that I might serve God and my country was what I aimed at.'

Presumably he had specific people in mind, but how do we recognise them? Did he know that John Barkstead, who he knew well and with whom he went into hiding, had made a fortune by taking huge bribes from Royalists and buying bishops' land cheaply?

The number of regicides who lost money while resisting their king was very small and Corbet was not one of them. He accepted a wage of £4 a week like all MPs, but was also in receipt of £1700 per year from the Long Parliament, a much higher figure than average.

Most regicides made money acquiring property from the vanquished king, bishop or Royalists, and many survived with their reputation intact.

163

John Hutchinson took the opportunity to acquire very cheaply some of the king's goods in 1649 – in his case, two Titian masterpieces, including the *Pardoe Venus* – but he did not buy them to admire them; he sold them on to continental agents almost immediately. This is how Charles I's exquisite collection ended up abroad, although to be fair, that is where most of it originally came from.

So, it's a tough call, but some regicides seem to have been motivated by money more than anything else. This did not preclude the holding of some principle, as without principle they would not have been able to inveigle themselves into the positions of influence to make the money. The easiest one to identify is the regicide **Humphrey Edwards**. He was a blatant turncoat who was determined to put himself where the money was.

In February 1637, during the early days of Charles's I war against the Scottish Presbyterians, Edwards was appointed a gentleman pensioner to the king. This sounds like a sedate and unchallenging sinecure, but the role involved guarding the king's person, and so Edwards was one of the armed guards who invaded the House of Commons in January 1642 to arrest the five most troublesome MPs. He received no reward from Charles, who was on this occasion a better judge of character than he is usually given credit for.

His role was mostly passive until 1648, when Edwards survived Pride's Purge, and attended every session of the trial. At a time when other regicides were given important tasks that suited their temperament, Edwards was in a team of three who made sure the king was reasonably comfortable in his captivity; the rationale being that Edwards was one of the few regicides that Charles would have recognised and accepted as a person of quality. After the execution he spent most of his time as an MP overseeing the sale of Church land and squabbling indecorously for other offices of profit. He seemed to have no more influence after the relatively early date of 1651.

Noble says that revenge was his reason for treason against his king, and that he did not 'have any one striking feature of his character'. He also wonders why very obscure men like Edwards were mentioned on the revenge paperwork, and he speculated that it was a way of finding those who were in hiding or pretending to be dead. Everybody knew Cromwell, Ireton, Bradshaw and Pride were dead, but you had to be an obscure figure like Edwards for there to be any doubt. There was no doubt, though; he was dead by 1658.

William Cawley of Chichester seems to have been an enigma – part sectarian administrator and part property speculator – and the final judgement is hard to make. He was the son of a wealthy brewer, in a family without any obvious Puritan or rebel inclinations, although he lived in a county that was predominantly Puritan and Parliamentarian. He was married, and though his wife's name is unknown, sources suggest that she was a Royalist during the civil war. His brother was an archdeacon in the Church of England. After the death of his father, John, in 1621, William became one of the richest men in the western part of Sussex.

Cawley had some principles, even when there was no profit in it. He resisted the kind of money-making activities that alienated the gentry from their king. One long-forgotten law was Distraint of Knighthood, which required any gentlemen who earned £40 or more from agricultural rents to be knighted by the king. Cawley failed to turn up to Charles's coronation in 1626, and was then investigated by the king's commissioners who allowed him to compound (pay a fine) for the relatively large sum of £14, nearly fifty per cent more than the going rate. In 1635 and 1636 Cawley refused to pay ship money, another medieval resurrection designed to raise money and circumvent the calling of a Parliament.

So it was not a surprise that Cawley declared Chichester for Parliament early in the conflict, but he had no answer to the 1,000 Royalist troops who took the town with little resistance in November 1642. Cawley fled to Portsmouth and did not return until December when a Parliamentary army retook the town. Cawley's main contribution was to allow the Parliamentary cannon to be trained on the North Gate from his own almshouses. When the town was taken, the cathedral was 'cleansed of popery', and the silver located from its hiding place and sold for the war effort. In August 1643 he was appointed by the House of Commons one of the commissioners 'for demolishing superstitious pictures and monuments' in London.

Cawley was the most important man for the next decade in Chichester and was also a very active committee man in Westminster. He was appointed to several Commons committees, including those responsible for the army, the advance of money, for plundered ministers and for compounding. These suggested a man who was religious zealot yet still keen to be at the centre of events when money and property were being assessed and transferred.

As a member of the Committee for Compounding with Delinquents, Cawley would be dealing with Royalists who had already had everything taken away from them by sequestration. A fine, usually of about three years' income from rents, would be sufficient, but there was considerable scope for the MPs to abuse their power. The Committee for Plundered Minsters sounds very charitable, but as the Parliament gained the upper hand, it was mostly a job that involved rooting out scandalous priests and distributing their income amongst more worthy people. As a member of the committee for the advance of money, his job was not to organise the loans demanded by Parliament, but to track down and fine those who had not paid. Once again, he was in a position to arbitrarily judge the extent of the crime and decide what the fine should be.

Much of the actual dirty work would be done by local committees, and Cawley was able to oversee his own work by becoming the chief sequestrator for Sussex, alongside such dubiously motivated regicides as Anthony Stapley, John Downes and Peter Temple. Cawley was one of the regicides tainted with whispers of corruption, but popular enough to be voted onto the first two Councils of State. Cromwell, however, had little time for him.

After the execution, he was one of the regicides identified as a friend of Henry Marten and Thomas Scot, which suggests some republican leanings. These were confirmed when he pulled out of national politics during Cromwell's single person rule, although his interest in property continued. He bought land previously belonging to the Crown in West Hampnett, and from the sequestered Royalists in Wartling in Sussex. It is hard to know how much of his activity was motivated by opportunistic greed, as Crawley was active in buying property even before the civil war.

He made the correct decision to flee the country in 1660, ending up in Vevey, Switzerland, in the company of Edmund Ludlow, who quite liked him. His own son, William, was an MP in the last Protectorate Parliament, and the Convention Parliament in 1660 which brought the king back. This did not help the family. Cawley's property was forfeited to the Duke of York. Most regicides had their property given to the future James II, most of which was sold on for ready money. However, it seemed that Cawley was one of the more fortunate of the regicides. His property may have been sequestered but he was financially comfortable in Switzerland.

Cawley had always wanted to be buried in the chapel of the almshouse he had founded in Chichester. This may or may not have happened. In the nineteenth century a lead case with a male skeleton was found in a vault under the floor of the chapel. Some believed that this could be Cawley's body, secretly smuggled home. It would be an appropriate end for a mediocre man of modest principles who always seemed to get his own way.

Gregory Norton (1603–1652) did not have a track record of opposition to the monarchy like Cawley, although they were born a year apart and lived through the same political events. He was made a baronet by James I and held a position as a minor official at the court of King Charles I. Norton supported Parliament on the outbreak of the First Civil War from his local base in Sussex and was a recruiter MP for Midhurst in 1645. He emerged as a radical Independent with a particular interest in Irish affairs (he seems to have spent some of his early life there). He was active in the legal proceedings against King Charles in 1649, sitting as a member of the High Court of Justice and signing the king's death warrant as the fiftieth signature.

During the Commonwealth, Norton was associated with the republican Henry Marten, but he also came under suspicion of profiteering from the sale of confiscated Royalist estates and properties, especially in regard to Richmond Palace, where he was reputed to have bought the furniture at a price so discounted that it was tantamount to theft. Noble, with his noted lack of neutrality, put it like this: 'As a reward for this nefarious butchery he was gratified with Richmond Palace and much of his majesty's furniture at a very inconsiderable price.' Norton disinherited his son, Henry, because he opposed the trial and execution of the king. When Norton died he left the bulk of his property to his friend and fellow regicide, Humphrey Edwards, which was not much of a character reference.[1]

John Downes was a man in the shadows during the civil war; described as 'feeble' by Veronica Wedgwood. He was vaguely of the Puritan persuasion, and Puritan support secured him his seat in Parliament in 1641. He had no track record of opposing the king before that.

Between 1641 and 1648 he was a minor member of the Independent faction but became more active after Pride's Purge. Although never a soldier, he was appointed to the powerful army committee. He was a confidante of Cromwell and seems to have made a fortune dealing in the confiscated Royalist estates. He had been appointed the auditor of the Duchy of Cornwall by Charles I and held this post for the first three years of the civil war, using it as a vehicle to make money from property.

Downes had one claim to fame, which he used ruthlessly when the Restoration happened and Royalists were bent on revenge. During the trial at Westminster Hall the king was about to put forward another plan for the peace of the kingdom, so he said, and Judge Bradshaw refused permission for it to be heard. The king's plan would have involved a joint meeting of the Commons and Lords, and Ludlow speculated that it would involve the king's abdication and replacement by his son. We will never know, as it was not allowed, but it does not sound like Charles. The commissioners who knew him best also knew this was more time wasting and prevarication.

Downes then interrupted proceeding with his famous plea, 'Have we hearts of stone? Are we men?' This stopped the trial, which added little to its credibility. Downes wanted to hear what the king had to say. He viewed any sentence as unjustified if the king would not be heard, a right that was given to the lowest of people in any court. In Downes' own words, 'Cromwell did answer with a great deal of storm.' Downes did not know the king, Cromwell told him; Charles was one of the most hard-hearted men on earth.

Perhaps Downes could be given the benefit of the doubt. It was not clear what the exact purpose of the trial was, and perhaps the people who organised it did not fully know. Downes may have thought, not unreasonably, that the trial was a last-ditch attempt to make the stubborn king offer enough compromise, and it is possible that Downes believed that this was what the king was doing even at this late point. However, that's a lot of doubt to benefit from, especially as Downes seemed to possess few obvious principles himself.

Downes was in tears, and Bradshaw saw this (or rather Downes made sure that he saw it). Downes' conscience did not mean that he was ready to relinquish the church lands that he had bought cheaply, much of it during Parliament's fire sale of bishops' land to raise the money for getting the king back from the Scots.

Despite his choreographed doubts about the trial, Downes did a lot of unnecessary attending. He did not absent himself as a High Commissioner, like many did, and most did not turn up at all. The leading regicides were scraping the barrel by including Downes in the first place, and were only doing so in order to give legitimacy to the process. He was present to see the sentence announced and there were at least nine other major players in the room who did not sign the execution warrant, without any ill effects.

Downes was thought guilty enough to be exempted from the pardon in 1660, and was in the first swathe to be indicted in October. He simply pleaded not guilty and agreed to be tried by God and his country. It could also be that he had heard objections being rejected by stronger characters like Harrison and decided not to resist. At his trial, he claimed to be a man outside the system who had been swept along by threats and intimidation. Nevertheless, knowing that his name was on the document, he asked the court if they were able to see any distinctions between himself and the others who had signed.

They could see no such distinctions and he was imprisoned in Newgate. In April 1663 he had petitioned the Lord Mayor of London to persuade the king for money and wished 'to be thrust into some hole where he may more silently be starved'.[2] There is no evidence that the mayor saw this passive-aggressive begging letter, never mind the king. He died in the Tower of London in 1666.

Daniel Blagrave had one of the more successful civil wars. He prospered, with no obvious principles to get in his way. Like most of the lawyers, he saw little fighting, but did well as an administrator and apparatchik, supporting the new regime until the end, and managed to escape to (what is now) Germany and remain free, living to the respectable age of sixty-eight.

He was not the most famous of his immediate Blagrave family. His father was Alexander Blagrave, the chess master, and his younger brother, Joseph, was a renowned astrologer and herbalist whose books were still being taken seriously two generations later. His uncle, John Blagrave, was a famous mathematician and one of Tudor England's most accurate cartographers, renowned for his learning, piety and generosity to the poor. John Blagrave died without children and bequeathed his Southcote manor to his eight-year-old nephew, Daniel. There is still a Blagrave Street in Reading, but it commemorates John, not our lawyer regicide.

Reading had been taken by the Royalists in November 1642. When the Earl of Essex tried to recapture it, Blagrave's house was used as the military headquarters for what was to be the first artillery attack of the civil war. At this point Blagrave lost Southcote, which was a sacrifice that many on both sides faced, but does not prove the existence of a point of principle. He did not fight in the civil war, but accumulated money and power instead. He seemed to be neither Puritan nor republican, and other motivations are hard to find. Like many apparatchiks he spent the First Civil War on the parliamentary committees for Reading, fulfilling the post of treasurer. He was Recorder of Reading, second only to the mayor, and was elected recruiter MP for the town in June 1648, though he was accused of using bribery to secure votes.

He seems to have all the hallmarks of the corrupt. While in Berkshire he was Treasurer of the County Committee. He was keen to gain appointments on committees and commissions and wrote frequently to the Royalist and astrologer Elias Ashmole for predictions about his career and whether Parliament would be prorogued. The position of astrology in the seventeenth century was ambiguous; it was often condemned, especially by Puritan theologians, but was also widespread. Its popularity with Blagrave makes him even less of a credible Puritan.

In July 1651 he was appointed Commissioner for Forfeited Estates, sequestering delinquents and selling confiscated church lands. He was appointed by the Parliament to the office of Exigenter of the Court of Common Pleas, said to have been worth £500 per annum, and also became a Master in Chancery. He was also Parliamentary Treasurer for the county of Berkshire and, in 1654, was named one of the commissioners for the ejection of scandalous and inefficient ministers, in which capacity he was accused by his enemies of using undue severity and of proving a vexatious persecutor of the clergy.[3]

During the rule of Oliver and Richard Cromwell, Blagrave seemed content with politicking and money-making in Berkshire. He was not a significant figure, but was watched by the Thurloe's secret service (though thousands of people were being monitored). In 1660, as the Commonwealth fell apart, the local Presbyterian gentry in Reading made removing Blagrave from office a priority. He was so far from the centre of events that he was able to get a seat in the 1660 Convention Parliament, a largely Royalist replacement for the Long Parliament. He must have felt that the rising clamour for revenge would eventually engulf him, and he fled the country in 1660, dying in Aachen in 1668.

Chapter 19

Cowards and Adulterers

Gregory Clement, Gilbert Millington, Michael Livesey,
Peter Temple

A Puritan army that wins three exhausting wars, executes a king and attempts a moral reformation of society has no place for cowardice and adultery, but given human nature there was a fair amount of both amongst the regicides. Cowardice and adultery do not mean that there were no other motives for regicide; but for these four men, it was their most obvious characteristic.[1]

Our best-known adulterer was **Gregory Clement**. He is the faintest of regicides, but probably not one of the greyest, and is famous not for his signature (he was the fifty-fourth at that point where they were scratching around a little) but for the alleged erasure of it later. Two theories exist about his blurry signature: his name was (incompletely) erased in 1652 because of his scandalous behaviour, or that it had been added on top of another signature that had been removed. Common sense suggests the first, and this is backed up by some of the great historians of the civil war, such as S.R. Gardiner and Veronica Wedgwood.

He was a member of the Puritan-dominated Rump Parliament from the moment of its purging to his expulsion for adultery with a maidservant in 1652. He was lucky merely to be purged, as the Rump had passed an adultery act in 1650 making Clement's transgression (and incest and fornication as well) a capital offence. After the law, prosecutions for adultery fell as juries failed to convict even with compelling second-hand evidence, but Clement was found *in flagrante*. He was unlucky to be caught, and some reports say that he may have been set up by Thomas Harrison after a political disagreement.

Another less passive man may have been indignant that he was stitched up by someone known for their vanity and flamboyance, but Clement was never one for making a fuss. He does not seem like much of a man of action, apart from this adultery in 1652, aged fifty-six. Clement was fornicating in Greenwich because he had acquired a house there a year earlier: Crowley House, a fine new building built at the cost of £5,000 by the ultra-loyalist Sir Andrew Cogan. Clement was able to buy it for the bargain price of £832. Cogan had built his house (and warehouse) by 1647, and had paid his fine to Parliament, but he then took part in an abortive rising in London during the Second Civil War.[2] In the subsequent orgy of revenge, he was declared an enemy of Parliament and all his property sequestered and sold. Clement also had a reputation for buying bishops' lands cheaply. If it wasn't for his adultery he would have been placed in the chapter for the plain greedy.

Clement was from a moderately significant Plymouth family and made his money in international trade in the East Indies – where he seemed to have fallen foul of the authorities with his unscrupulous practices – and later as a London merchant. There seems to have been no real formal education and no gentry route into the establishment, but he made a success of his business. He was very wealthy by 1640, and like many men with the same profile, he became a supporter of Parliament. He was the recruiter MP for Fowey in Cornwall in 1646 and was generally known to be 'diligent'.

Little is known about his life between 1652 and 1660. He may have withdrawn from politics out of a sense of shame, but, as later events bore out, he could have been sulking. In 1660 he was top of nobody's list to be apprehended, but Clement made it very easy for the authorities, partly due to his own incompetence and greed, but mostly through terrible luck.

He had lain low in a poor part of town to await events, but had drawn attention to himself by ordering expensive and exotic food that was unknown to the inhabitants of Cheapside. The word got out, and a crowd gathered, but he was able to blag his way out of it, until somebody recognised his unique, high-pitched voice. Noble claims that it was a blind person who recognised his voice; a sad and ironic end for a man who had deliberately hidden in a place where nobody recognised his face.

He was in the Tower by the end of May 1660, where one of the inmates was Thomas Harrison; so it was not only the regime of solitary confinement that prevented a warm greeting between the two men. When Clement was searched, a book detailing his property and wealth was found, probably ending his chances of ever being pardoned.[3]

His behaviour at the trial was different to the others. He was neither defiant nor contrite, but managed an unsatisfactory mixture of the two. He soon changed his initial 'not guilty' plea to guilty, and surrendered meekly without giving the court any trouble. Others in the trial, like Harrison and Carew, had fought back with various attempts to make a point rather than plead. He may have pleaded guilty because better men than him had failed. Edmund Ludlow thought so, and, while partisan, was probably correct. Another theory was that his family had persuaded him to plead guilty, and that he resented them when this plan to save him failed.

When his execution came, on 17 October 1660, he was on the first sled with Thomas Scot, a position in history that he did not really deserve. He maintained his silence until the very end, according to the same hostile source. His enemies said, 'His guilty conscience and his ignorance would not suffer him to make any plea at the bar or any speech or prayer at the gallows.'[4]

Some commentators believed that his shame was greater because he had not stood up for what he believed and therefore did not deserve a martyr's death. This does not sound like the man. On this one occasion we may wish to believe the words of the judge at his trial, 'Gregory Clement is hardly worth mentioning.'

Another high-ranking lawyer with a moderate track record of opposing the king was **Gilbert Millington**. He went to Peterhouse, the Inns of Court, then married and inherited his late father's substantial Nottinghamshire estates in the period 1614 to 1620. He was one of the few lawyers who was prepared to take on the paperwork and administration for the trial of the king and was a useful fig leaf at the time, but he was the least important of a very unimpressive legal team. The only thing that can be said in his favour is that he took an unnecessary risk out of something approaching principle. As a leading London lawyer he could have made nearly as much money without risking his neck, or that of his king.

He practised as a barrister but was never a soldier, although he did work, and argue, with John Hutchinson as governor of Nottingham Castle. Meeting John Hutchinson also meant meeting his wife, Lucy, who, almost inevitably, did not like him. She decreed him a poor administrator who incompetently handled the money that was meant for the town, with a strong suggestion of corruption. On this occasion it was an opinion shared by others.

It got worse. Millington was also guilty of 'poor conversation', meaning the company he kept rather than the way he talked. He had an equally disreputable friend called White: 'not only conniving at and permitting wickedness in others, but themselves conversing in taverns and [...] houses of ill repute, till at last Millington and White were so enamoured that they married a couple of ale house wenches.' He was, according to Lucy Hutchinson, a man of sixty, professing religion, and having but lately, 'buried a religious matronly gentlewoman, and married a "flirtish" girl of sixteen'. The proviso here, of course, is that the other regicides did not have Lucy Hutchinson to judge them. They may have been as bad, but were probably not.

According to Noble, Millington was later shunned by Puritans. Noble accuses him of being motivated by money. The accusation is that, as a member of the Committee for Plundered Ministers, he siphoned off money for himself. He would probably have been included in the greedy regicides had he not been more famous for his sexual misdeeds (which strictly speaking was fornication rather than adultery, because his wife had died and he was single). He also claimed money from Parliament for the destruction of his house in Nottingham by the Royalist Earl of Newcastle, to be taken from his sequestered estates. A figure of £1,713 was accepted by Parliament, but only Millington knew how accurate that was.

He pleaded for his life in 1660, and twisted in the wind a little. He tried to make his case rather than plead guilty or not guilty. When he later got his chance, his mitigation was that he was old, deaf and weak, which had not been the case eleven years earlier. He eventually pleaded guilty, claimed intimidation, and blamed the conveniently dead, 'I will confess myself guilty every way; I was awed by the powers then in being.' He was rewarded with six more years of life at Mont Orgueil Castle on Jersey alongside regicides Smith, Temple and Waller.

With **Michael Livesey** we are scraping the barrel a little. Veronica Wedgwood described him as 'ambitious, irresponsible and reputed a coward', and he almost certainly wins the prize for the least worthy regicide. Historian Christopher Hibbert called him 'arrogant, quarrelsome and pusillanimous'.

Although he lacked positive personal characteristics, he did have some principles. In November 1642, in an attempt to divide his enemies, the king issued a general pardon with exceptions, and Livesey made it

174

to that list. Livesey was a 'traitor and stirrer of sedition'. There was only one other person from Kent on the list of exceptions, which was more a list of the king's personal enemies than a roll call of those who had objections in principle. It was a list of the obnoxious, and Livesey made the cut.

Livesey was mostly a bureaucrat in Kent, a county that saw little fighting in the First Civil War. In December 1642 he secured and removed the loyalist High Sheriff of Kent, Sir William Brockham, who was attempting to obey the king's commission. By thwarting him, Livesey was able to secure Kent in a posture of defence for most of the First Civil War, and as a happy consequence, he become the new High Sheriff of Kent himself.

Livesey saw some action in the south of England, at the siege of Chichester and also at Arundel, where he seemed to have watched the fighting rather than take part. After that point he developed a track record of either running away from battle or refusing to obey orders, and largely getting away with it. Many of the regicides made their mark when the New Model Army was formed, but Livesey was the opposite. He refused to serve and his regiment was taken over by Henry Ireton.

In September 1645 he was elected the recruiter MP for Queenborough, Kent, and identified himself with the Independents and republicans. In 1647 he was one of the fifty-eight MPs and peers who fled Westminster for the protection of the army when Presbyterian mobs threatened his safety. Bigger and braver figures like Ludlow did the same, so it is hard to condemn him for this.

During the Second Civil War, rebellion broke out in Kent, a county secure for Parliament during the first war. The Royalist rebellion by men like the Earl of Holland was powered by war weariness and hatred of an expensive Puritan army and its policies. People of Kent now had the New Model Army billeted on them. The spark of the rebellion was an attempt by the people of Canterbury to reinstate the Christmas celebrations, which had been recently abolished. Livesey did his bit in Kent and Sussex. He also defeated the Earl of Holland's rebels and prevented them from threatening London, though he was fortunate that the Earl's desire to march on London from Kingston-on-Thames had to be downgraded to an attack on Reigate Castle due to the small number who responded to his call to arms. Coward or not, he did his bit, and a few months later he was, unsurprisingly, spared from the army purge.

His name is fifth on the death warrant. Historians have argued about the way signatures were collected, but it is clear that he was one of the twenty-five or so who signed quickly, without being actively sought out or persuaded. He remained in frontline politics, but, like most republicans, he opposed the establishment of the single man rule of Cromwell in 1653. He returned to his local base and served as High Sheriff of Kent again, where he seemed to continue to make money. Noble called him the 'plunder master of Kent'. He was still taking promotions from the dying Commonwealth as late as 1660. As a man who failed to turn his coat, for whatever reason, he chose to flee the country rather than submit himself to the new regime. His exact location was never ascertained, but his wife was described as a widow very soon afterwards.

Peter Temple was a relatively undistinguished regicide; a man of local reputation who was regarded as a bit of a coward. He came from moderately prosperous Leicestershire gentry, but had the misfortune of being the third son in the family, and so would have been expected to look after himself. Like many in his predicament, he was guided into an apprenticeship, in his case as a linen draper, but was saved from this average existence by the death of his two older brothers.

There is no sign of activity or motivation until 1643, when he took part in the administration of his own county. He held a military commission under Lord Grey of Groby, a much more famous regicide, but was accused of cowardice when he left Leicester for London at the approach of the king's army in May 1645. However, he was elected recruiter MP for Leicester in November 1645, with Grey being the other member as well as his political mentor and boss.

Temple is identified as an Independent and supporter of the army in the period 1647–49. Despite this, his religious toleration did not extend that far, as he seemed to have actively persecuted Baptists during the Commonwealth. He had some motivation: he was from a Puritan family – his father, Edmund, was a Puritan – and it seems that Temple had nothing more to do with the central Government after Cromwell became Lord Protector.

Temple was one of the first wave of regicides tried in October 1660. Like most of them, he pleaded not guilty, and when found culpable asked for the benefit of the king's proclamation, which extended some form of mercy to those who handed themselves in. His death sentence was commuted to life imprisonment, and he died in the Tower of London in December 1663. His estate in Leicestershire was forfeited and bestowed upon James, Duke of York, like many of the other regicides. Noble describes him as an 'ignorant, opinionative person who was the tool of Cromwell', and suggested that it would have been far better if he had risen no higher than his natural position as an upmarket shopkeeper. Prosecuting council commented, 'there were some worse than he, but he was bad enough', which seemed both fair and a little damning about his significance.

Chapter 20

Suspect Motivation

John Danvers, Simon Mayne

If Mauleverer, Bourchier and Chaloner can be acquitted of bad faith, there are still regicides whose motivation is more than a little suspect, or very difficult to perceive. The accolade for the most unlikely regicide goes, narrowly, to **John Danvers** of Chelsea and Wiltshire. Not only does Danvers not fit into any category – religious, political or personal – he seems to be the exact opposite of the normal profile for a king-killer.

He was an older regicide, old enough to be knighted by James I in 1609. His early life was one of 'interests', those arcane intellectual pursuits of the privileged, architecture and horticulture, and was more famous for his Italianate gardens in Chelsea than any opposition to the king. He had travelled through France and Italy in his youth, where his companion, one Thomas Bond, said that the locals came out into the street to admire him because he took such exquisite pains with his appearance. He was a paid-up ally of the ecclesiastical establishment, an aesthete and a spendthrift, and nothing about him was Puritan or political. The historian A. L. Rowse did him down a little when he called Danvers an 'aristocratic playboy'. Danvers was serious about his garden, and his reputation endures in horticultural circles to the present day, but he was a most unlikely regicide.

Danvers married Magdalen Herbert in 1608, and in doing so became the stepfather of the metaphysical poet George Herbert. Magdalen died before him in 1627, unsurprisingly as she was forty and Danvers twenty when they married. The commemorative sermon was read by John Donne. Francis Bacon was also a friend, and spent much time in Danvers' lovely gardens. When Bacon wrote his *History of Henry VII* he showed it first to Danvers and James I, and it was apparently Danvers who provided the better critique.[1]

So why did he sign the death warrant? Veronica Wedgwood, in her book discussing the motivations of the regicides, commented that 'nobody on either side had much to say about John Danvers', and then logically (but unhelpfully) said nothing else about him. His conflicts with the monarchy seem to have been largely about money. He inherited a lot from various marriages to heiresses, but seems to have frittered it away.

He refused to contribute to the king's expedition to Scotland in 1639, a decision possibly caused by principle, but just as possibly by resentment. He was an MP and colonel from 1640, but his activities in both war and Parliament seemed to be limited to his home county of Wiltshire. This was common enough as most regicides fought only in their own region, but there seems to have been no real motivation to do more.

Danvers would have been one of the eight commissioners at the High Court of Justice who King Charles told his servant, Herbert, that he recognised; in the modern sense of 'knowing who he was'. Some of the others – Cromwell, Ireton, Harrison and Deane – he had met during the crisis of 1647, while Danvers had been a member of his Privy Council.

Amongst the regicides Danvers was not popular as he was seen as a weak, vain man who was easily seduced by being part of the great enterprise. Clarendon, the Royalist, had similar thoughts. Had Danvers lived beyond 1655, he would have been a Cromwellian, accepting all changes in government. It mattered little to men of no principle the source of the power that they were flattering.

Simon Mayne was probably the least effective of all the regicides. In the small pond of his county he was a big fish, but was ineffective on the Westminster stage, and the only thing of note was his signature on the execution warrant. He was Buckinghamshire gentry and studied at the Inner Temple, but not university. He lived close to Thomas Scot and Richard Ingoldsby, and it was as the junior party to Scot that Mayne became the recruiter MP for Aylesbury in 1645, at the same time that Henry Marten was governor. Aylesbury was well known for its disloyalty to the king – a Puritan town in a very Puritan county – and Mayne did the paperwork there. A hostile source noted that he was a great committee man, 'wherein he licked his fingers; one of his Prince's cruel judges and a constant Rumper to the last.'[2]

Mayne was, therefore, drawn into regicide through his association with more prominent people. He knew Oliver Cromwell quite well through knowing Cromwell's father, Robert. Cromwell at some time visited Mayne, and Cromwell's sword and scabbard are still at Dinton Hall, Buckinghamshire, given to Mayne as a present after the Battle of Edgehill or Naseby. He survived until the Restoration and was tried for treason alongside more prominent men. He used the standard argument that he was forced to sign the warrant, a position backed up by the fact that he played almost no part in politics after 1649.

He was a committee man, interested in the Sequestration Committee in Buckinghamshire and picking up a few bargains along the way. Sequestration and Committees for Compounding gave bureaucrats considerable power. Royalists who compounded (paid a fine) for their delinquency would have the level of their fine decided by their wealth and how compromised they were, and it was the Puritan committee men who decided both of these. Mayne was not notoriously greedy, religiously fanatical or excessively republican, and remains an enigma, though not a particularly interesting one.

In 1660 Mayne's response was not to flee the country, surrender as a martyr, or justify himself in court. Instead, he ran away and hid in a secret room under the eaves of Dinton Hall to avoid arrest for High Treason. It was reached by a tunnel lined with tapestries, as was the room itself. He was found by the authorities quite easily despite these precautions. He had, after all, hidden himself in his own house, the first place that would be searched.

He would have won any prize for being the most ineffectual liar. He claimed that he had absented himself (by hiding again) on Saturday, 27 January 1649, when the execution was announced and affirmed by those present. This was easily disproved by witnesses. At the trial Mayne argued that it was fellow Buckinghamshire man Thomas Chaloner who had made him sign, although he only hinted at the name in court. His case was not helped by his being the fortieth name on the warrant while Chaloner was the fifty-first.[3] He originally pleaded not guilty, but changed his mind and threw himself upon the mercy of the court, 'I am an ignorant weak man in the law.' He also claimed intimidation, 'a gentleman plucked me down by the coat and, saith he, you would rather lose your estate than take away the king's life?' You did not need much law to know that the most sensible answer to this question was,

'No, I would rather lose my estates.' He also claimed that he was on no committees and that his wife made him do it.

Mayne knew the other Buckinghamshire regicides, especially Richard Ingoldsby. They both came from the village of Dinton, which had provided twice as many regicides as the entire county of Lancashire. Both men were part of the local justice system in their county and jointly employed a legal clerk, John Bigg. There is a legend, without supporting evidence, that Bigg was one of Charles I's executioners. Another story, more factual, was that he was so upset after the Restoration of the king that he became a hermit and lived in a cave. Bigg became an early tourist attraction, and was supplied with food and drink. His clothes were never changed and consisted of pieces of leather nailed together, and his shoes were the same (there is a pair in the Ashmolean Museum in Oxford). He seemed to have paid a bigger price that his two regicide employers, but at least is slightly better known in history than Simon Mayne.

During his life there was little evidence of motivating principles, but they can be seen a little in death: he had the typical Puritan funeral, without ostentation or excessive grief. He still rests at Dinton parish church after dying in April 1661. There is a family memorial, established in 1628, but his name is missing. Mark Noble said that he was a man of 'no great depth of judgement and violent passions.'

Chapter 21

The Strained Quality of Mercy
Adrian Scrope, Richard Ingoldsby

Charles II was in Brussels when word of his father's execution reached him. His courtiers had already intercepted the news, and wished to be gentle with the delivery, but the messenger was constrained by courtly etiquette and began his announcement with 'Your Majesty'.

Charles was eighteen and, quite understandably, incandescent with fury. His proclamation, issued immediately afterwards, reverberated with impotent rage: 'We are firmly resolved, by the assistance of Almighty God though we perish alone in the enterprise, to be a severe avenger of his innocent blood which was so barbarously spilt and which calls aloud to Heaven for vengeance.'

If he ever achieved vengeance it would be swift and severe; or so he said when he was a traumatised young man. He had a decade in the wilderness to reconsider this punitive attitude. His hopes of an uprising were temporarily raised, then dashed when Cromwell died. His new offer of pardon for all bar those directly responsible for his father's death was offered, but failed to spark Royalist rebellion or republican contrition. A year later, and apparently no nearer a restoration, the new offer was a pardon for most of the regicides on the condition that they exiled themselves. Charles II had fallen considerably in status and power since 1649. There was no reason to believe that if he was ever restored he would have much scope for revenge.

The Commonwealth fell apart very gradually, and Restoration of the Stuarts was not as inevitable as is seemed in retrospect, so the surviving regicides had no idea what their punishment would be, and indeed what specific crimes would be punished. Justice did not turn out to be very equitable, although it is difficult to work out how it could have been, given the bloodlust of the Royalist parliaments, the vacillation of the new king, and the general ethos of nepotism and corruption amongst those who were making life and death decisions.

Although it was clear by March that Monck was now set on restoring the king, it was not so clear that the Restoration could be achieved successfully. General George Monck suggested that nobody should be executed. This was a sign of Monck's pessimistic view of the king's political strength; but the stronger the monarchy became, the more people would die.

Charles II's Declaration of Breda of 4 April 1660 issued a general pardon, with exceptions to be decided by Parliament. The declaration was made public on 1 May. The next day Parliament declared that government ought to be by king, Lords and Commons, and Charles II was invited to return. On 8 May Charles was proclaimed king. Allowing Parliament to decide who was executed and otherwise punished was a master stroke; it absolved him of work and responsibility and passed both to a new Royalist Convention Parliament that was ready to be very severe. It was now clear that the king would be restored unconditionally. Some MPs remembered that before Pride's Purge the two sides were about to agree on the Treaty of Newport, which would have diluted his power. This was now forgotten, and Charles was held back only by whatever voluntary restrictions he was prepared to put on himself.

The number of regicides to be executed started at five, and increased quickly to seven. These would be chosen from those who had been present when the sentence of death was passed, and who stood up to show their consent. This included ten people who were present but did not sign the warrant, and two people who were not present and did sign the warrant: Thomas Chaloner and Richard Ingoldsby. So many had to be excluded from punishment. It could not include those who went on to support the regime militarily or politically in the years after 1649 because that would include many others whose cooperation was needed to secure power after the restoration. It would include Monck himself.

The key question was who should be condemned to death. Signing the execution warrant itself was not the only consideration. In fact, the document itself was not found until 26 July. The choice was made a little more difficult because the obvious culprits – Cromwell, Ireton, Bradshaw, Pride, Grey and Ewer – were dead. With so much treasonable activity since 1642, who should be executed for treason? The main criterion seemed to have been how repentant they were. The first two people that came to mind were the Fifth Monarchists. Harrison, Jones and Carew were also obvious choices as they hated all monarchies, not just the restored Stuarts. Also candidates were the lawyers, Say and Lisle, and the loud-mouthed and reckless Thomas Scot. Ludlow and Barkstead were next, and Barkstead was chosen probably because he had upset rather more people in London than Ludlow had in Ireland. Amazingly, there was no room on the list for Henry Marten at this stage.

Lots of influence and nepotism muddied the waters. There was a real possibility that the body of Thomas Grey would be dug up and punished, and it was his surviving father who stopped this from happening. Those who still had influence with the new regime used it. Some, like Bulstrode Whitelocke, the lawyer who had originally refused to countenance the regicide but continued to work with the new regime, nearly ruined himself with bribery, but saved his life and estates.

It was clear that whoever was exempted from pardon would potentially face the death penalty. Another five were added soon after, and then another twenty. At this point, Parliament put the limit at twenty, which seems to have saved the life of poet and Cromwellian propagandist John Milton, whose words had done more to hasten the execution than the majority of regicides. Hugh Peters, Cromwell's firebrand Puritan chaplain was added to the execution list as a man more hated by Royalists more than most surviving regicides.

A week after his triumphant return to London on 6 June, the king's proclamation declared forty-nine people guilty of treason: 'so much for their prospect of a fair trial,' commented lawyer and historian Geoffrey Robinson.[1] They were given fourteen days to hand themselves in 'under pain of being exempt from any pardon or indemnity both for their respective lives or estates'. Most of the regicides who surrendered did so under the impression that obeying the fourteen-day rule would definitely lead to a pardon, while in the king's eyes the proclamation had the opposite meaning: a failure to appear would guarantee their condemnation.

The document was deliberately ambiguous; its author, Clarendon, admitted as much. The ambiguity of the wording did the trick. Eighteen regicides surrendered and two – Dixwell and Ludlow – remained in touch with the authorities. Eleven people who had not handed themselves in were added to the primary death list of twenty-three. Then Daniel Axtell and Francis Hacker were added to the list. In any case, Parliament was to make the final decision about whether execution would take place, which added another level of uncertainty.

One regicide who surrendered was **Adrian Scrope**. As he had not been active in defending Cromwell or resisting the Restoration, he could have reasonably expected mercy. Scrope was middle-ranking Oxfordshire gentry, with the traditional two years at university and then the Inns of Court. He raised a troop of horse for Parliament early in the war, and his only major engagement in the First Civil War was his presence at Fairfax's breaking of the siege of Bristol.

He was present in June 1647 when the army took control of the king to ensure that no 'side agreement' was made between him and the Presbyterian-dominated Parliament. Scrope became governor of Bristol in the 1650s. Bristol was the only substantial port whose loyalty Cromwell doubted, so Scrope's appointment indicated Cromwell's high level of trust. The Bristolians were less trusted though, and demolition of the castle began in January 1655. After 1655, Scrope worked for the Protectorate as an administrator in Scotland, but when Cromwell died he seemed to have done nothing in the subsequent crisis of 1659–60.

The execution of Adrian Scrope showed the weaknesses of the punishment process in 1660. His grisly execution was a bit of an injustice. He obeyed the instruction of 6 June, and on 20 June he was discharged with a large but not unmanageable fine and a ban from public office. It was the Lords that insisted on his trial and execution. Scrope had been betrayed by Richard Browne, a former Cromwellian major-general, who he should have been able to trust. When challenged about the legality of the trial, Browne testified that Scrope had said 'some are of one opinion, some of another'. Never in history has such a bland statement led to such terrible consequences. This non-committal comment was made after the return of the king, when only those who were publicly contrite could save their lives and estates. Scrope had overestimated the desire of minor figures like Browne to clear their name by enthusiastically denouncing others. Browne had been the man who had taken custody of the king in 1647 when the Scots sold him to Parliament. He had just become Lord Mayor Elect of London, and was ambitious enough to condemn Scrope to the gallows.

Even the regicides' enemies had some compassion. Noble, in his *Lives of the Regicides*, states: 'It was a thousand pities that if so many were to die as public examples; some of the others were equally guilty of the King's death, and whose lives were a disgrace to any cause, were not substituted in his stead'. In other words, there were far worse than Scrope, and none of them were executed as horribly.

Scrope died with dignity at Charing Cross, on the same platform as Jones and Scot, two men who had done far more damage to the Stuart monarchy than Adrian Scrope. Scot, who was forbidden to make a speech, was allowed instead a prayer, which turned out to be very long and sounded suspiciously like a speech.[2] Jones was briefer. Scrope asked for the judgment of God to prevail. Unlike some of the others, Scrope's death brought more tears than jeers. His death added to the growing feeling that the executions had gone too far. Ludlow described the death of Scrope as a result of the 'lust of Nero', establishing a distinction between the virtue of republican Rome and the evil of the later emperors. His estates were confiscated for a year before being returned to his son, Thomas, in 1662.

Scrope came out badly from the process. At the other end of the spectrum was **Richard** 'Honest Dick' **Ingoldsby**. Ingoldsby was one of the chief mourners at Cromwell's funeral in 1658. Ingoldsby supported the offer of the crown to Cromwell in 1657. He was Cromwellian establishment and the Protector's cousin. He should have expected severe punishment.

His involvement in the execution of the king was much greater than Adrian Scrope. His family background was pro-Parliament: his father and at least six of his brothers were active on the Parliamentarian side during the civil war.[3] He sprang into action against the king quite early. In 1642 his connection led to a captaincy in John Hampden's regiment of foot, and he was promoted to colonel in the New Model Army. His kinship with Oliver Cromwell would have smoothed the way, but it would not have been enough without his own commitment and competence. He had a distinguished battle record. He helped secure Taunton, Bristol and Bridgewater for Parliament and was present at the surrender of the king's forces at Oxford in 1646.

After the war his career followed the same path as Ireton, albeit at a lesser level. He was elected to Parliament for Wendover in October 1647, as a New Model Army officer. In the quarrel between Parliament and the army in 1647 Ingoldsby's regiment took the army's side. His regiment also petitioned in favour of punishing the king and halting the negotiations aimed at a generous settlement with him.

He remained loyal to the new regime even when soldiers under his command did not. In 1649 his regiment was one of those that supported the Leveller soldiers at the Bishopsgate mutiny, and for a time he was held prisoner by his own men. Ingoldsby worked with Cromwell to crush the Levellers, and in 1651 he was present at the defeat of Charles II at the battle of Worcester. Ingoldsby was a constant pillar of both the Commonwealth and Cromwell's Protectorate. He was on the Council of State in 1652 and a compliant member of both of Cromwell's Parliaments. When Cromwell re-instated the Other House, Ingoldsby was a member. His loyalty to the Cromwell dynasty continued after Oliver died in 1658 and he supported his son, Richard, as Lord Protector.

Richard Cromwell had few friends amongst those who had risked their life in battle, but Ingoldsby was one of them and Cromwell was grateful. When pressed by the officers to promote more people like them, Richard Cromwell replied, 'Now here is Dick Ingoldsby who can neither pray nor preach yet I will trust him before ye all.' Cromwell was a hunting and fishing Hampshire squire, not a leader, and in this case, clearly not a diplomat. His comment would have deeply annoyed the religious sensibilities of those present. Richard's comments were in response to the accusation that Ingoldsby was not only ignoring the merits of the godly but actively promoting moral reprobates. It was clear to the godly and republican officers present that neither Ingoldsby nor Richard Cromwell was 'one of them'.

In early 1659 Ingoldsby was still supporting Richard Cromwell's Protectorate but it was failing fast. When Richard fell, 'Honest Dick' would fall with him. In April 1659, when the majority of the army regiments led by Charles Fleetwood deposed Richard Cromwell, Ingoldsby remained loyal to him knowing, correctly, that he was now in the minority and would lose his commission. He was out, and Okey and Ludlow were back in. So when the latter were attainted for high treason a year later, Ingoldsby had created sufficient distance from them to survive.

With a track record like this, he should have expected at the very least a lifetime of isolation and imprisonment in Jersey, Tangier, Northumberland or the Isle of Man, and a confiscation of his property. Not only did he keep his estates, he held on to the land and property he had acquired during the Protectorate. He was created a Knight of the Bath at the coronation of Charles II on 20 April 1661. He was re-elected MP for Aylesbury in the Cavalier Parliament, and held the seat there until his death twenty-five years later.

How did he manage it? It was a mixture of luck and good judgement, as these things always are. His first piece of good luck, or good judgement, was that he broke with the army-dominated Rump Parliament in one fell swoop. While other people had faded away, or invested in secretly helping a few selected royalists, Ingoldsby changed sides quickly, fully and energetically.

It is easy to criticise Ingoldsby for this *volte face*, but he was taking a risk. Despite the mayhem caused by disagreements between army and Parliament, he was seriously isolating himself in April 1659. There was still no prospect of a royal return; partly due to the pusillanimity of most Royalists, who did nothing much to help Charles II until it was clear that victory was a possibility; a self-defeating philosophy that men like Ingoldsby were prepared to challenge.

When Ingoldsby took part in the Royalist uprising known as Sir George Booth's Rebellion, in August 1659, he did not regard himself as a turncoat. Booth, with advice from his king, did not declare for monarchy (it was regarded as too early for that) but for an end to sectaries, army rule and for some sort of full and free Parliament: perhaps the Parliament before Pride's Purge or a new election. Ingoldsby had had enough of the republicans and sectaries who had brought instant instability after Oliver Cromwell's death, and now wanted, like most people in the country, a government based on precedent and legality. The uprising failed after some success in Cheshire for a few weeks. Other regicides helped to stop it: Scot, the spymaster, rooted out the secondary rebellions, and Ludlow was preparing to send a regiment of horse and one of foot to help crush them. He had created even further distance between himself and the 'extremists'.

Ingoldsby's support of a free Parliament made it easy for Monck to offer him command of a regiment in February 1660. By this point it was clear that Monck was restoring a Parliament that would back the king, and Monck knew that Ingoldsby wanted the same thing. They had had similar histories; confidants of Cromwell, both with solid achievements that advanced the new regime, both popular with their soldiers, and neither of them with any time for the religious fanatics. The only difference between them was a signature on a death warrant. This difference explained the disparity of their rewards after the Restoration: Ingoldsby kept what he had, while Monck became the Duke of Albemarle and moved into Hampton Court.

Ingoldsby was sent by Monck to suppress the last-gasp republican uprising of John Lambert in April 1660. Ingoldsby met Lambert's forces near Daventry, arrested him as he tried to flee, and brought him in triumph to London. He had earned his indemnity as far as the king was concerned. A week after his victory at Daventry, Ingoldsby was thanked by the House of Commons for his very important role in the defeat of the final republican forces. In the topsy-turvy world of Restoration justice, a mere two weeks later he was back in Parliament, tearfully begging for his life.

This paradox can be explained. It goes back to Charles II's angry decrees of 1649, threatening universal revenge. More than a decade later, this was impossible. Too much time had passed, and too many people had worked with, and profited from, the Cromwellian regime. Many were even judges at the trial of the regicides. Thomas Harrison was able to remind them of this because he had no interest in saving his own life. Justice was demanded for the murder of the king, not your attitude afterwards. Harrison had boycotted Oliver Cromwell's funeral because he hated him, and Ingoldsby had been there and shed tears, but this difference not matter as much as the events of January 1649.

The focus on revenge, therefore, had to be on people who facilitated the execution, in a narrow timespan from 1648 to 1649, and Ingoldsby was one of those. He still had to answer the same question as the other regicides: why did you sign? His defence was similar to that used by others – naivety, youth and ignorance – with an outrageous but unique mitigation that he was physically forced to sign the warrant by Oliver Cromwell, who guided his hand on to the warrant.

> As soon as Cromwell's eyes were upon him, he ran to him, and taking him by the hand, drew him by force to the table; and said, though he had escaped him all the while, he should now sign that paper as well as they [...] he refused but Cromwell and the others held him by violence; and Cromwell, with a loud laugh, taking his hand in his, and putting the pen between his fingers, with his own hand wrote Richard Ingoldsby.[4]

This was nonsense. His signature is confident and free flowing, and, like all the other signatures, is accompanied by his seal, which must have been stolen for his story to be true. However, this fabrication was accepted when other similar and often more plausible excuses were laughed out of court. The establishment wanted him to be saved. His claim to have always been a Royalist had some support in his later actions, and the fact that he had not attended a single day of the trial worked in his favour. He lived out the rest of his life as a solid, but not particularly trusted Member of Parliament, dying in 1685, just as the revolt against the Stuarts was starting again.

Chapter 22

Reluctant to Kill, or Just Reluctant to Die?

Hardress Waller, Henry Smith, George Fleetwood

Thomas Harrison, a man of principles, even if you disagreed with the principles themselves, was overjoyed when this sentence was passed on him in October 1660:

> The judgement of this court is that [...] you be led back to the place from whence you came, and from hence be drawn upon a hurdle to the place of execution, and there you shall be hanged by the neck, and being alive shall be cut down, your entrails shall be taken out of your body, and, you living, the same to be burnt before your eyes, your body to be divided into four quarters, and head and quarters to be disposed of at the pleasure of the King's Majesty, and the Lord have mercy on your soul.

This sentence was even worse than it seemed. It does not mention castration specifically, but it was always an option in the process. In a less Christian age we underestimate the shame of having your remains disposed of in a non-Christian way, buried in the grounds of a prison or scattered in chunks to the four corners of the kingdom. There is also the threat of eternal damnation. Harrison was without fear. He looked forward to his fate. He expected to be welcomed joyfully into Christ's kingdom.

'Only' nine people were eventually hanged, drawn and quartered – Thomas Harrison, John Jones, John Carew, Adrian Scrope, Thomas Scot, Gregory Clement, and the non-regicides Hugh Peters, Daniel Axtell and John Cook – but the regicides were not to know this in 1660. As the previous chapter showed, the number on the death list, initially five, was increasing by the week. This method of punishment was common enough for treason. In May 1658 Cromwell had three Royalist conspirators hanged, drawn and quartered in London. There was every reason to expect the same punishments in 1660.

Those regicides who gave themselves up on the Restoration of Charles II were required to explain their behaviour. Many, like Harrison, were unrepentant, but others did not want to die in that way, or at that age, and they had worked out that there were alternative punishments available for those who could put distance between themselves and the ringleaders. Some pleaded not guilty, then justified their actions, while others pleaded guilty. Their key mitigations were they were young, they were weak and had been bullied, or they did not understand what they were doing. It was mostly, if not entirely, claptrap.

When the trials started it was **Hardress Waller** and Thomas Harrison who were told to plead first. These men knew each other well. Harrison would have recalled that they were given joint responsibility to guard the king in the weeks prior to his execution, and he would have remembered that Waller was no less keen than he was. It was different now. It was widely believed by the prosecution that Waller would accept the legitimacy of the accusation and plead for his life, thus creating a momentum that would encourage the other prisoners to do the same. This would have speeded up the process rather than changed the result, but it was still important to the authorities that events moved quickly. Waller pleaded guilty and later did enough grovelling to confirm Ludlow's view that he would do anything to save his life, and the estates that he had accumulated.

Waller was an unusual regicide in many ways. He was the only one who turned his coat during the war itself. Waller was Kentish gentry, and was knighted by Charles I in 1629, inheriting land in Castletown, County Cork in the 1630s. He did not join the Parliamentary side until 1644. Before that date he spent most of his time in Ireland, mostly opposing the king's policies there.

Waller's conversion to the Parliamentary cause seemed sincere. He was at Naseby and at the Siege of Basing House (October 1645) where he led his regiment of foot against the most heavily defended part of the house and was wounded. He became an admirer of Oliver Cromwell and a supporter of the Independents. He was at the Putney Debates, did his bit in the Second Civil War by securing Devon and Cornwall, and was alongside Pride and Hewson when Parliament was purged. He was an active rather than passive judge during the trial and execution. He escaped to France in 1660, then thought better of it and returned for trial in October 1660. His plan was to plead guilty, beg for forgiveness, and hope he could avoid execution.

He did plead guilty, although it did not come very easily. At first he tried to prevaricate with 'I dare not say not guilty', but the court was not having it. As the first person to be tried, he was also the first person to suggest that the proceedings were as much of a 'show trial' as the one for the king. They had been given no legal advice, they did not even know the nature of the charges, nor even the time of the trial until the evening before. Most of the imprisonment had been in solitary confinement. At least he was brave enough to mention this. It was the first time the court had heard it, but not the last, and they were to become heartily sick of hearing it by the end.

He was one of the two on trial who peddled a penitent petition to Parliament. He was allowed to present it, but it was never read. The other regicide who used the same tactic was the equally unimpressive George Fleetwood. Then he produced his alibi, he had been elsewhere: 'My Lord my Condition differs from others. I am a Stranger. I have been thirty Years transplanted into Ireland which has made me unacquainted with the Affairs of the Laws here.'

This was an outrageous and ineffective defence. He had certainly been living in Ireland, but he not been quietly farming. He had helped to subjugate the country in 1650–51 and held various political and administrative posts. He knew what he was doing; he was helping Oliver Cromwell and he extended this aid to his son. He did nothing to help the Restoration and was still resisting in February 1660 when the fight was over. Though he was condemned to death, his cousin, Sir William Waller, interceded for him, and the sentence was commuted to life imprisonment on Jersey, where he died in 1666.

Some historians have not given these desperate men the benefit of the doubt, while others have defended their positions as sincere. One witness who works better for the prosecution than the defence is **Henry Smith** of Leicestershire. His claim to have fallen into regicide by accident was ludicrous. He was younger than most regicides and only finished his university and law education in 1640. He entered Parliament for his local power base of Leicestershire in 1647, as a candidate of Arthur Hasilrige and co-member with Thomas Grey, Lord Grey of Groby. He was identified as a 'friend of Henry Marten' early in the war when Marten was suggesting very early in the fighting that the king could be killed if this contributed to the general good.

In November 1648 Smith was one of the delegation of MPs that went to Windsor to persuade Henry Ireton to purge Parliament of the king's supporters rather that dissolve it, and he was consequently not purged. In the same month, he joined the Committee of Compounding in order to take action against delinquent loyalists. He attended every day of the king's trial and sentencing, and was active in the 1650s.

He was in the first tranche of regicides in October 1660. This was his defence: 'My lords, I shall not desire to spend your lordships time what I have done I did it ignorantly, not knowing what I did [...] I was ignorant of the law of the nation, I have not been bred to it I humbly desire your lordships to consider that what I did was done ignorantly not knowing the law.' This was a lame start. Smith had been at Lincoln's Inn, and may have even practised law, although most who went to the Inns did not. However, even a mere grounding in the law was sufficient to know that executing your king was treason.

He had other great arguments. Despite his commitment at the time, his memory was failing him now. He was asked if he remembered signing the execution warrant and attaching his seal. When he replied, 'I do not remember that I signed or sealed,' he was shown the execution warrant. His answers continued to be unconvincing. 'My lords, I confess the hands are like mine but whether they be so or no I know not.' All of those put on trial were shown the document, and admitting that it was their hand was enough to convict. Only Smith and Ingoldsby prevaricated, and of the two only Smith went for the weakest argument of all (Thomas Waite could not remember either).

He then went on to fail to remember that he was in the Painted Chamber, or that he had attended every single day of the trial. Smith, while still not remembering the event, was forced to go and explain why he had signed: 'There were those about me that were able to call me who were then in authority whom I dared not disobey if so I had been in danger also.'

Like most regicides, he went on to blame Cromwell and Ireton, who were both dead and could not contradict him. Luckily for Smith, the regicide who knew him best, Thomas Grey, Lord Grey of Groby, and with whom he fought in 1651 defending the new republic from an invasion by Charles II and the Scots, was also dead.

Other events that Smith was hazy about were the fact that he had been made the Governor of Hull, had foiled a Royalist plot in 1658, and been sincerely thanked by Cromwell's Council of State for his service. At no point in his later career did he turn towards the Royalists. He returned to Parliament in 1659 when the army brought back the Rump, which was a sign of his uncompromising attitude to monarchy and republican principles.

Smith then went on the blame his youth, and bad company. He confessed the error of his ways, rejoiced at the return of the king and begged for mercy, which was initially not given. Although sentenced to death, he was allowed to appeal and the sentence was commuted to life imprisonment. Smith was held at the Tower of London until 1664, and then transported to Jersey, where he is presumed to have died around 1668 in Mont Orgueil Castle.

Smith was marginal and unheroic. Noble, not to be relied on usually, suggested, 'He was seemingly a very poor weak man whose name and person was used just to fill up the number required', and on this occasion there may have been something in it. He may have been intimidated into signing the warrant, but many other, better men, refused to take part and were not punished. There can be no benefit of the doubt for Henry Smith, because there is no doubt to put his way.

It is possible to write a comprehensive history of the Civil War without mentioning **George Fleetwood** once. There *was* a Fleetwood in the civil war, Charles Fleetwood, a successful Puritan soldier who was important enough to be considered as Cromwell's successor in 1658. George was a gentlemen's son, like so many of those who signed the execution warrant. He was one of the six from Buckinghamshire, a county with many close-knit Puritan families. He was only five when he inherited the estate of The Vache, in Chalfont St Peter, after the premature death of his father. He was one of the youngest of the regicides (born 1623), and while being a less prominent regicide, deserves to be more than a historical footnote.

Apart from a general air of Puritanism, there is little to link him with opposition to the monarch before 1642, although he took to arms quite quickly. His youth was noted by the Royalists. In December 1643 one of their partisan news sheets stated that 'Young Fleetwood of The Vache' had raised a troop of dragoons for the Parliament. He would have been no more than twenty-one years old and his main interest was to defend Buckinghamshire. There was nothing dishonourable about this objective, and by doing so he blocked the advance of the king's army into London.

By late 1643 Fleetwood was on the committee administering his home county. This is, of course, less colourful than fighting at Marston Moor or Naseby, but in its way just as important. He was one of many regicides who did paperwork, most of whom were in the second rank. Many did good work, and George Fleetwood was recognised when he became recruiter MP for Buckinghamshire in July 1647. He had the normal profile of those who became regicides: he supported the New Model Army in its struggle with Parliament in 1648, and was appointed one of the commissioners for the trial of the king. He did not seem to be overly enthusiastic, attending only twice during the trial, but he was present when sentence was passed.

He was mostly back in Buckingham in 1649 and 1650 as a colonel of the county militia, and was chosen as a member of the eighth and last Council of State of the Commonwealth, from 1 November to 10 December 1653. He continued to serve after that date, and seemed to have no objection to Cromwell taking king-like powers. In 1654 he became one of Cromwell's local Ejector's, removing 'unfit' clergymen and schoolteachers from their posts. Fleetwood was certainly no republican: Cromwell knighted him in 1656, and in December 1657 summoned him to the Upper House, the new House of Lords that Fleetwood had worked so hard to abolish in 1649.

Fleetwood was a Cromwellian for most of his life, trusted by the Commonwealth that he repudiated in 1660. In 1655 his second cousin, Charles Fleetwood, was made a regional major-general, responsible for the security of the regime and a Puritan reformation of manners. In February George was made his deputy – for Buckinghamshire – and became an agent to suppress disorder, seek out Catholics and coordinate the army and civil power. On the moral front, he closed down inns, strangled chickens and killed bears to stop gambling, and enforced adultery laws. This was clearly what Fleetwood was able and willing to do, and Cromwell must have shared this opinion to give him the post.

In 1659, after the death of Cromwell and his replacement with his weak son, Richard, Fleetwood raised another troop of soldiers to secure his county during the Royalist rebellion of George Booth in August 1659. That was the end of his contribution to the regime. He changed sides at the last moment possible. When George Monck was marching south from Scotland to (as it turned out) restore the monarchy, he collaborated with the Royalists and was entrusted with the command of a regiment by Monck in the spring of 1660. He declared Charles II king on 11 May 1660 at York. It was this conversion – too late to save his liberty but soon enough to save his life – that allowed George Monck to intercede for him later.

At his trial he remembered to weep and beg forgiveness both before and after sentence. He had some advantages; unusually, he was indicted under the title of George Fleetwood Esquire, not with his current army rank, as was the case with the military regicides on trial. His father was still alive and he was well regarded by the new regime. There was a point in grovelling; he had a chance, and he was only thirty-seven. He was not a sixty-year-old regicide who was convinced of his cause and whose life was coming to an end anyway.

He claimed that his name had been added to the High Commissioners against his will and knowledge, and that he had been intimidated by Cromwell 'whose power, commands, and threats (he being then young) frighted him into court'. On the positive side, he had gained the support of General Monck. It was unconvincing, but circumstances coincided to the point where the establishment wanted to be convinced. He was eventually sentenced to life imprisonment in Tangier, newly available to the king as a distant place of punishment as it was part of the dowry of his new queen, Katherine of Braganza.

He died on 17 November 1672, in the obscure circumstances which mirrored his obscure life. The government-sanctioned *London Gazette* announced that 'sometime before his death his senses failed him', and, 'he was a constant frequenter of the church and expressed himself very penitent for his heinous crime'. Other sources suggested that he escaped to the USA and remained a staunch supporter of the 'good old cause'. Nobody knew the truth at the time, and nobody seems to have bothered to find out afterwards.

Conclusion

Mostly Men of Principles

'I tell you, it was a just act; God and all good men will own it.'

John Bourchier, 1660[1]

> If I believed the king had to die – I personally think that
> they should have murdered him. They would have been
> better off letting him try to escape and shooting him in
> the back, as some Parliamentarians planned. It wouldn't
> have been noble, and I'm not saying murder is ever a great
> thing, but there was no chance of putting a king on trial
> successfully in that era – especially a king to whom you
> have sworn allegiance as an army officer or MP. They
> chose the one method that didn't work: it was completely
> wrong for the job.[2]

This is the opinion of the historian Charles Spencer, a man with a
remarkably reasonable attitude to the regicides given his own royal
connections. There is room to disagree with every part of this statement.

Most of the regicides *had* come to the conclusion that the king had
to die, but they had come to this conclusion via religion, political theory
or desperate pragmatism. The country was at the end of its tether and
another war would have destroyed it, but murder could never have been
an option. Spencer was correct in the sense that it could have been done
easily. The fact that it was not done, and was actively discouraged, shows
that they were mostly men of principles. Murder was beneath them.

Assassination would have been easy. Trial and execution were by
far the greater risk, both at the time and later, should the monarchy be

197

restored, which of course proved to be the case. The regicides knew this. Spencer's view that it was impossible to put a king on trial is contradicted by the fact that they actually did it. They succeeded in the short term, failed in the medium term but succeeded in the longer term. They executed their king and Britain would never be the same again.

If they had been merely murderers, nothing would have been changed politically and they would have been forgotten. To their enemies, the trial made them no less murderers than if they had killed their king in a corner, but to elect for a trial suggests – correctly or incorrectly – that the king had broken the law, or more profoundly, that kings could break the law, because it was above them and not their servant, and that some actions were bad enough to dissolve oaths of allegiance.

Spencer suggests that the method used was 'wrong for the job', but that begs the question, what was the job? There was an element of greed and egotism, as the book has shown, but there were principles present, and they were noble ones; ones that we would not want to live without today: a limited monarchy, with power being distributed among many people who could be held responsible for their actions, parliamentary privilege, and religious toleration. Their religious and social views are alien to people today, but this does not mean that they did not, ultimately, do a favour to future generations.

Sir Harbottle Grimston, the judge in the first trial of the regicides, lambasted the fifty-nine. They were 'never to be remembered without tears'. That was an understandable reaction in 1660, but, knowing what we know today about freedom in faith and politics, perhaps we should say that they should never be remembered without gratitude?

Bibliography

Primary Sources

Anon, *The Trials of Charles the First, and of Some of the Regicides* (1839).

Anon, *The history of king -killers; or, the 30th of January commemorated* (1719).

Anon, *The Speeches and Prayers of John Barkstead, John Okey, and Miles Corbet* (1662).

Caulfield, J., *The High Court of Justice* (1820).

Corbet, M., *The Speeches and Prayers of John Barkstead, John Okey, and Miles Corbet* (1662).

Deane, J., *The Life of Richard Deane* (1870).

Dictionary of National Biography, 1885–1900 (via Wikisource).

Finch, H., *The Indictment, Arraignment, Tryal and Judgement, at Large, of Twenty-nine Regicides* (1662).

Granger J., *Biographical History of England: From Egbert the Great to the Revolution* (1824).

Hutchinson, L., *Memoirs of the life of Colonel Hutchinson* (1806).

Hyde, E., Earl of Clarendon, *History of the Rebellion* (1690).

Ludlow, E., *Memoirs* (1690).

Neal, D., *The History of the Puritans* (1863).

Noble, M., *The Lives of the English Regicides two volumes* (1798).

Rushworth J, *Containing the Principal Matters Which Happen'd From the Beginning of the 1645 to the death of Charles I* (1721).

Walker, C., *History of Independency* (1650).

Whitelocke, B., *Memorials of the English affairs* (1752).

Wood, A., *Athenae* Oxonienses (1691).

Secondary Sources

Adair, J., *By the Sword Divided.*

Aston, M., *Broken Idles of the English Reformation.*

Beckett, I., *Wanton Troopers: Buckinghamshire in the Civil Wars 1640–1660.*

Birch, I., *Baptists, Fifth Monarchists, and the Reign of King Jesus.*

Braddick, J., *The Oxford Handbook of the English revolution.*

Carlton, C., *Going to the Wars.*

Carlyle, T., *Works.*

Christenson, R., *Political Trials: Gordian Knots in the Law* (R. Lilburne).

Elmer, P., *Witchcraft, Witch-hunting, and Politics in Early Modern England.*

Fraser, A., *Cromwell, Our Chief of Men.*

Gentles, I., *The English Revolution and the Wars in the Three Kingdoms, 1638–1652.*

Greaves, R. L., *Deliver Us from Evil: The Radical Underground in Britain, 1660–1663.*

Hobson, J., *Following in the Footsteps of Oliver Cromwell.*

Hodkinson, R., *Cromwell's Buffoon: The Life and Career of Regicide Thomas Pride.*

Hooper, A., *Black Tom: Thomas Fairfax and the English Revolution.*

Hopper, A., *The Reluctant Regicide? Thomas Waite and the Civil Wars in Rutland.*

Jenkinson, M., *Charles I's Killers in America: The Lives and Afterlives of Edward Whalley and William Goffe.*

Jordan, D. and Walsh, M., *The King's Revenge.*

Manganiello, S., *The Concise Encyclopaedia of the Revolutions and Wars of England, Scotland and Ireland.*

Peachy, J. (ed), *The Regicides and the Execution of Charles 1.*

Plowden, A., *In a Free Republic.*

Purkiss, D., *The English Civil War – A People's History.*

Rees, J., *The Leveller Revolution.*

Robertson, G., *The Tyrannicide Brief: The Story of the Man who sent Charles I to the Scaffold.*

Simpkinson, C., *Thomas Harrison: Regicide and Major-general.*

Schofield, J., *From Cromwell to Cromwell.*

Spencer, C., *The Killers of The King.*

Tomalin, C., *Samuel Pepys, The Unequalled Self.*

Wallace, D.C., *Twenty-Two Turbulent Years 1639–1661.*
Walsh, M. and Jordan, D., *The King's Revenge: Charles II and the Greatest Manhunt in British History.*
Wedgewood, V., *The Trial of Charles I.*
Woolwych, A., *Britain in Revolution 1625–1660.*
Worden, B., *The Rump Parliament.*
Worden, B., *The English Civil Wars.*

Websites

www.historyofparliamentonline.org
https://web.warwick.ac.uk/english/perdita/html (John Hutchinson)
https://keith -perspective.blogspot.com (A Trumpet of Sedition)
https://www.robert -temple.com
www.turtlebunbury.com (Ewer)
https://www.british-history.ac.uk/
https://www.le.ac.uk (Thomas Grey)
http://bcw-project.org/ (British Civil War, Commonwealth and Protectorate)

From www.jstor.com:

Gee, H., *The Derwentdale Plot, 1663. Transactions of the Royal Historical Society* (1917).
Bittle, W., *The Trial of James Nayler and Religious toleration in England* (1984).
Jenkinson, M., 'Regicides on the Run', *Huntington Library Quarterly* (2013).

Notes

Chapter 1: The Morning Stars of the Regicide

1. Hewson, Blakiston and Cromwell also fall into this category.
2. Not Just Wilberforce (Amnesty International).
3. Lancashire: Its Puritanism and Nonconformity (R. Halle).
4. English Puritanism and the Shaping of New England Culture (S. Foster).
5. Other regicides on the same committee were Scot, Purefoy, Millington and Marten.
6. History of the Rebellion (Clarendon).
7. Glimpses of our ancestors in Sussex (C. Fleet).
8. Hull provided two regicides: Pelham and Alured, both honoured with plaques; Pelham at the Hull Truck Theatre and Alured at Charterhouse.

Chapter 2: The Chief Regicide

1. Athenae Oxonienses (A. Wood).
2. The Trials of Charles the First, and of Some of the Regicides (Anon).
3. Baptist Reporter and Missionary Intelligencer (1856).
4. The English Civil War – a People's History (D. Purkiss).
5. Henry Ireton and the English Revolution (D. Farr).

Chapter 3: The Gentry Soldiers

1. wiki.bcw-project.org (British Civil Wars, Commonwealth and Protectorate, 1638–60).
2. The Life of Richard Deane (J. Deane).
3. A Biographical History of England: From Egbert the Great to the Revolution (J. Granger).
4. The Humble Petition of Several Colonels of the Army Causes, Character, and Results of Military Opposition to Cromwell's Protectorate (B. Taft).

Chapter 4: The Brewer, the Servant and the Cobbler?

1. Cromwell's Buffoon: The Life and Career of the Regicide, Thomas Pride (R. Hodkinson).
2. Deane and Ingoldsby also signed this document.
3. Complete Collection of State Trials, Volume 2 (F. Hargrave).
4. Selected members were Carew, Tichborne and Stapley; Cromwell and Harrison were ex-officio members. See chapter on Tichborne and Harrison for more about the Barebones.

Chapter 5: Metropolitan Militia Men

1. Thomas Pride (see Chapter 4) falls into this category as well.
2. A Second Narrative of the late Parliament (1658).
3. Baptists, Fifth Monarchists and the Reign of King Jesus (I. Birch).
4. Works of the Camden Society, Volumes 84–85.
5. Calendar of State Papers, Domestic Series.
6. www.robert-temple.com/articles/owen_rowe.pdf
7. The Indictment, Arraignment, Tryal and Judgement, at Large, of Twenty-nine Regicides (1662) (H. Finch).
8. bishopslydeardbenefice.org/lydeard-st-lawrence-st-lawrence
9. Of Englishe Dogges (Abraham Fleming, 1596) described the Bandog as a 'vast, stubborn, eager dog of heavy body'.
10. www.stgeorgeswindsor
11. Annals of Windsor: Being a History of the Castle and Town; Volume 2.

Chapter 6: Turning Point 1648

1. Reports and Transactions, Volume 9, by Cardiff Naturalists' Society.
2. Ibid.

Chapter 7: The Main Lawyer

1. The Trials of Charles the First: And of Some of the Regicides.
2. White King (L. de Lisle).

Chapter 8: Two Regicide Lawyers

1. www.robert-temple.com/articles/augustine_garland.pdf
2. Ibid.
3. Ibid.

Chapter 9: The Main Republican

1. Brief Lives (J. Aubrey).
2. The Statesmen of the Commonwealth of England (J. Forster).

Chapter 10: Hardcore Republicans

1. The Trial of Charles I (V. Wedgwood).
2. Select and Remarkable Epitaphs on Illustrious and Other Persons Volume 2 (J. Hackett).
3. Memoirs (E Ludlow).
4. sourcebooks.fordham.edu/mod/1644cromwell-marston.asp

Chapter 11: Two Well-documented Men?

1. Early Modern Ireland, 1534–1691.
2. thehistorywoman.com/tag/edmund-ludlow/
3. Autobiography and Gender in Early Modern Literature (S. Seelig).
4. www.nottinghamcityofliterature.co
5. Dictionary of National Biography, 1885–1900 (C.H.Firth).
6. A Guide to the Civil War in Nottinghamshire (I. Brown).

Chapter 12: The Main Religious Fanatic

1. Two great Fifth Monarchy Women and prophetesses were Anna Trapnel and Mary Cary.
2. Others strident millenarians were John Okey and Robert Tichborne.
3. Memoires of the Reign of King Charles (Sir P. Warwick).
4. This is a Montero, a fashionable hat with flaps to protect neck and ears. It was worn by both Fairfax and Prince Rupert, but clearly rare enough for the king to notice.
5. Bishop Burnet's 'History of His Own Time'.

Chapter 13: The Fanatics

1. Cromwellian Gazetteer (P. Gaunt).
2. Bishop John Williams died 1650; a man who fell out with both sides and perhaps may have been right about Jones.
3. Inedited Letters of Cromwell, Jones Bradshaw and other regicides (J. Mayer).

4. See Chapter 5, note 7.
5. Select Views in Leicestershire, from Original Drawings (J. Throsby).

Chapter 14: The Cromwellian Major-Generals

1. Dairy of John Evelyn, 25 December 1657.

Chapter 15: The Cromwellians

1. Dover Historian website
2. History of Three of the Judges of Charles I (E. Stiles).
3. It Happened in Connecticut (D. McCain).
4. Ezra Stiles and the Monument for Colonel John Dixwell (C. Lutz).
5. The Major-generals in the North; Cromwellian Administration in the Northern Counties during the English protectorate (S. Harper).
6. Thurloe State Papers.
7. Chaloner, Crawley, Constable, and Blakiston were also accused of being 'sectaries'.
8. James Nayler in the English Civil Wars (Digital Commons).
9. www.historyofparliamentonline.org
10. Dutch Puritanism: A History of English and Scottish Churches (K. Sprunger).
11. www.sussexhistory.co.uk/glimpse-ancestors/sussex -ancestors

Chapter 16: Committee Men

1. http://caldecotehall.weebly.com/history.html
2. politics, Society and Civil War in Warwickshire, 1620–1660
3. Edgehill and Beyond: The People's War in the South Midlands, 1642–45 (P. Tennant).
4. Historical Memoirs relating to the Independents (B. Hanbury) 1660.

Chapter 17: Unprincipled, Choleric Malcontents?

1. Music at Ripon Cathedral (Various).
2. The Tourist's Guide; Being a Concise History and Description of Ripon.
3. The Private Journals of the Long Parliament: 2 June to 17 September 1642

Chapter 18: Mostly about the Money

1. Westminster 1640–60: A Royal City in a Time of Revolution (J. Merritt).
2. Calendar of State Papers, Domestic Series, Volume 11.
3. Edited from Leslie Stephen's 'Dictionary of National Biography' (1886).

Chapter 19: Adulterers and Cowards

1. Also Henry Marten, Robert Tichborne (adulterer and coward respectively).
2. The Strange Case of Lord Pigot (S. Bhattacharya).
3. The Killers of the King (C. Spencer).
4. See Chapter Five, note 7.

Chapter 20: Suspect Motivation

1. The Story of Lord Bacon's Life (W. Dixon).
2. The Mystery of the Good Old Cause (1660).
3. www.robert-temple.com/articles/simon_mayne.pdf

Chapter 21: The Strained Quality of Mercy

1. The Tyrannicide Brief: The Story of the Man who sent Charles I to the Scaffold (G. Robertson).
2. Ibid.
3. parliamentonline website.
4. The History of the Rebellion.

Conclusion

1. Memoir (E. Ludlow).
2. BBC History Magazine (October 2014).

Index